THE NAKED COMMUNIST

THE NAKED COMMUNIST

Cold War Modernism and the Politics of Popular Culture

ROLAND VÉGSŐ

Fordham University Press

NEW YORK   2013

Library of Congress Cataloging-in-Publication Data

Végső, Roland.
  The naked communist : Cold War modernism and the politics of popular culture / Roland Végső. — First edition.
     pages cm
  Includes bibliographical references and index.
  ISBN 978-0-8232-4556-7 (cloth : alkaline paper)
  ISBN 978-0-8232-4557-4 (paper : alkaline paper)
  1. Anti-communist movements—United States—History—20th century. 2. Anti-communist movements—United States—Philosophy. 3. Cold War—Political aspects—United States. 4. Popular culture—Political aspects—United States—History—20th century. 5. Aesthetics—Political aspects—United States—History—20th century. 6. United States—Politics and government—1945–1989. 7. Anti-communist movements in literature. 8. Cold War in literature. 9. American literature—20th century—History and criticism. 10. United States—Intellectual life—20th century. I. Title.
  E743.5.V44 2013
  973.91—dc23   2012027146

Printed in the United States of America

15 14 13   5 4 3 2 1

First edition

A book in the American Literatures Initiative (ALI), a collaborative publishing project of NYU Press, Fordham University Press, Rutgers University Press, Temple University Press, and the University of Virginia Press. The Initiative is supported by The Andrew W. Mellon Foundation. For more information, please visit www.americanliteratures.org.

To the memory of my father, Dr. Károly Végső (1940–2010)

Contents

Acknowledgments

I would like to start by thanking my mentors at the English and Comparative Literature Departments of the State University of New York at Buffalo for their unfailing guidance and inspiring friendship: Joan Copjec, Ernesto Laclau, David Schmid, Tim Dean, and Rodolphe Gasché. At the same time, I would like to acknowledge the direct and indirect contributions of all of my friends and foes at UB's Center for the Study of Psychoanalysis and Culture. You know who you are. Furthermore, I am also indebted to the two readers of the manuscript, Donald E. Pease and Michael Tratner, for their helpful comments and friendly criticisms. Needless to say, I am also grateful for the support of my colleagues at the English Department of the University of Nebraska-Lincoln. Special thanks are due to Sorin Radu Cucu and Marco Abel for their friendship. In the end, all this would have been impossible without Emily Hammerl.

Parts of Chapter 7 have been published previously as "The Importance of Being Ugly: Anti-Communist Anti-Imperialism" in *Comparative American Studies* 6.4 (December 2008): 374–387.

Introduction

Those familiar with the history of American anti-Communism will immediately recognize that I borrow my title from Cleon W. Skousen's *The Naked Communist* (1958).[1] The book belongs to the same genre as J. Edgar Hoover's better-known classic, *Masters of Deceit* (1958), and it presents to a general audience a history of Communism in conjunction with the practical knowledge necessary to fight its expansion.[2] For Skousen, an ex-FBI agent, the nakedness of this Communist has a precise meaning. As he explains in the preface, the book "attempts to present the Communist in his true native elements, stripped of propaganda and pretense. Hence the title, 'The Naked Communist.'"[3] The title refers to the "naked truth" itself, which is expected to come about as the result of a successful critique of ideological mystifications and which offers pure presentation in place of deceitful representations.

But when I quote Skousen's title, I intend to repeat it with a significant difference. As Skousen's own career shows, the first revelation of truth leaves something to be desired. In 1970, he authored the companion piece to *The Naked Communist* under the title *The Naked Capitalist*, in which he argued (in the form of an extended review of Carroll Quigley's *Tragedy and Hope*) that the Communist conspiracy was a mere tool in the hands of an even bigger conspiracy run by rich capitalists.[4] Of course, this shift from the Communist conspiracy to something resembling contemporary theories of the New World Order might appear to be a historically predictable move. But we could also interpret the "naked capitalist" as the answer to the inherent ambiguity of the "naked Communist," since it replaces an unstable earlier version of the truth with a new kind of certitude.

Thus, the irony of Skousen's title is that it presents an unstable figure of ideological demystification which leads to secondary acts of demystification. From the perspective of the second book, the nakedness of the Communist does not refer to the direct revelation of "truth" but to yet another seductive illusion that was first mistaken for a truth. The inherent danger of such demystifications is that they threaten to open up an infinite series of further demystifications. Hence the necessarily double figure of the naked Communist: it is simultaneously an object of knowledge and an object of desire. As an object of knowledge, it functions as the central figure of a potentially infinite discursive machine whose objective is the dissemination of anti-Communist knowledge. As an object of desire, however, it functions as an agent of seduction. It puts an end to the potential infinity of demystifications by introducing the possibility of "truth" into the domain of mere knowledge. This distance separating *The Naked Communist* from the *The Naked Capitalist* provides us with a first definition of ideological truth: truth occurs when a desire for truth interrupts a potentially endless series of demystifications.

Unlike Skousen's title, therefore, mine intends to evoke both of these meanings as it tries to call attention to the internal dialectic of ideological knowledge. But I evoke here the figure of the naked Communist as one possible historical manifestation of a general problem of modernity. My argument is based on the assumption that the political ideologies of modernity were determined in a fundamental manner by four basic figures: the world, the enemy, the secret, and the catastrophe. Whereas the "world" names the totality that functioned as the ultimate horizon of modern politics, the three other figures define the necessary limits of this totality. The naked Communist is an easily recognizable figure of this "enemy" whose identity was determined in a fundamental manner by the secrecy that was associated with it and the global catastrophe that it threatened to bring upon us.

Although these four figures have formed a number of different historical constellations, I try to highlight their enduring presence in the modern imagination through the detailed analysis of one concrete historical example: American anti-Communist politics of the 1950s. Within this historical context, my primary objective is to describe the internal mechanisms of what we could call an "anti-Communist aesthetic ideology." By "aesthetic ideology," I mean a specifically modern invention that names the complex relation between art and politics in our age. This is why I argue that in order to understand the politics of literary modernism in the United States, we have to analyze the terms of its institutionalization during the 1950s by the discourse of "Cold War liberalism." In this liberal discourse, however, anti-Communist popular culture emerged as a political "symptom" of modernism for two reasons: on the level of politics, Cold War liberalism strove to define itself as the opposite of conservative anti-Communism; on the level of aesthetics, its fundamental gesture was the rejection of mass culture in the name of modernism. It is in this sense that I call anti-Communist popular culture the ideological "other" of modernism.

By focusing on the problem of "aesthetic ideology," I aim to reverse the logic of some of the by-now familiar canonized readings of Cold War culture. Scholars of the liberal "end of ideology" consensus of the 1950s are always quick to point out that the depoliticization of the aesthetic field in fact served clearly definable political purposes. But what is usually missing in these accounts is a reflection on the contrary movement: after the apolitical has been revealed to be political, we must also acknowledge the fact that the allegedly political is structured by a set of apolitical assumptions. This is why, as I will argue, our relentless search for the "political unconscious" must also be accompanied by the equally rigorous search for the "aesthetic unconscious" of seemingly innocent political statements.

* * *

The first half of *The Naked Communist* is devoted to the theoretical and historical foundations of my reading of anti-Communist fictions. Based on an interrogation of the concept of "aesthetic ideology," I argue that the historical problems discussed in later chapters can be interpreted in terms of a "post-Althusserian" theory of representation.[5] I argue that representation must be understood as a form of *division* introduced into a terrain of ontological inconsistency. But the effects of this division can be experienced as a meaningful totality only if an act of *exclusion* clearly establishes the limits of representation. Due to this exclusion, therefore, ideological identification is always marked by a number of inherent limits. The articulation of these limits is essentially an "aesthetic" issue in the sense that they define the basic coordinates of a field of experience, which can then emerge as a field of representation. Politics is, thus, essentially aesthetic in nature to the degree that it is the communal management of these inherent limits.

After the theoretical introduction, I examine anti-Communist aesthetic ideology in two steps: first, I analyze its political (Chapters 2 and 3) and then its aesthetic (Chapter 4) components. In my second chapter, I concentrate on the instances when the American anti-Communist discourse of the 1950s provides a reflection on the limits of representation. I examine the recurrent rhetorical and discursive strategies of official American anti-Communist politics. As I argue, Cold War anti-Communism primarily legitimized itself by reference to a number of privileged moments when representation reached a certain limit. In Chapter 3, I examine the three most important figures marking these limits: the unreadable *enemy* (a radical formal indeterminacy combined with the most rigid determination of content: we cannot identify the enemy by external traits, but we know for sure what the enemy wants); the *secrets* of the national security state (most important: the secret of the A-bomb as an American property); and the absolute *catastrophe* (caused by the enemy who stole our secrets). The enemy, the secret, and the catastrophe mark the moments when representation reaches a certain limit and, therefore, it is by reference to them that this discourse establishes the proper domain of representation.

In Chapter 4, I show that it is more than just a coincidence that this politics and its theory of representation coincide with the institutionalization of a certain modernist aesthetics in which literature as such is theorized as the probing of the limits of representation. This modernism, however, is based on the exclusion of "popular literature" as mere propaganda from the field of high art. Therefore, I argue that according to the basic coordinates of anti-Communist aesthetic ideology, anti-Communist popular fiction occupies a paradoxical position: although this ideology claims that art as such is anti-Communistic, it reduces anti-Communist art to a contradiction in terms by excluding it from the field of pure art.

In the second half of *The Naked Communist*, I examine the way the culture of anti-Communism defined the "world" as the ultimate horizon of political imagination. As I argue, the constitution of this new totality depended on a threefold articulation: it had to define the unity ("one world") as well as the internal ("two worlds") and the external limits of the world ("three worlds"). In the last three chapters, I show that the primary function of nuclear holocaust novels was to establish the unity (or the "oneness") of the world, whereas spy novels and popular political novels about the Third World established, respectively, the internal and external limits of this totality. These three genres allow me to demonstrate the way the necessary limits of representation are thematized in popular fiction. These last three chapters contain parallel examinations of popular fiction and the critical category of modernism as it was employed in the 1950s. Through this series of juxtapositions, I examine the ways in which both "high art" and its "other," mass culture, participated in the very same cultural work on establishing the legitimate limits of representation. Thus, the last three chapters follow the same structure and can be broken down into the four sections. First, I examine the idea of the world in relation to the given genre discussed in the chapter. Next, I explore the relation of modernism to the foundational ideological figure of the examined genre. This is followed by a brief overview of some of the most popular texts of the given genre. Finally, I conclude these chapters with a reading of particular authors.

Chapter 5 explores the historical ties between modernism and the rise of atomic holocaust fiction. It argues that catastrophe functions in both as a fundamental aesthetic and a political figure for the unrepresentable. In Chapter 6, I continue my parallel examinations of popular culture and modernism by highlighting the figure of the secret. In my discussion of the modernist poetics of difficulty in juxtaposition with contemporary spy fiction, I concentrate on the motif of the stolen secret. I argue that the ideological function of modern spy fiction was to legitimize political secrecy, which immediately divided the world into two complementary units: the public domain of representative democracy and its necessary supplement, the world of secrecy. In the final chapter, I discuss the relationship between the aesthetics of modernism and the politics of modernization. Through a reading of the popular political novels of the 1950s, I examine the "global imaginary" of middle-brow anti-Communism.

PART I

ANTI-COMMUNIST POLITICS

1 /   The Aesthetic Unconscious

Aesthetics, Ideology, Critique

Since the end of the eighteenth century, "aesthetics" and "ideology" have inhabited overlapping theoretical domains, but the combination of the two terms into a unified concept ("aesthetic ideology") is of relatively recent vintage. Why this delay? Why did we have to wait until the second half of the twentieth century for the birth of this concept? In order to answer this question, we should first note that even a brief survey of the contemporary uses of the term will show us two completely different applications. More often than not, popular usage relies on this category simply to name the political dimension of the circulation (the production, exchange, distribution, and reception) of artistic products. The stronger philosophical meaning of the term, however, derives from the critique of "aesthetics" that has formed an important philosophical current of Western thought over the last two centuries. In the latter sense, the birth of "aesthetic ideology" amounts to the philosophical renunciation of the mastery of philosophy over art. From a theoretical perspective, however, one significant question still remains open: what can the simultaneous historical emergence of these two divergent meanings teach us about the meaning of modernity?[1]

Our first question, therefore, concerns the historical conditions of this conceptualization. In this regard, it is customary to cite the more or less parallel emergence during the eighteenth century of modern aesthetics (Baumgarten), ideology as the science of ideas (Destutt de Tracy), and transcendental philosophy as critique (Kant).[2] The interesting thing about the modern inception of aesthetics, ideology, and critique is that their moments of birth do not fully reflect the later uses of these categories. As is well known, Baumgarten's aesthetic theory is a science of sensory perception; and de Tracy's ideology is not the science of "false consciousness" but the study of the representations of the world in the form of ideas. This dual study of particular perceptions and universal ideas was, then, bridged by Kant's theory of transcendental imagination, which ultimately found its justification in a critique of aesthetic judgment. The latter, however, was not exclusively a theory of art, since its ultimate goal was to define the teleology of nature.

Thus, the familiar meanings of these three categories, as we tend to use them today, are mostly post-Kantian inventions. This historical move, however, introduced certain ambiguities that are still with us. As a philosophical discourse, aesthetics simultaneously names a general theory of experience (mostly concerned with sensory perception) and a theory of art (understood as a specific form of experience). Ideology refers either to ideas constitutive of subjectivity or to a false consciousness which can be replaced by authentic ideas. Finally, critique names the descriptive investigation of "conditions of possibility" as well as the normative application of standards deducible from these conditions.

The prehistory of "aesthetic ideology" was, thus, marked by the tacit assumption that "aesthetics" and "ideology" are two separate entities in ever-changing relations with each other, while "critique" involves their proper separation. Upon further reflection, we find that the identities of the two terms predetermined this history, depending on which of the two was considered to be the primary category. When the stress fell on "ideology," we found ourselves in a classic Marxist problematic. In this sense, "aesthetic *ideology*" refers to the fact that culture, since it belongs to the sphere of superstructure, is always determined (at least in the "last instance") by a more fundamental structural moment. At its worst, aesthetic experience is a false escape from ideology and, as such, an exemplary instance of ideological mystification. At its best, it is the transparent transmission of a good ideology and, as such, not really aesthetic at all. On the other hand, if we choose "aesthetics" as the master term, we find ourselves in the midst of the classic problems of Romanticism. In this sense, the autonomy of the aesthetic is the only viable model of just political organization. Aesthetics is still ideological, but art is the only "good" ideology that could effectively establish the harmony of an "aesthetic state." Aesthetics here names the nonideological instance that fully realizes the essence of ideology.

Within the horizon of this prehistory, then, we can speak only of the "politicization *of* art" or the "aestheticization *of* politics." These two basic paradigms were most famously formalized in the concluding sentences of Walter Benjamin's "The Work of Art in the Age of Its Technological

Reproducibility." Here, Benjamin offers us a choice between (fascist) aestheticized politics and (Communist) politicized art.[3] Regardless of whether such interpretations actually exhaust Benjamin's meaning, these two options and their corresponding political values became the tacit presuppositions of a wide range of subsequent enquiries. As a result, even today "aesthetic ideology" is often condemned as the inappropriate introduction of artistic practices into nonartistic fields. Whichever route the critic chooses to follow (and in this respect it has not proven to be decisive if a combination of the two was professed), the decisive point remains that the ideological problem always emerges at the point of intersection of two supposedly autonomous domains. So the difficult task that we have inherited from Benjamin consists of severing the ties between structural possibilities and political programs: what if the mutual interactions of aesthetics and politics lack an inherent political meaning?

This is why Althusser's theory of ideology is a crucial turning point in this history, since it redirects the theorization of ideology to the "original" meaning of aesthetics and, thereby, performs an important approximation of the two categories. For Althusser, ideology is to be located on the level of the very constitution of subjectivity and "lived experience." In this sense, ideology is "aesthetic" because it accounts for the very possibility of experience. Henceforth, ideology will always be aesthetic, even if the ambiguity of the latter category leaves the question open of how we move from a theory of experience to a theory of art. Schematically speaking, the Althusserian theory of ideology is concerned with the problem of reproduction and argues the following: (1) ideology is eternal (it has no history because it is omni-historical); (2) it is an imaginary representation ("ideology = an imaginary relation to real relations"); (3) it is realized in material practices; and (4) it interpellates individuals as subjects. Concerning the last point, Althusser speaks of a "double constitution": "the category of the subject is only constitutive of all ideology insofar as all ideology has the function (which defines it) of 'constituting' concrete individuals as subjects."[4]

This dual constitution has at least two significant consequences. First, ideological recognition implies the misrecognition of the real conditions of reproduction. But, as Althusser argues, reproduction is actually the condition of production (for without the reproduction of the conditions of production there would be no production). Thus, ideology always functions as the disavowal of the conditions of a particular mode of production and, as such, it is also the disavowal of the conditions of the constitution of subjectivity. In the same movement, ideology constitutes a subject and covers up the traces of this constitution. The second point concerns the possibility of ideology critique. For, if the subject is constitutively ideological, the move beyond ideology must take place from within ideology.[5] Such is the role of science constituted by the knowledge of ideological mechanisms.

But "real art" has a very similar function even if it must be distinguished from science. Althusser's theory of art can be derived from his essentially aesthetic theory of ideology. In "A Letter on Art," Althusser writes:

> When we speak of ideology we should know that ideology slides into all human activity, that it is identical with the "lived" experience of human existence itself: that is why the form in which we are "made to see" ideology in great novels has as its content the "lived" experience of individuals. This "lived" experience is not a *given*, given by a pure "reality", but the spontaneous "lived experience" of ideology in its peculiar relationship to the real. This is an important comment, for it enables us to understand that art does not deal with a reality *peculiar to itself*, with a *peculiar domain* of reality in which it has a monopoly (as you tend to imply when you write that "with art, knowledge becomes human", that the object of art is "the individual").[6]

The important point here is that the function of "authentic" art is an internal critique of ideology. As Althusser argues, unlike science, art does not make us conscious of its object (in the form of concepts). Rather, by establishing an "internal distance" in relation to the ideology that functions as its very condition, art can make this ideology visible, perceptible, and sensible. Nevertheless, art cannot be established as a radically autonomous field outside ideology. All it can do is render visible the conditions of its own constitution (which are disavowed in ideology). In other words, Althusser simultaneously rejects the humanist ideology of art (which claims that art is the autonomous expression of human essence) and the absolute ideologization of art. Thus, Althusser's significance for this history of "aesthetic ideology" was to question the autonomy of the two fields. On the one hand, he performed a significant approximation of the aesthetic and the ideological through his theory of the ideological constitution of subjectivity. On the other hand, he rejected the radical autonomy of art and redefined it as the internal limit of ideology.

More recently, the two most instrumental books in popularizing the term "aesthetic ideology" were Paul de Man's *Aesthetic Ideology* and Terry Eagleton's *The Ideology of the Aesthetic*.[7] In their symmetrical opposition, they reproduce the two paradigmatic options of the prehistory of the category. While de Man moves from a critique of aesthetics as a philosophical discourse toward politics, Eagleton moves from a set of political convictions toward an aesthetic theory of art. In spite of all their differences, however, their discourses are structured by the same opposition: materiality (in Eagleton's case the materiality of the body, in de Man's the materiality of the signifier) is opposed to ideology. In this respect, they are both heirs to the Althusserian redefinition of ideology, since the problem of aesthetics and ideology has to be discussed in relation to the very constitution of experience. What concerns us the most, however, is that they both effectively claim that the basic paradigm of ideology is a kind of aesthetic distortion. If ever so indirectly, they both argue that ideology as such is inherently aesthetic.

De Man's "non-phenomenal linguistics" locates the problem of "aesthetic ideology" at the heart of a recognizably Kantian problematic, that of the "phenomenality of the non-phenomenal."[8] As a result, the aesthetic cannot be equated with art, as it unavoidably leads to phenomenological questions about the constitution of objectivity as such. As de Man insists, since for Kant the function of the *Third Critique* is to establish the link between theoretical and practical reason, aesthetics assumes a double role: on the one hand, it is a particular philosophical discipline devoted to the study of art; on the other hand, inasmuch as aesthetic theory also fulfills a more general mediating role, it is also "critical philosophy to the second degree, the critique of the critiques."[9] Thus, "aesthetics" simultaneously functions as a theory of art and an attempt by "a universal system of philosophy" to establish its very own systematicity.[10] As a result, it is "a phenomenalism of a process of meaning and understanding, and it may be naïve in that it postulates (as its name indicates) a phenomenology of art and literature."[11] At the same time, "ideology" names the tropological movement whereby something essentially nonphenomenal is given a sensible form. In de Man's famous definition, ideology "is precisely the confusion of linguistic with natural reality, of reference with phenomenalism."[12] But this confusion of linguistic reference and phenomenological intuition is essentially of an aesthetic nature: "Intuition implies perception, consciousness, experience, and leads at once into the world of logic and of understanding with all its correlatives, among which aesthetics occupies a prominent place."[13] Therefore, aesthetics is inherently ideological simply because it is concerned with the phenomenology of art; and ideology is inherently aesthetic, as the confusion of reference and intuition is the constitutive move of aesthetic discourse.

For Eagleton, the category of the aesthetic functions as the condition of impossibility of bourgeois ideology and its corresponding definition of the subject. As a condition of impossibility, this ideological definition of the work of art simultaneously renders possible the hegemony of bourgeois ideology and establishes the preconditions of its radical critique. From this perspective, the single most important quality of the aesthetic in the age of its complete commodification is its "autonomy," which becomes the ultimate model of the freedom the bourgeois subject. The latter, however, is best understood as the internalization of the law (the historical move from the primacy of physical coercion to spiritual consent and willing subjection to the law). Therefore, the aesthetic remains an essentially contradictory category which, on the one hand, functions as "a genuinely emancipatory force," on the other hand, signifies "internalized repression."[14]

In this respect, Eagleton's reading of the Kantian aesthetic judgment is revealing. As is well known, for Kant the peculiarity of aesthetic judgment lies in the fact that it is simultaneously subjective and universal without the mediation of concepts. For Eagleton, this is precisely the structure of ideological mystification, since the latter displaces a purely subjective judgment to the level of a universal law which, nevertheless, cannot be formulated with the conceptual clarity of reason:

> The aesthetic, one might argue, is in this sense the very paradigm of the ideological. For the peculiarity of ideological propositions might be summarized by claiming, with some exaggeration, that there is in fact no such thing as an ideological proposition. Like aesthetic judgments for Kant, ideological utterances conceal an essentially emotive content within a referential form, characterizing the lived relation of a speaker to the world in the act of appearing to characterize the world.[15]

At this moment, the political ambiguity of the aesthetic surfaces again. On the one hand, the spontaneous universality of aesthetic judgment promises to establish a noncoercive community of aesthetic consensus. On the other hand, however, under the guise of this spontaneous universality, the aesthetic justifies a specific form of coercion. This ambiguity, however, also means for Eagleton that "aesthetic ideology" carries no inherent political value, and as the condition of impossibility of bourgeois ideology, it can simultaneously establish and transcend what it renders possible.

Thus, aesthetic ideology enters history at the moment when the autonomy of the aesthetic and the ideological can no longer be maintained. The coming of age of aesthetic ideology is dependent on the perception of a certain tautology: aesthetics is inherently ideological because ideology is essentially aesthetic. But the question of the heteronomy of these two fields remains a crucial problem. While an Althusserian position would argue for their relative autonomy in the name of a "determination in the last instance," a properly post-Althusserian position will have to start with the assumption of what Étienne Balibar called the "heteronomy of heteronomy" (that is, the ultimate impossibility of reducing the moment of heteronomous determination to an a priori given, in itself autonomous moment).[16] From this moment, critique is the investigation of the institution of the field of the interactions of ideology and aesthetics without the normative prioritization of any of the two terms in an a priori fashion.

The Distribution of the Sensible

What sets Jacques Rancière's work aside in the contemporary debate about aesthetics is precisely his unequivocal rejection of what he calls "this great anti-aesthetic consensus."[17] He is clearly unapologetic in his efforts to recover a different meaning of the term: "Aesthetics is not the fateful capture of art by philosophy. It is not the catastrophic overflow of art into politics. It is the originary knot that ties a sense of art to an idea of thought and an idea of the community."[18] With a single stroke, the prehistory of "aesthetic ideology" is brought to an end. In place of "an aestheticization of politics" or "a politicization of aesthetics," we are proffered the "originary knot" that makes the interactions of art, thought (pure concept or mere ideology), and politics possible in the first place. It is this displacement of the problem that renders Rancière's work especially relevant for us.

The central category of Rancière's program is the "distribution of the sensible" (le partage du sensible), which is best understood as a politicized version of Kant's "transcendental aesthetics."[19] It is based on a singular definition of both politics and aesthetics. As Rancière explains: "Politics, indeed, is not the exercise of, or struggle for, power. It is the configuration of a specific space, the framing of a particular sphere of experience, of objects posited as common and as pertaining to a common decision, of subjects recognized as capable of designating these objects and putting forward arguments about them."[20] Rancière calls this level of political engagement "primary aesthetics" and opposes it to actual "aesthetic practices."[21] Thus, politics as the primary aesthetics of the social is above all of the counting of the "parts" of the community, "which is always a false count, a double count, or a miscount."[22]

Rancière's definition of politics is, therefore, fully dependent on this miscount which disavows the radical equality of all speaking beings. The miscount is based on the "double use of logos" which means that speech carries a double burden: on a basic level, speech is communication between speaking beings who are acknowledged to be such by a particular distribution of the sensible; at the same time however, speech is also an account of speech in the sense that it also defines the very limits of the access to speech.[23] Rancière designates the lot of those who are not counted as capable of speech as the "part of those who have no part."[24] Thus, the distribution of the sensible allows for two alternative logics of being together: the policing of a given order of the sensible (of the sayable and nonsayable, the visible and the invisible, etc.) is contrasted with the redistribution of the sensible through the interruption of the normal order. For Rancière, however, only the latter constitutes a proper political act: politics occurs when the disavowed radical equality of all speaking beings interrupts the normal flow of things. In a genuine political act, a mass of men without qualities identify with the whole of the community in the name of the wrong done to them (the miscount that reduced them to the part of no part). The *demos* is the nothing that wants to become everything. This is the "all or nothing" logic of the miscount of democracy.

As Rancière argues, critiques of aesthetic ideology are often based on the mistaken assumption that the relations among artistic practice, a generalized concept of art, and the philosophy of art are necessary (rather than contingent). Even those who acknowledge this contingency tend to assume that the role of "aesthetics" was precisely to misrepresent this relationship as necessary. But Rancière reverses the traditional sequence according to which an artistic practice is followed by its conceptualization when he argues that the latter is actually constitutive of the former. Aesthetics, therefore, is not the philosophical appropriation of an artistic practice, but one of the "conditions of possibility for what artistic practices can produce and for what aesthetic gazes can see."[25] This move from a philosophy of art to a condition of possibility means that aesthetics is now part of what Rancière calls "a general regime of art," which consists of three components: "modes of production of objects or of the interrelation of actions; forms of visibility of these manners of making or doing; and manners of conceptualizing or problematizing these manners of making or doing and these forms of visibility."[26] Creation (or, in a more general sense, production), perception, and thinking are tied together at their roots in a system of mutual determinations.

The fact that aesthetics is redefined as a condition of possibility, however, does not mean that it is impossible to speak of historical determinations of the aesthetic. For example, Rancière claims that the specifically modern "aesthetic regime of art" is brought about by the birth of an idea: "the idea that the sensible is the presentation of an in-sensible which, strictly speaking, is the thought of thought."[27] This new regime is constituted by a division within the field of the visible: in Hegelian terms, mere seeming (*Schein*) must be distinguished from the appearance (*Erscheinung*) of the idea (the in-sensible). The assumption is, of course, that the field of human perception mostly consists of objects that are mere sensations. But the identity of certain special objects can be split between their sensible forms and what these sensible forms render visible. This way, visibility is split (or redoubled) between mere visibility and the visibility of the invisible. But if thought (the invisible) can appear in a sensible form, the act of appearance divides the field of the intelligible as well as that of the sensible: appearance separates the sensible from the in-sensible as well as thought from nonthought. Within this aesthetic regime, as Rancière argues, the function of art is precisely to provide the sensible surface where this double split can take place.

The historicity of the "originary knot" of aesthetics and politics is, thus, described by Rancière in the following terms: "It retains the principle from the Kantian transcendental that replaces the dogmatism of truth with the search for conditions of possibility. At the same time, these conditions are not conditions for thought in general, but rather conditions immanent in a particular system of thought, a particular system of expression."[28] As we can see, this double move concerns the very status of the transcendental: "I thus try at one and the same [time] to historicize the transcendental and to de-historicize these systems of conditions of possibility."[29] As a result, the central problem of a critique of "aesthetic ideology" is to locate "the originary knot" as an immanent condition in a particular system of expression.

At this point, however, the question emerges: How can we separate this "primary aesthetics" from actual "aesthetic practices"? A quick way to describe Rancière's theoretical project in general would be to call it a political phenomenology of the disavowed conditions of the constitution of the social. Rancière's central presupposition is that the function of "the distribution of the sensible" is a given of human existence: since there is a constitutive limit in human experience, it is always configured through the legislation of the boundaries separating the visible from the invisible and the sayable from the unsayable. But it is not entirely clear how we can distinguish this inalienable function from its actual manifestations. And here we encounter a decisive complication of Rancière's thought: although he seems to insist on the difference between the two levels, at the same time his whole thought is predicated upon the categorical rejection of the languages of classical metaphysics and ontology. As a result, he does not present a systematic attempt to account for the emergence of the "ontological function" of the distribution of the sensible.

Thus, it is an important fact that Rancière's defense of "aesthetics" is based on an equally passionate critique of "political philosophy." Rancière identifies three basic forms of the philosophical misappropriation of politics: archipolitics (Plato), parapolitics (Aristotle), and metapolitics (Marx). These three categories represent three different ways of misappropriating the true meaning of the political. In the case of archipolitics, true politics is rendered impossible by the idea of the realization of the essence of the community. Archipolitics is the complete achievement of the *phusis* as *nomos* in the tangible coming into being of the community's law, the complete realization of the *arche* of the community. It provides a logical solution to "the part of no part" and thereby replaces the democratic institution of politics with the saturation of the social without a remainder.[30] As its name suggests, parapolitics displaces the political onto other nonpolitical activities. For parapolitics, it is not the *arche* but the original division of the *arche* of the community that must be realized as its *nomos*, but in such a way that the properly political nature of this division is masked. Metapolitics, in turn, defines politics as a social "symptomology" (as ideology critique) that detects a sign of untruth in every political distinction.[31] As the truth of the "lie of politics," metapolitics aims to go beyond politics (primarily through a scientific complement) and therefore its aim is the final elimination of politics. The three prefixes (*arche, para,* and *meta*) represent three different logics of the disavowal of politics: one is "below" politics (in the sense that it is its origin); the other is on the same level but "on the side of" or "beside" politics; and the third is "beyond" politics.

These three politics correspond to three different aesthetics, which we could call by analogy: archi-aesthetics in Plato, para-aesthetics in Aristotle, and meta-aesthetics in modernism. To be more precise, Rancière distinguishes three different regimes of art: the ethical regime of images (Plato), the poetic or representative regimes of the arts (Aristotle), and the aesthetic regime of art (modernism). The ethical regime is best exemplified by the Platonic ban on art as simulacrum (the mere imitation of imitation). As Rancière argues, in Plato's case we cannot speak of "art" in the same way we use this term today, because the arts meant for him simply "ways of doing and making."[32] Therefore, the opposition of the true arts (imitation of ideas) and mere simulacra (imitation of imitation) reduces the aesthetic to an educational function. This also means that art is supposed to participate in the realization of the *arche* of the community. The regime of representation is based on the *mimesis/poeisis* opposition. As in the case of Aristotle, the arts are now submitted to a hierarchy through a number of rules in such a way that the autonomous concept of "art" is still not possible. Rancière calls this "a regime in which art in general does not exist but where there do exist criteria of identification for what the arts do, and of appreciation for what is or is not art, for good or bad art."[33] Finally, aesthetic modernity emerges in Rancière's scheme as a form of "meta-aesthetics," since it establishes a peculiar paradox: art's autonomy (or, its radical singularity summarized by the statement: "art is art") becomes a form of heteronomy ("art is nonart"). To be more precise, modernity simultaneously asserts the unique nature of art and attempts to identify it with life.

In Rancière's formulations, however, we always lose something: none of the three political philosophies allows us a proper articulation of the political or the aesthetic. In other words, the question of "primary aesthetics" cannot be raised by any of the regimes in the proper form.[34] In a certain sense, we could think of these three political and aesthetic regimes as three different logics of the disavowal of the ontological function within particular ontic domains. At the same time, however, we have to be careful not to establish too tight a correspondence between these political and aesthetic logics. Rancière's point is not to set up a direct correspondence between these domains. Rather, we get here a first glimpse of the possible articulations of the way a "primary aesthetics" is institutionalized in different forms of political and aesthetic practices. The proper object of a critique of aesthetic ideology is, then, precisely this move from the originary knot to particular aesthetic and political regimes.

What could be the best term for this move? We have seen that Rancière categorically rejects formulas heralding the aestheticization of politics. But is there anything that he offers in place of aestheticization? One possible answer to the question is the "autonomization of aesthetics": "There never has been an 'aestheticization' of politics in the modern age because politics is aesthetic in principle. But the autonomization of aesthetics as a new nexus between the order of the logos and the partition of the perceptible is part of the modern configuration of politics."[35] It is important to point out that Rancière's rejection of the "aestheticization of politics" does not mean that he is blind to the interactions of politics and aesthetics. Rather, as he argues, "The core of the problem is that there is no criterion for establishing an appropriate correlation between the politics of aesthetics and the aesthetics of politics. This has nothing to do with the claim made by some people that art and politics should not be mixed. They intermix in any case; politics has its aesthetics, and aesthetics has its politics. But there is no formula for an appropriate correlation."[36] As we can see, these arguments form three essential steps. First, on the ontological level, Rancière reasserts the "primary knot" of aesthetics and politics and claims that "politics is aesthetic in principle." Then, he claims that although politics and aesthetics are separate fields on the ontic level, they always interact. Finally, however, he adds that the actual content of this relation on the ontic level (constant interaction) cannot be logically deduced from the ontological function. As a result, "there is no criterion for establishing an appropriate correlation between the politics of aesthetics and the aesthetics of politics."

What does this seemingly contradictory rejection of the "aestheticization of politics" and the simultaneous assertion of the unavoidable intermixture of aesthetics and politics show us? First, it makes clear that the process of "aestheticization" is not the interaction of two independent domains (a process in which one overtakes the other), but the activation of an inherent potential *within* politics itself. Aestheticization only makes sense if it is internal and not external to politics. At the same time, we can also see that the autonomization of aesthetics (which falls within the field of politics itself) remains a contradictory project: aesthetics becomes an independent domain from politics, but for Rancière this very process of autonomization is a political problem. As a result, Rancière argues that the autonomization of aesthetics is its very own cancellation: "the contradiction constitutive of the aesthetic regime of art . . . makes art into *an autonomous form of life* and thereby sets down, at one and the same time, the autonomy of art and its identification with a moment in life's process of self-formation."[37] Simply put, if autonomization is the undoing of the originary knot (since it falsely represents two fields tied together at their origins as if they were independent), it nevertheless remains an interminable project.

Following Rancière's lead but moving outside the proper limits of his project, we could define our terms in the following manner. Let us call the process of autonomization the move whereby an ontological function is divided and then disavowed in the form of its very own institution as an apparently independent ontic field. In this sense, for example, the institution of particular aesthetic practices will always imply the misrecognition of what Rancière calls "primary aesthetics." Similarly, the institution of a particular political regime in the form of a "police" order will always amount to the disavowal of politics proper. At the same time, let us call aestheticization and politicization the move from the ontological function to an ontic actualization. In other words, let us argue that these two categories do not define "horizontal" relations between already established autonomous fields with clearly defined identities, but rather a "vertical" movement *within* the objects of the respective fields. This is why, for example, Rancière insists that nothing is political in itself but anything may become political.[38] For us, this means that an inherent ontological function can be realized in any object, but then politicization takes place within the object and not between an object and an already established autonomous field. Thus, while both autonomization and aestheticization/ politicization imply a move from an ontological to an ontic level, there are some crucial differences to consider. While autonomization is an attempt to establish an independent field and therefore it establishes relations *between objects*, aestheticization/politicization take place *within objects*. Furthermore, autonomization works by way of a disavowal of an ontological function, aestheticization/politicization function as reactivations of the same function.

The Distribution of the Insensible

In order to introduce the category of representation to this discussion, let us consider Alain Badiou's critique of Rancière's *Disagreement*. First, we should note that Badiou readily admits that his own project shows important similarities with Rancière's. In fact, it is precisely because of these similarities that, in the final analysis, Badiou's critique of Rancière turns out to be so categorical. For Badiou, the irksome problem is that the similarities hide essential differences. Badiou summarizes Rancière's argument by calling it "a democratic anti-philosophy that identifies the axiom of equality, and is founded on a negative ontology of the collective that sublates the contingent historicity of nominations."[39] But while Badiou speaks about their common ontological premises (their shared interest in counting, the void, the whole, nomination, etc.), he faults Rancière for reducing these ontological insights to "a historicist phenomenology of the egalitarian occurrence."[40] As a result, Rancière's project is neither properly philosophical (since he does not explicitly formulate his ontology), nor properly political (since he fails to provide an effective definition of politics in the present).

Since the foundation of this critique is an ontological disagreement, let us first consider this aspect of Badiou's thought. One of the fundamental categories of Badiou's ontology is "presentation": "being is what presents (itself)."[41] Although it is not part of Badiou's terminology, we could argue that the central category of his ontology is actually "failed presentation." By failed presentation, however, I do not mean that presentation fails to achieve its goals and therefore nothing is ever presented. Contrarily, the point is that presentation is successful to the degree that it also presents something unpresentable. Thus, the failure of presentation simply means that presentation also presents the unpresentable. Rather than being an external limit (which would imply that presentation fails to present something presentable), this failure is actually an internal limit of presentation in the sense that the field of presentation is always riddled by the void.

We can derive all of the basic categories of Badiou's ontology from this internal limit of presentation. Let us, then, distinguish three levels of this ontology: the void (the unpresentable), the multiple (presentation), and the one (representation). The philosophical problem is to establish the relations of these three terms. But while in the ontological sense we move from the void toward the one, in the phenomenological sense we have to reverse this movement and work our way back from the one to the void. In other words, while the rigor of Badiou's thought in *Being and Event* is such that he can literally deduce everything from nothing, he also argues that in reality our starting point is always a fully structured situation and, therefore, we have to deduce the existence of nothing from our experience of the world.

Let us first briefly outline the "phenomenological" line of reasoning. When we speak of "everything," we mean here a fully structured situation under the sway of what Badiou calls the "state of the situation," which establishes the principle of counting the elements of the given situation as one. But, as Badiou argues, we always know that the "one" is an effect of an operation. Therefore, we have to suppose that what the state of the situation represents under the rule of the one was once merely presented on the level of the structure of the situation and must have been multiple. This is how we can move from the phenomenological experience of representation to the level of presentation. This move involves the retroactive deduction of the existence of the multiple from the fact that the one fails to constitute itself in a consistent manner. But then the question emerges: Why is the reduplication of the logic of presentation necessary in the first place? Why is the presented also necessarily represented? This is where the supposition of the void appears: representation is necessary because there is something in presentation that must be covered up. And what needs to be covered up is precisely the failure of presentation, the void (the unpresentable). From this perspective, then, our phenomenological starting point will always have to be the failure of representation, which should ultimately lead us to the retroactive presupposition of the void.

But the phenomenological primacy of the failure of representation corresponds to the ontological primacy of the void (the failure of presentation). This is why Badiou has to show that "the absolutely primary theme of ontology is therefore the void": "*the sole term from which ontology's compositions without concept weave themselves is necessarily the void*."[42] The problem is that although being is what presents (itself), it is irreducible to what is being presented. Being is neither the multiple nor the one. Rather, being is subtracted from existence (the domain of presentation and representation). The void, "the unpresentable of presentation," is only accessible as the "proper name of being."[43] This means that in spite of the fact that being is unpresentable, it is still not alien to thought. However, it is only accessible through a declarative act of nomination. Since Badiou's ontology is based on the assumption that everything is a multiple and that any multiple is always a multiple of multiples, the question emerges whether it is possible to institute a foundational act of counting which would put an end to this infinite regression. Badiou's answer is straightforward: "But where to start? What is the absolutely original existential position, the first count, if it cannot be a first *one*? There is no question about it: the 'first' presented multiplicity without concept has to be a multiple of nothing."[44] The void, therefore, is the foundational term of all ontology, since "it is the first multiple, the very being from which any multiple presentation, when presented, is woven and numbered."[45] It is in this sense that Badiou's ontology can derive everything from nothing.

If our ontological starting point is always "nothing" (which is subtracted from presentation as the unpresentable of presentation), we can also assert the centrality of failed presentation. We can see that the void, as the unpresentable, is always a retroactive deduction from the failure of presentation, while the one is the anticipated closure of failed presentation in representation. In other words, the void is the supposed cause of the failure of presentation, while representation is the remedy to this failure. This is why Badiou's system consists of three levels of constitution: the pure multiple, the structure of the situation (consistent multiple), and the state of the situation. Pure presentation presents multiples without a count. But as we have seen, the failure of presentation also institutes the first count of nothing. As a result, there is no situation without a count and every presentation is always already structured. But the structure of the situation is at odds with the void, the failure of presentation: "The apparent solidity of the world of presentation is merely a result of the action of structure, even if *nothing* is outside such a result. It is necessary to prohibit that catastrophe of presentation which would be its encounter with its own void, the presentational occurrence of inconsistency as such, or the ruin of the One."[46] The problem is that something escapes the count that institutes the structure of the situation: the count itself. Therefore, as Badiou argues, the count itself needs to be counted on the level of a metastructure (the state of the situation): "In order for the void to be prohibited from presentation, *it is necessary that structure be structured*."[47] This is how both the necessity and impossibility of representation can be derived from the ontological fact of nothing.

Based on the centrality of failed presentation, we can now map out Badiou's typology of being which consists of four basic categories: the void (neither presented nor represented), normal terms (both presented and represented), singular terms (presented but not represented), and excrescent terms (represented but not presented). Badiou calls these categories "the most primitive concepts of any experience whatsoever."[48] We can see then that "representation" functions here as the internal division of presentation, since it enacts the very institution of Badiou's threefold typology. Without a split between presentation and representation, we could not speak of normalcy, singularity, and excrescence. But without the errancy of the void we could not speak about representation either. And since it is representation itself which institutes the internal division of experience, it is also the principle of representation which achieves the distributions of these very terms. It is by counting certain terms as normal that the state of the situation establishes the principles of singularity and excrescence. At the heart of representation, therefore, we have to locate a constitutive exclusion. Contrasting this system with Rancière's, we could speak of this exclusion in terms of a distribution of the insensible.

We can see that representation primarily manifests itself in the form of the distribution of different terms within the field of presentation. But if every situation has its own state, we are always already within a regime of representation. As a result, experience is always already divided between presentation and representation. This division of the field of experience suggests that properly speaking only two terms fall immediately within the field of representation: normal and excrescent terms. At the same time, we can suppose that beyond or below representation, we find the void and singular terms. This dual division of the field of experience, however, leads to a set of related questions. The most important of these is whether it is possible to distinguish presentation from representation *from within* the field of representation? To put it differently, does the metastructure of the situation render visible anything other than the normal terms of a situation? This question has two important components. On the one hand, we have to ask if it is possible to distinguish normal and excrescent terms within the field of representation. On the other hand, if it is not possible to distinguish presentation from representation, how could we separate singular terms from the void itself? Ultimately, the question is whether we imagine the relationship of presentation to representation as a radical break (complete externality) or rather as a more refined "dialectical" relation of sorts.

In order to draw the consequences of this separation of presentation and representation, let us first examine Badiou's critique of the classic Marxist theory of the State. This problem involves a more consistent separation of the ontological state of the situation from the State of a historico-social situation. As Badiou argues, Engels's argument could be paraphrased by claiming that the bourgeoisie represents normalcy (since "it is presented economically and socially, and re-presented by the State"), the proletariat represents singularity (because it is presented but not represented), and the State represents excrescence (because it is always in excess of the situation).[49] According to this logic, then, Engels has to define politics as the universalization of singularity in order to do away with excrescence (the State) as such. The goal of politics is, then, to establish presentation without representation. Badiou, however, shows that this argument is fundamentally flawed:

> The two major parameters of the state of a situation—the unpresentable errancy of the void, and the irremediable excess of inclusion over belonging, which necessitate the re-securing of the one and the structuring of structure—are held by Engels to be particularities of presentation, and of what is numbered therein. The void is reduced to the non-representation of the proletariat, thus, unrepresentability is reduced to a modality of non-representation; the separate count of parts is reduced to the non-universality of bourgeois interests, to the presentative split between normality and singularity; and, finally, he reduces the machinery of the count-as-one to an excrescence because

he does not understand that the excess which it treats is ineluctable, for it is a theorem of being.[50]

It appears that Engels confuses ontological functions with concrete ontic contents. As a result, politics cannot be properly defined in relation to the dialectics of void and excess, since Engels cannot distinguish singularity (non-represented) from the void (unrepresentable). Furthermore, he can only define the (antagonistic) relation of the normal and the singular as an empirical accident that assumes the form of a "false universality" (and which, therefore, can simply be "corrected"). Finally, since he cannot properly separate representation (the count-as-one) from one of its forms (excrescence), the difference between normalcy and excrescence itself is made ambiguous. Ultimately, this confusion leads to a mistaken sense of politics, which believes that it can do away with a structural moment (excrescence) in the name of pure presentation.

Engels's erroneous identification of ontological functions with ontic contents, however, leaves us with a few questions. Would it be possible to assume that Engels's mistake is ideological? That is, can the fact that his three terms (the proletariat, the bourgeoisie, and the State) cover the totality of the field of experience be an effect of a particular regime of representation? Were there really no other possible elements in the situation analyzed by Engels? If there were, we could argue that these three categories themselves are results of a particular regime of counting. This, however, would mean that besides particular contents, the *positions* of normalcy, singularity, and excrescence are also marked *within* the field of representation. In other words, in Engels's system, besides being a normal element, the bourgeoisie comes to represent normalcy as such; besides being a singular element, the proletariat comes to represent singularity as such; and besides being an excrescent element, the State comes to represent excrescence as such. To put it differently: when the proletariat is identified with singularity as such, its name comes to signify within the field of representation the *possibility* of singularity. This conclusion, however, raises a new question: Although singular elements fall outside the field of representation, would it be possible to claim that the possibility of singularity is marked within representation by the split identity of one of these singular terms?

Let us consider the name "proletariat." The singularity of the proletariat does not mean that, for example, in nineteenth-century England the proletariat was effectively invisible, only that it was represented as the element whose exclusion was constitutive of bourgeois order. It was the very exclusion of the proletariat that rendered the presentation/representation split possible in the first place. To be more precise, the proletariat was represented as incapable of representing itself. Therefore, it was represented as inherently unrepresentable without an external agency (since it did not belong to its essence that it be represented). This shift of emphasis implies that in spite of the fact that it was without representation, the singularity of the proletariat was actually marked within the field of representation by a name: it was counted as "one" even if it was the one that does not count. The problem is that radical singularity means that the singular terms have absolutely no access to the field of representation. But if the possibility of singularity (the possibility that certain elements remain outside representation) is always marked within the field of representation, it becomes possible to represent elements *as* singular elements. Another way of saying the same thing would be to claim that the split between normalcy and singularity must be marked within the field of the normal: the field of representation institutes itself through an act of exclusion (some presented elements of the structure are not counted again by the metastructure), but the exclusion must be represented within the totality that is created by this act of exclusion.

This conclusion, however, has important consequences for our definition of representation. The principle of representation can be summarized by the following statement: since there is an inherent limit to presentation, experience must be divided. Although representation apparently introduces a new unity ("the one exists"), it actually divides the field of failed experience so that the one can at least appear in a restricted field. In order to exorcise the field of presentation of its void, representation divides this field (between normal and singular terms) and introduces an excessive dimension (mere representation without presentation). The fact, however, that representation is primarily the configuration of the field of experience in such a way that the inherent failure of presentation cannot manifest itself does not mean that we could define representation as an additional layer of presentation superimposed over the primary order of presentation (the natural state of things). Rather, representation is the act of division that produces an excess to cover up the void.

But how do we know that this exclusion is constitutive? It is precisely Badiou's distinction between the "natural" and the "historical" situation that establishes this point. Since for Badiou the natural situation is the domain of pure normalcy ("Nature is what is normal"), the historical situation is constituted by the division of normal, singular, and excrescent terms.[51] History comes about as a result of the separation and dislocation of presentation and representation (which no longer fully overlap as in the case of Nature). Therefore, there is no historical situation without an excess of representation over presentation, which also means that there is no history without exclusion. The primary target of this exclusion is, of course, the void. The objective is precisely to render the appearance of the void within presentation impossible: exclusion is supposed to make up for the failure of presentation by restoring it to itself in the field of representation. The problem, however, is that the void as such cannot be excluded, since it does not have an a priori determined structural location. In this sense, exclusion is always a failure. In fact, the only things that can be effectively excluded are particular elements of the structure of the situation that, in themselves, have no special relation with the void. This is why the exclusion of the void has to assume the form of a substitution: in place of the void, a presented term must be excluded which assumes the role of the embodiment of the void. Engels's mistake, then, appears in a new light: it is indeed a theoretical mistake to reduce the void to presentation, but it is a political necessity that one particular element embodies this void.

Exclusion and the Limits of Representation

As we can see, we are moving in the direction of a definition which holds that representation is fundamentally an *exclusion* of the void and the simultaneous *division* of the field of presentation. However, given the fact that "representation" is an overdetermined philosophical category, it might be necessary to introduce a few distinctions here and address the difference between the object and the signifier. A potential source of this complication is that, in its common usage, the term "representation" can refer to the constitution of the field of objectivity by a subject as well as to the process of signification. In order to locate the structures of the constitutive exclusion and the concomitant reflection on the limits of representation on both levels, I will cite here Slavoj Žižek's concept of the "sublime object" and Ernesto Laclau's definition of the "empty signifier." In spite of their differences, these two theories show that both the object and the signifier are products of a fundamental exclusion.

What renders Laclau's work especially relevant for this discussion is his thesis according to which there is no totality without exclusion. Simply put, for Laclau, subjectivity and objectivity are always articulated through the signifying practices of a discursive totality. Already in *Hegemony and Socialist Strategy*, Laclau and Mouffe defined their theoretical project as a radicalization of the Althusserian concept of totality. The problem with Althusser was that the theoretical possibilities opened up by the concept of overdetermination were short-circuited by his concept of "determination in the last instance."[52] In other words, while Althusser reduced totality to a determination by the economy, Laclau and Mouffe wanted to extend the logic of overdetermination to include all identities. This emphasis on overdetermination means that the problem is not only the logical deconstruction of the relation between the elements of a totality but the deconstruction of the very identity of these elements as well. What had to be affirmed was the "incomplete, open and politically negotiable character of every identity."[53]

The centrality of the category of "discourse" means that for Laclau "every object is constituted as an object of discourse," and "every subject position is a discursive position."[54] "Discourse" here designates a relational totality that articulates elements into moments of a structure. But since the process of articulation is never entirely fulfilled, the transition from elements to moments is never complete. Consequently, objectivity and subjectivity always partake of the constitutive openness of discourse. The impossible closure of discourse is guaranteed by the overdetermination of all identities and assumes the forms of a constitutive antagonism. This, however, does not mean that the closure of totality is entirely missing. Rather, Laclau argues that it is present as an absent fullness, which can be embodied by impossible objects. This is the logic of hegemony, which implies that a particular object will assume a role incommensurate with its particular identity and start to function as the embodiment of the absent fullness of a particular totality.

In fact, we could even argue that in Laclau's works the constitution of objectivity and signification as totalities follow a similar logic. On the level of signification, Laclau's seemingly contradictory starting point is that an empty signifier is a signifier without a signified, which nevertheless remains a sign. How is this possible? The answer concerns the limits of signification. Laclau summarized his argument in five points, which are the following.[55] First, if we follow Saussure in assuming that language is a mere differential system of signs, we have to assume that the meaning of a particular sign will always be dependent on the system it forms a part of. In that case, however, the totality of the system of signification is actually involved in every act of signification. Second, in order to conceive of this totality, we have to define the limits of signification, because what institutes a totality is precisely its difference from its outside. The problem is that this externality cannot be conceived as yet another difference internal to the system of signs. Third, if this outside cannot be conceived in terms of a neutral difference, the limit of the system has to assume the form of a radical *exclusion*. But this exclusion initiates a subversive dialectic between equivalence and difference: with regard to the excluded element all the differential identities within the totality appear to be equivalent. Fourth, this means that totality is always a locale of a tension between equivalence and difference. Rather than a positively given fullness, we are dealing with a failed totality, an impossible but necessary object. Finally, although this impossible object is beyond conceptual determinations, it is not beyond representation: a particular difference within totality can assume the role of representing totality as such. It is precisely this hegemonic articulation that is performed by an empty signifier. Laclau concludes: "With this it should be clear that the category of totality cannot be eradicated but that, as a failed totality, it is a horizon and not a ground."[56] Thus, every totality is a result of a hegemonic articulation.

We could say that while at the heart of Laclau's argument we find a critique of the Althusserian definition of totality, Slavoj Žižek's works are explicitly framed by a critique of the Althusserian definition of ideology. Žižek redefines the Althusserian subject as well as the Althusserian object. Concerning the subject, Žižek argues that we need to move beyond the logic of interpellation (which can only address the levels of imaginary and symbolic identification and thus only deals with the lower half of Lacan's graph of desire) toward the logic of fantasy, which covers up the constitutive lack in the Other, "pulsating around some unbearable surplus enjoyment."[57] To put it differently, what is missing from the Althusserian theory of the subject is a reckoning with the Lacanian real. As a result, this subject before subjectivation cannot be reduced to being mere substance, since its very being is constituted by the failure of substance to constitute a consistent field of objectivity. The logic of the "sublime object" implies that the domain of objectivity cannot establish its consistency without the supplement of an excessive dimension, that of the "object a" (the object more in the object than the object itself). For Žižek, then, what is missing in Althusser is the subject beyond subjectivation as well as the object beyond objectification. The point is that neither the field of subjectivity nor that of objectivity can be articulated in their ontological consistency without the intervention of an ideological operation.

In fact, one of the most important philosophical building blocks of Žižek's works consists of the reversal of classic definitions of the subject/substance relationship. As Žižek's Hegelian argument goes, as a first step, the subject comes to recognize the constitutive split between essence and appearance and conceives of essence as irretrievably withdrawn from the field of "mere" appearance. As a second step, however, we have to recognize that the split between essence and appearance is not a mere external obstacle, which denies us access to essence, but belongs to the very essence of essence. This way the split between essence and appearance is internalized in essence. But as Žižek argues, this second step is still misleading because it reduces appearance to a moment of the internal mediation of essence. Therefore, the crucial final reversal ("determinate" reflection) consists of the recognition that essence is nothing but the internal split of appearance: "'essence' itself is nothing but the self-rupture, the self-fissure of the appearance."[58] This means that the essence/appearance split itself has to appear in the field of appearance: one particular phenomenon has to embody the nullity of phenomena. These points are relevant for us because they show how we can move from the ontological presupposition of failed presentation to the idea that "totality" always exists in the form of a particular element (a part) representing an absent fullness (presentation without the void).

This is why, at the center of Žižek's theory of ideology, we find the notion of the "sublime object." His starting point is the Hegelian critique of the Kantian theory of the sublime. The core of this debate concerns the constitutive limits of representation. From Hegel's perspective, the problem with Kant's sublime is that it defines the beyond of representation as a positive reality. The Thing-in-itself is beyond phenomenality and is only accessible through the effects that it produces within the field of representation, but "in-itself" it is nevertheless a positive piece of reality. The limit of representation assumes the form of a transcendental surplus beyond phenomenality. For Hegel, however, the excess over representation does not present anything other than itself: it is pure negativity embodied in an object. The internal reflection of essence implies that the limit of phenomenality is not a fully constituted essence outside of phenomenality (since essence fails to constitute itself in an unmediated immediacy), but an internal blockage of representation that embodies the internal split of essence. The sublime object, therefore, hides nothing: it embodies the "determinate nothing" which is the failure of essence.

What concerns us the most here is that the *limits* of representation assume the form of *objects*. These are the objects that Žižek calls "object in subject."[59] The point is that the fields of subjectivity and objectivity are both constituted by the failure of representation. As Žižek argues, the positive condition of the constitution of the subject is the failure of its representation (the subject is the retroactive effect of the failure of its own representation) which also means that "the failure of representation is the only way of representing it adequately."[60] But this is precisely the alienating failure that must be already reflected within substance as the failure of the full constitution of objectivity. The failure of the full constitution of objectivity, however, is not external to its field, since it is always embodied by particular objects. Thus, the ideological constitution of the subject is impossible without certain objects that embody the very limits of representation. In this regard, Žižek speaks of three different types of objects, which correspond to the three basic orders of Lacanian theory (the real, the imaginary, and the symbolic). First, he speaks of the real as *object a*, the absent object (the Hitchcockian MacGuffin) which is pure semblance in that it is a void in the symbolic order. Second, we have the symbolic object characterized not by its absence but its presence as an object of exchange. This object embodies the lack in Other. Finally, Žižek discusses the imaginary objectification of the real in the form of an oppressive object that embodies enjoyment. Thus, his typology allows us to speak of the limits of representation in terms of objects that are themselves representations.

In spite of their differences, then, Laclau's theory of totality and Žižek's theory of ideology do have something in common: in both cases failed presentation (the lack in Being or the impossible self-constitution of essence) provides the negative ontological foundation for the institution of particular totalities by way of an excess that marks the internal limits of representation, and an impossible object stands in for an absent fullness. This also means that our earlier categories (normalcy, singularity, and excrescence) remain operational. When representation institutes itself in the form of a cut within the field of failed presentation, the exclusion of the singular terms leaves a trace in the field it makes possible: this trace is excrescence itself. In other words, if exclusion creates the possibility of the excess of representation over presentation, excrescence is the very effect of the exclusion of the singular. But the way to imagine this excess is not as some sort of a transcendental dimension, but rather as an internal torsion of representation. The split between presentation and representation institutes a totality which, in order to constitute itself as a totality, has to mark its own limits. In order to do so, it has to produce "pure representations" marking these limits. The problem of excrescence can be located on this level: the internal limit of representation assumes the form of a representation without presentation.

The common psychoanalytic foundation of Laclau's and Žižek's theories surfaces here. For isn't the best example of excrescence the Freudian Thing or the Lacanian object a? Imagine the ontological status of the lost object: as a *lost* object, it is without presentation (because it is lost forever); but as an object, it is still internal to the field of representation. This is why Laclau argues that the "logic of the *objet petit a* and the hegemonic logic are not just similar: they are simply identical. . . . The only possible totalizing horizon is given by a partiality (the hegemonic force) which assumes the representation of a mythical totality. In Lacanian terms: an object is elevated to the dignity of the Thing."[61] Using Laclau's terms, we could say that whatever is excluded from a particular hegemonic articulation appears from the perspective of this articulation as a singular term. In case some of these elements successfully enter the chain of equivalences composing this hegemonic articulation, they will become normal terms. They are both presented and represented in the sense that their identity is always split between their particularity and the hegemonic universality that counts them as one. Excrescence is the dimension of this mythical totality (the universality of the "one") which only exists by way of an internal fold of representation.

In order to draw some of the consequences of these points, let us return for a moment to Engels. We could say that when Engels identified the proletariat with singularity, the bourgeoisie with normalcy, and the State with excrescence, his mistake was that he did not recognize these categories as results of hegemonic articulations. To put it differently, we all know that "the proletariat" was not the only element excluded by the bourgeois state. Therefore, other singular entities must have been present in the situation besides the proletariat. But the fact that the proletariat could appear as the very embodiment of singularity meant that it assumed a hegemonic position. Similarly, we could argue that all three categories follow the same logic: the proletariat is one singular term that represents the universality of the excluded; the bourgeoisie is one normal category that represents the universality of the count (of normalcy); and the bourgeois State is one excrescent element that can represent the universality of the community (and represents excrescence as such). As Laclau argues, from the point of view of a hegemonic totality, one excluded element will have to assume the role of "pure negativity" (proletariat), while the system has to represent its own systematicity, "pure being" (the State).[62] Thus, we can always expect a similar threefold distribution of names (proletariat as pure negativity, bourgeoisie as being, the State as pure Being), since we could argue that the role of ideology is precisely the designation of these names in order to establish a particular totality.[63]

The Aesthetic Unconscious

So what can we conclude on the basis of these discussions? Most important, it was the history of "aesthetic ideology" that has revealed to us the necessity of a theoretical shift of perspectives: today, we must turn from popular discussions of the "political unconscious" to what we could call, without insisting on terminological orthodoxy, the "aesthetic unconscious."[64] This new category will allow us to question some of the most pervasive implications at the heart of the current uses of the "political unconscious": namely, that the unconscious *is* politics (rather than potentially politicized); that politics is always unconscious (rather than partially determined by the unconscious); and that politics and aesthetics can be clearly separated on the level of the unconscious (rather than forming an "originary knot").

The basic shortcoming of the concept of the "political unconscious" is that it assumes a clear separation of the aesthetic and the political and argues that the political dimension of aesthetic production is to be situated in one particular location. This assumption is only partially true. The problem is that it endorses the standard view of the aesthetic: since the aesthetic falsely believes that it is a pure apolitical field, its inalienable political dimension must be located in its unconscious. In case after case, discussions of the political unconscious prove that seemingly innocent aesthetic statements are in fact political. But they often fail to ask the other question: what if seemingly pure political statements are actually aesthetic? That is, the unconscious *of* the political itself (a different kind of political unconscious) can turn out to be aesthetic in nature. This claim, however, can hold water only if it refuses to be a mere reversal of the hierarchy. The deconstruction of the political unconscious implies that the aesthetic unconscious is not simply the secret aesthetic component of political statements; rather, it must designate the zone of indistinction in which the aesthetic and the political are both truly unconscious and not yet distinguishable.

It is in this sense that the concept of the aesthetic unconscious can be used to introduce at least two new dimensions to our discussions. On the one hand, it allows us to rethink the very concept of representation as a form of division. At the same time, however, it also allows us to move beyond Rancière's "distribution of the sensible," since we have found that this division consists of the exclusive-inclusion of the insensible within the field of representation. Thus, Badiou's ontology allows us to speak of the "distribution of the insensible" in terms of the institution of the field of representation over the terrain of failed presentation. As we have seen, in Badiou's system, the failure of presentation is the result of the operations of the unpresentable void. The unpresentable, therefore, accounts both for the failure of presentation and the necessity of representation (whose role it is to cover up the failure of presentation). The split between presentation and representation, in turn, defines the ontological foundations of the limits of representation. Yes, representation establishes the hegemonic universality of the "one" and therefore its primary function appears to be unification. But this is precisely the ideological effect of the one. What representation first accomplishes is a mere cut that divides the field of failed presentation and excludes certain elements with the intention of containing the void. The "distribution of the insensible" does not mean that representation can and will always be divided. It means that representation *is* first and foremost division.

In the language of psychoanalysis, this idea is best articulated by way of the concept of the *Vorstellungsrepräsentanz*: the very field of representation comes about through the exclusion of an element that stands in for the impossible Thing. Therefore, the *Vorstellungsrepräsentanz* constitutes representation from nothing (the Thing is lost forever), by standing in for this nothing (and not by substituting for something), which renders the repetition of this lost thing (which is nothing) possible. Representation is not the reproduction of a positive reality on another level, but rather the effect of the primary signification of the lack in being. Furthermore, based on Badiou's typology of being, what our discussion of Laclau and Žižek aimed to show was that the limits of representation are *internal* to representation. Or, to put it differently, the limits of representation are themselves representations. In other words, if there is nothing beyond the limits of representation, the effects of the exclusion that constitutes a given totality will have to appear inside the system. This is why we claimed that the distribution of ontological terms (normal, singular, and excrescent elements) will appear within the field of representation: the positions of their universality will be marked by names within the field of representation. These are the names that designate the constitutive limits of representation.

* * *

The following chapters will provide an extended examination of the way this theory of aesthetic ideology can be applied to a concrete historical situation: early Cold War America. Our central question will be the following: What is anti-Communist aesthetic ideology? As we have seen, this question immediately leads us to the problem of primary aesthetics. What we need to examine is the way the symbolic framework of American democracy had to be instituted so that "politics" and "art" (as autonomous fields) could immediately appear as expressions of the truth of anti-Communist ideology. The fundamental exclusion of anti-Communist ideology is, of course, directed against "the Communist." In other words, anti-Communist ideology establishes a field of social visibility in which particular entities can appear because "the Communist" assumed the role of pure negativity.

My thesis will be that this ideology marked the limits of representation by a set of clearly definable objects, which are the following: the world (totality), the secret (singularity), the enemy (normalcy), and the catastrophe (excrescence). The radical transformation of American politics after World War II led to its redefinition as a form of "world politics." The problem, however, was that this world could not be easily construed as a unity. We encounter here the inherent ambiguity of the term "world," which simultaneously means a particular ideological unit ("the free world") and the globe (which supposedly consisted of three worlds). In this sense, the ideological gambit of the Cold War was to simultaneously assert that although we live in one world, this world is divided into three worlds. The fields of normalcy, singularity, and excrescence had to be marked inside this new concept of totality. The problem is that none of these terms possesses an already given political value (that is, we cannot derive the political meaning of a term from the mere fact that it appears as a singular term in a given situation). Therefore, all three domains became terrains of political contestation.

The field of singularity (presented but not represented) became simultaneously the underworld of subversive conspiracies and the locale of the core of American identity. This is where the problem of secrecy enters our argument. Secrecy was defined by anti-Communist ideology as simultaneously dangerous yet necessary. On the one hand, secrecy was the dangerous "beyond" of American democracy, the domain of subversive conspiracies. At the same time, it also functioned as the guarantee of the very democratic framework and the exclusive domain of sovereign power. While the secret could be defined as what is presented but not represented, the ideological figure of the catastrophe functioned as what is represented but not presented. In other words, the new global concept of totality led to an ambiguous construct of universality that simultaneously promised "doom or deliverance": utter destruction or complete victory. In this sense, the image of the absolute catastrophe came to mark the condition of impossibility of the symbolic order as such. Finally, the enemy appeared on the level of normalcy in the crevices of the split between presentation and representation. A peculiarity of anti-Communist ideology was its obsessive concern with the problem of the simulacrum. The exclusion of the enemy from the field of representation had an ambiguous effect: if the enemy is capable of perfect imitation, it is impossible to tell the excluded element from normal elements.

Anti-Communist discussions of "art" followed a similar path. The visibility of true art depended on an exclusion. As is well known, one of the most striking features of the art criticism of the fifties was the politicized separation of highbrow, middlebrow, and lowbrow cultures. In other words, in order for true art to become visible, a set of divisions had to be introduced to the field of artistic practices. Once again, the success of the constitutive exclusion was threatened by the logic of the simulacrum: between art (high-modernism) and non-art (mass culture) the domain of the mere simulacrum of art (kitsch) appeared. While high art was often defined in excess of representation (as a transcendence of realistic representations), mass culture was habitually dismissed for being too "low" for current standards of representation. Although the middlebrow tried to lay claim to the proper field of representation by renouncing both of these extremes, it was nevertheless undermined by the threat of the simulacrum. Once again, the normal and its mere imitation became hard to tell apart. The following discussions will focus on the way the anti-Communist ideology of the "the vital center" articulated these two exclusions (the political exclusion of Communism from the proper field of politics and the aesthetic exclusion of mass culture from the field of art) as parts of the same political program.

2 /   Anti-Communist Politics and the Limits of Representation

Anti-Communist Politics

Any consideration of Cold War anti-Communism has to start with the acknowledgment that anti-Communist discourse, even in America, long predates the Cold War.[1] Although in Europe anti-Communist politics was already fully formed by the middle of the nineteenth century, in America it was the turn of the century that saw the full emergence of this kind of political discourse. The political attacks on undesirable radicals reached their first peak in the general reaction to anarchist violence and later in the persecution of the so-called Wobblies. But it was only in the wake of the Bolshevik Revolution that anti-Communism became a significant force in American politics. As Richard Gid Powers has argued, by the early 1920s the basic stereotypes of both the dangerous Communist and the conservative countersubversive infringing on the constitutional rights of innocent citizens were fully established.[2] The first Red Scare of 1919 and the Palmer Raids of 1920 are responsible for the former; the investigations of the illegal activities of the Justice Department pursuing subversives of all breeds, as detailed in Felix Frankfurter's *Lawyers' Report* (1920), are responsible for the latter.

Thus, the novelty of post–World War II American culture was not the mere existence of anti-Communist politics, but rather its position among the available political discourses. Through a conservative hegemonic articulation, this discourse became the central organizing principle of political culture.[3] It emerged from a series of potential discourses as the one that named the totality of legitimate political discourses for the organization of social order. By the 1950s, a political force that did not affiliate itself in one way or another with the cause of anti-Communism lost its legitimacy in the race for the wide-ranging support of the American people. And this is where the constitutive exclusion of this political field becomes clearly visible. The legitimate field of political opinions and actions was created by a double movement. On the one hand, the exclusion created the "universality" of the legitimate field (since anti-Communism by definition applied to all legitimate forces). On the other hand, everything that fell on the other side of this frontier was subjected to different forms of depoliticization and criminalization.

In spite of its central position, however, it would be a mistake to suppose that anti-Communist politics named a monolithic block that could be easily reduced to a unified political program. Taken at its most extreme formal generality, anti-Communist politics was without a concrete content. A whole spectrum of different political positions could be compatible with it. So it is important to emphasize that early Cold War politics in the United States was to a large extent a struggle *within* the anti-Communist community (rather than a conflict exclusively between anti-Communists and their opponents) for the very definition of the meaning of "anti-Communism." Since politics by definition had to take place within the register of anti-Communism, the strongest force within the field also had the power to influence the symbolic framework of politics by investing "anti-Communism" with a specific meaning.

For a long time, the consequences of this plurality of anti-Communisms have been all but ignored in historiography. Although today it might appear evident that "rather than a single anticommunism, there have been a multitude, with different objections to communism," the systematic analysis of these differences was not on the agenda until relatively recently.[4] One of the most consistent examinations of such a plurality was carried out by Richard Gid Powers, who described the struggle among anti-Communists in the following terms:

> During the five critical years between the end of World War II and the Korean War, anticommunists of all persuasion jostled for power: countersubversives, religious and ethnic anticommunists, liberals, and socialists. The anticommunist orthodoxy that emerged as the Cold War consensus combined the objectives of the liberal internationalist who dominated the foreign policy establishment with the ideas and values of liberal and left anticommunists. Excluded from this consensus, however, were those unmollified isolationist anticommunists still furious over being brown-smeared during the war by liberals allied with the progressive left. During the late forties, these

vengeful countersubversives were able to expand their base within the Republican party until, with the outbreak of the Korean war, they could push themselves to the center of American politics, to take revenge against the same liberal anticommunists who were the architects of the free world's defense against communism.[5]

This historical example illustrates a crucial theoretical point: the constitutive exclusion that establishes the universality of a legitimate political field does not fully determine the identity of this universality in a univocal manner. In other words, the exclusion creates a contested field of universality which forever remains the battlefield of competing political forces. Nevertheless, in order to give a recognizable schematic shape to this struggle, I will concentrate here on the two general poles identified by Powers: the political conflict between liberal orthodoxy (the co-called "Cold War liberalism") and its countersubversive opponents.

Cold War Anti-Communism

In order to better understand the ideological stakes of this conflict, three important historical changes have to be considered. First, the fact that America for the first time in its history found itself in an active, leading role in an international political theater implied a significant reversal: the primacy of foreign policy over domestic politics. This reversal turned anti-Communism into a truly global politics. Second, since participating in international politics meant an engagement in an enduring conflict on a global level, we witness during this period the consolidation of the militarization of American politics. The novelty of the Cold War was that, for the first time in its history, it redefined American anti-Communism as an actual *war*. And third, due to the peculiar nature of this militarization which assumed nontraditional forms, culture took upon itself a crucial political function. Since total war was equated with nuclear annihilation, the Cold War became also a war for the minds and hearts of people, that is, a *global cultural war*. Thus, anti-Communism established two competing paradigms: the (conservative) militarization of politics and the (liberal) aestheticization of politics.

As Daniel Bell has argued, one of the most important changes in American political culture during the postwar years was the institutionalization of the primacy of foreign policy over domestic policy. The reversal of political primacies, according to Bell, was a result of the peculiarly American phenomenon of "status anxiety" (since class antagonism is not really applicable to American society), which proved to be fertile ground for the "new threat" of extremist excesses: "These elements of moralism, populism, Americanism, and status anxieties achieved a peculiar congruence in the fifties because of the changed nature of American politics: the emergence of foreign policy as the chief problem of politics. The politics of the 1930's were almost entirely domestic, and the sharp political conflicts of that decade were around economic issues, and the divisions in interest-group terms."[6] This primacy of foreign policy meant that, at least in theory, all domestic issues had to be handled with an eye on the international threat of Communism, and in case of a conflict of interests, foreign policy decisions had to be given priority.

The primacy of foreign politics, however, also justified the militarization of American anti-Communism. Of course, as Michael S. Sherry reminded us, "militarization" was neither restricted to America nor was it exclusively a Cold War phenomenon. Following his analysis, we could say that the early phase of the Cold War witnessed the full institutionalization or, in his term, the "consolidation" of militarization, even if the process was not explicitly apparent to contemporary observers.[7] Sherry insists on this point: "Just as empire did not look imperial to most Americans, the militarized state did not look militaristic."[8] Taken in this broader sense, militarization does not imply a direct military coup d'état that forces martial law over a whole country. Rather, we have to understand this militarization as a *political logic* that defines the meaning of politics as doing war, and therefore subordinates all political issues to the exigencies of the Cold War. This is how the logic of war slowly eroded prior conceptions of politics.

In order to understand the nature of this militarization, however, it is important to note that recent historical scholarship has paid increasing attention to the "unconventional Cold War." For example, Gregory Mitrovich argued that "the Cold War struggle, particularly from 1948 to 1956, began as a true war between the two camps with one side destined to emerge victorious over the other. . . . It was a war fought, however, by non-military methods—psychological warfare and covert action."[9] Mitrovich provides here yet another formulation of the fundamental predicament of the Cold War: it is a war which cannot be fought as a traditional war. As a consequence, militarization itself had to proceed through nonmilitary methods and, therefore, primarily meant the extension of the logic of war to nonmilitary cultural terrains. The most important tool of this nonmilitary warfare was the notorious "psychological warfare" which, as Kenneth A. Osgood argued, "had become, in essence, a synonym for *Cold War.*"[10] Whatever other form this historical change might have assumed, what we need to remember is that at the same time politics entered the process of militarization, the very meaning of "war" also changed.

The conclusion we have to draw from this ambiguous extension of the meaning of military categories is that during the Cold War the very meanings of the terms "war," "politics," and "culture" have undergone important changes as they became increasingly difficult to separate.[11] As part of this nonconventional warfare, culture itself became a political weapon. From the perspective of American intellectual history, one of the most enduring historical documents of this transformation remains Lionel Trilling's *The Liberal Imagination*. In his preface, Trilling recorded the same historical change: "It is the wide sense of the word [politics] that is nowadays forced upon us, for clearly *it is no longer possible to think of politics except as the politics of culture*, the organization of human life toward some end or other, toward the modification of sentiments, which is to say the quality of human life."[12]

This redefinition of politics as a "politics of culture" calls attention to the fact that Cold War politics was not only a "politicization of culture" that appropriated cultural products for the cause of anti-Communism. In fact, what is more important is the reverse move: the politicization of culture was accompanied by a redefinition of politics according to an "aesthetic principle." It is here that Arthur Schlesinger's *The Vital Center* (1949) and Trilling's *The Liberal Imagination* (1950) emerge as complementary pieces involved in the same redefinition of liberal politics.[13] But while Schlesinger provides a political and historical analysis with strategic but only occasional references to art, Trilling's book is an exemplary case of literary criticism that moves toward political conclusions. In other words, Schlesinger's interest appears to be a certain "politicization of the aesthetic," while in Trilling's case we get an example of the reverse process, namely, the "aestheticization of politics." Schlesinger's interest in art does not explicitly go beyond the common observation that the repression of art is one of the most obvious symptoms of totalitarian politics. This is how the aesthetic becomes the touchstone of a free society: the correct political organization of the social will always allow the aesthetic field to develop according to its own laws. Contrary to the attempts of totalitarian systems, the purely aesthetic essence of art should not be reduced to a politics external to it. Nevertheless, for Schlesinger, the two fields (aesthetics and politics) still remain clearly separated fields.

In Trilling's book, however, we can easily trace the opposite movement, since he depicts artistic literary activity as the ultimate model of correct liberal political action. Trilling formulates the connection between politics and art in the following way:

> The job of criticism would seem to be, then, to recall liberalism to its first essential imagination of variousness and possibility, which implies the awareness of complexity and difficulty. To the carrying out of the job of criticizing the liberal imagination, literature

has a unique relevance, not merely because so much of modern literature has explicitly directed itself upon politics, but more impor-
tantly because literature is the human activity that takes the fullest
and most precise account of variousness, possibility, complexity, and
difficulty.[14]

The passage makes it clear that the redefinition of the liberal imagination (where "imagination" is to be understood in the strong sense as the
very constitution of the basic terrain of political activity on the level of an
imaginary horizon) is the primary political task of the moment. In the
background of this redefinition, we find the disillusionment of a whole
generation with 1930s leftist radicalism. At the same time, we can also
see that literature plays an essential role in the redefinition of the liberal
imagination. But—and this is the crucial point here—the role of literature
is not defined on the level of mimetic representation. Rather, we get here
a functional definition of literature. To put it differently, it is not a realist
aesthetics that can bring liberalism back from the other side of dangerous
illusions, but understanding politics as essentially a literary activity. And
not just any literary activity: Trilling's language also prescribes a concrete
aesthetic program to the degree that it speaks of "variousness, possibility,
complexity, and difficulty" as aesthetic values transcending naïve forms of
realism. Therefore, literature (defined on this functional level as a human
activity) becomes the ultimate model for correct liberal politics. For Trilling, literature is not simply a special case of political action—it is political
action par excellence.[15]

More important, however, Trilling derives the necessary aestheticization
of liberal politics from the constitutive paradox of liberal democracy: namely,
that it wants to institute freedom by limiting it. This is why "imagination"
has to be understood as equivalent to the field of representation established
within the democratic framework. As Trilling explains, the necessary self-
criticism of liberal politics is based on the following insight: "So that when
we come to look at liberalism in a critical spirit, we have to expect that there
will be a discrepancy between what I have called the primal imagination
of liberalism and its present particular manifestations."[16] The source of the
paradox is the irreducible difference between the primal imagination and its
particular manifestations: "Its characteristic paradox appears again . . . for
in the very interests of its general primal act of imagination by which it
establishes its essence and existence—in the interests, that is, of its vision of
a general enlargement of freedom and rational direction of human life—it
drifts toward a denial of the emotions and the imagination."[17]

It appears then that the function of criticism and literature is to "liberate"
the liberal imagination from its self-imposed limitations by reactivating its

primal imagination. Politics, therefore, is necessarily aesthetic in nature, since it must reactivate the primal imagination in order to reconsider the limits of a given field of representation from the perspective of the original institution of the democratic framework. But if the constitutive paradox of liberal democracy is that it institutes freedom by limiting it, the function of this aestheticization of politics is to guarantee that the limit remains always displaceable. Rather than a simple given, this limit must be an object of interpretation. The aesthetic critique of liberal politics proposed by Trilling automatically leads to the conclusion that liberalism can be truly liberal only if it is auto-critique. To put it differently, liberalism must first and foremost be a critique of liberalism itself.

Thus, we can articulate here some of the basic coordinates of early Cold War anti-Communism. As a first step, anti-Communism had to be elevated to the level of the signifier that names the totality of legitimate political opinions. This articulation created the field within which politics as such could take place. But within this field we witness the interaction of two different political logics: the militarization and the aestheticization of politics. The first attempts to define the essence of politics as participating in a paradoxical war that must proceed through nontraditional means. The second defines the essence of politics as an aesthetic activity concerned with the very institution of a field of representation. The two logics, as we can see, are not always easy to separate, but they were clearly based on different definitions of "representation." The analysis of this conflict between the two definitions will allow us to account for the crisis of representation characteristic of Cold War anti-Communism.

The Cold War and the Crisis of Representation

As Ernesto Laclau argues, we always find a "crisis of representation" at the root of a populist outbreak.[18] A crisis of representation, however, can assume two different forms: it can either be the local crisis of a particular demand that finds no institutional representation; or it can be the crisis of the very principle of representation that established a particular field of social visibility. In the first case we assume that the lack of representation can be corrected without endangering the symbolic framework of representation; in the second case, we face a more radical crisis that threatens this symbolic framework itself. In other words, whereas in the first case certain elements from the other side of the antagonistic internal social frontier threaten to penetrate the field from which they were excluded, in the second case the emergence of a heterogeneous element threatens the field of representation as such. In the early Cold War context, the first kind of crisis corresponds to the internal conflicts of Western democracy;

the latter—more radical—form of crisis is represented by the menace of Communism.

In order to examine the crisis of political representation, we have to emphasize that the very figure of the "Cold War" refers to a "permanent crisis." The paradoxical logic of militarization was fully dependent on a crisis that was "permanent" not because it would never end, but because this militarization sustained itself by maintaining a permanent state of exception.[19] To put it differently, the crisis is not permanent *de facto* but *de jure*. It lasts precisely as long as the politics that aims to solve it is maintained. In other words, while the Cold War is often defined as a crisis of certain democratic institutions, it was in fact also the very institutionalization of the rhetoric of crisis. Giorgio Agamben argued that twentieth-century totalitarianism introduced the logic of the permanent state of emergency into politics: "modern totalitarianism can be defined as the establishment, by means of the state of exception, of a legal civil war that allows for the physical elimination not only of political adversaries but of entire categories of citizens who for some reason cannot be integrated into the political system. Since then, the voluntary creation of a permanent state of emergency (though perhaps not declared in the technical sense) has become one of the essential practices of contemporary states, including so-called democracies."[20] In the present context, we should add to Agamben's analysis that one of the most important steps in the institutionalization of the "permanent state of exception" within the framework of democracy occurred precisely in response to the Cold War. For the latter is a permanent crisis which defines itself as a war on the level of international politics, while on the domestic front it assumes the form of a "legal civil war."

One of the most striking features of early Cold War historical documents is the unremitting pervasiveness of a rhetoric of global crisis. In the somewhat melodramatic language of Whittaker Chambers—the Communist defector whose autobiography became one of the classics of anti-Communist literature—this was a "total crisis":

> The world has reached that turning point by the steep stages of a crisis mounting for generations. . . . The last war simplified the balance of political forces in the world by reducing them to two. . . . All the politics of our time, including the politics of war, will be the politics of this crisis.
>
> Few men are so dull that they do not know that the crisis exists and that it threatens their lives at every point. It is popular to call it a social crisis. It is in fact a total crisis—religious, moral, intellectual, social, political, economic. It is popular to call it the crisis of the Western world. It is in fact a crisis of the whole world. Communism,

which claims to be a solution of the crisis, is itself a symptom and an irritant of the crisis.[21]

If we follow Chambers, we have to conclude that "total crisis" really means that everything partakes of the same historical crisis: in other words, crisis defines the norm of this new historical era. First, politics itself is identified as a management of this universal crisis which is even more primary than the logic of war. Then, the crisis is defined as being total both in the sense that it involves all spheres of human activity and in the sense that it affects the whole globe. The role of anti-Communism is clarified when Chambers calls Communism a symptom of this crisis: while Communism embodies this crisis precisely as a symptomatic false solution to it, anti-Communism is going to be a politics of this crisis by waging war on its symptom.

In fact, Arthur Schlesinger was also quick to point out that the Cold War is essentially a "permanent crisis."[22] He argued, however, that the ideological conflict between Communism and capitalism is not the cause of this crisis: "The crisis of free society has assumed the form of international collisions between democracies and the totalitarian powers; but this fact should not blind us to the fact that *in its essence this crisis is internal.*"[23] This time the crisis is permanent and internal. Schlesinger argues that the dilemma of the "age of anxiety" is based on a historically determined existential predicament. This historical determination, however, is not the conflict known as the Cold War, but the much broader history of industrialization: the internal crises of modernity as such. In fact, the United States and the Soviet Union were both products of this history. In Schlesinger's own terms, the "dilemma" of history must be distinguished from the "problem."[24] He calls the dilemma the fact that "man today must organize beyond his moral and emotional means" and "this basic dilemma projects itself to us in the middle of the twentieth century in terms of the conflict between the United States and the Soviet Union."[25] Schlesinger then explains the relation of the dilemma and the problem in the following terms:

> The USA, the USSR, the strength of industrialism and the weakness of man cannot be evaded; they make up the problem; and there is no point, in General Marshall's phrase, in "fighting the problem." We must understand that the terms of the problem do not exhaust the dilemma of history; but we must understand equally that men in the middle of the twentieth century can strike at the dilemma of history only in terms of the problem.[26]

Chambers and Schlesinger demonstrate here an important aspect of anti-Communist politics. As a first step, they both historicize the crisis and therefore include the politics of anti-Communism in a wider historical and political framework. Unlike more unregenerate anti-Communists, they both claim that the crisis cannot be reduced to the Communist threat. Schlesinger insists on this point: "[The United States and the Soviet Union] are not the cause of the tensions. Nor does either nation have the secret of their solution. Nor will the destruction of one by the other usher in utopia."[27] Thus, as Communism is displaced from being a cause to being a symptom of the crisis, Schlesinger effectively claims that fighting the symptom (problem) will not lead to utopia (a solution to the dilemma). Nevertheless, Schlesinger's claim does not fully reject the politics of the symptom. It is very important that he claims that "men in the middle of the twentieth century can strike at the dilemma of history *only* in terms of the problem." This exclusive position of the problem recasts the politics of the center as a more enlightened version of the politics of the symptom. Although anti-Communism as an end in itself is rejected, it is legitimized as a means toward a more comprehensive end, since it is the only legitimate means.

If we consider this crisis in more concrete terms as it relates to the everyday experience of politics, we could borrow a term from Timothy Melley, calling it an "agency crisis."[28] The general awareness of crisis simply recorded the effects of a number of historical transformations that affected the very structure of political life. The sudden "globalization" of politics through Cold War anti-Communism led to the conclusion that traditional models of political behavior were no longer viable. Schlesinger, for example, speaks of "new ambiguities": "Left and right were adequate to the political simplicities of the nineteenth century, when the right meant those who wished to preserve the existing order and the left meant those who wished to change it. But the twentieth century, here as elsewhere, introduced new ambiguities."[29] Similarly, C. Wright Mills opens *The Power Elite* (1956) with the diagnosis that today ordinary men "often seem driven by forces they can neither understand nor govern" and therefore they feel that "they are without purpose in an epoch in which they are without power."[30]

But one of the most compelling accounts of this crisis is to be found in David Riesman's *The Lonely Crowd* (1950). In Riesman's analysis, the historical shift from "inner directed" to "other directed" personality also leads to an experience of the "incomprehensibility of politics."[31] According to his nostalgic construction, during the nineteenth century "men were masters of their politics," which constituted "a comparatively well-defined and indeed often over-defined and constricted sphere."[32] But as Riesman hastens to add:

Politics today refuses to fit into its nineteenth-century compartment. With the mass media behind it, it invades the privacy of the citizen with its noise and claims. This invasion destroys the older, easy transitions from individual to local, local to national, and national to international interests and plunges the individual directly into the complexities of world politics, without any clear-cut notion of where his interests lie.

At the same time politics becomes more difficult to understand in a purely technical sense, partly because it invades previously semi-independent spheres like economics, partly because of the growing scope and interdependence of political decisions. . . . The incomprehensibility of politics gains momentum not only from the increase in its objective complexity but from what is in some respects a drop in the general level of skills relevant to understanding what goes on in politics.[33]

Riesman very clearly registers here the crisis as the result of the historical transformation of politics. What is striking about these lines is that they depict this new experience of politics as being simultaneously *compulsory* and *incomprehensible*. According to this description, a new experience is forced upon the individual that remains alien to his or her traditional sphere of experience. As the mass media invade the privacy of the citizen, politics is forced upon the individual against his or her will. Politics is no longer contained in its proper public space. It overflows these boundaries and threatens to demand the whole life of the individual. But then we also learn that this experience is incomprehensible partly because Cold War politics dissolves the traditional differences between the local and the global. In the Cold War, to do politics means participating in global anti-Communism. The transition from "individual to local, local to national, and national to international" level is too quick, because the primacy of foreign policy demands that every political act contain a certain universal anti-Communist component whose content must be derived from the global situation. Therefore, "incomprehensibility" also registers the discontent that it is not always clear how local interests are being represented in the politics of global anti-Communism.

Following Frederick M. Dolan's suggestion, we could call the politicized split between essence and appearance that underlies the experience of the incomprehensibility of politics "Cold War metaphysics."[34] According to Dolan, this metaphysics introduces into the discourse of politics a radical break between reality and deceptive appearance. Politics is therefore organized by a general fear of simulation that is used by both extremes of the political spectrum: "The right-wing articulation of simulation as fear of communism, and the left-wing articulation of simulation as fear of consumer capitalism, are equally workable (or unworkable) attempts to think, judge, and protest the transition to a society of sheer artifice, where the model, as in Baudrillard's influential formulation, not the original, is the only source of authority."[35] Simulation is thus the generalized name given to the crisis of representation that is supposed to be solved by politics.[36] But the interesting thing about simulation is that it is not a crisis of representation because of a lack of representation (according to which someone's interests are not being represented). The case is precisely the opposite: simulation is an excess of representation which misrepresents the represented (and threatens to do away with it altogether). The ideological concern of anti-Communist politics is precisely the restoration of "representation" to its original function. If the crisis is that of representation, the task is to define the proper limits of representation against both harmful extremes: the lack of representation (which is undemocratic and leads to social discontent) and the excess of representation (which is a deceitful practice pursued by the enemies of democracy).

To illustrate these points, we could refer here to the locus classicus of the anxiety concerning the split between essence and appearance and the subsequent "unreadability" of the enemy: Jack Finney's 1955 novel *The Invasion of the Body Snatchers*. Dr. Miles Bennell returns to his hometown of Santa Mira, California, only to find that an alien race invaded the town and systematically and conspiratorially replaced people by their exact replicas. One of the first encounters with the dubious signs of alien invasion is described to us when Bennell is called to the house of a friend who is convinced that her Uncle Ira is not really Uncle Ira:

> Wilma sat staring at me, eyes intense. "I've been waiting for you today," she whispered. "Waiting till he'd get a haircut, and he finally did." Again she leaned toward me, eyes big, her voice a hissing whisper. "There's a little scar on the back of Ira's neck; he had a boil there once, and your father lanced it. You can't see the scar," she whispered, "when he needs a haircut. But when his neck is shaved, you can. Well, today—I've been waiting for this!—today he got a haircut—"
>
> I sat forward, suddenly excited. "And the scar's gone? You mean—"
>
> "No!" she said, almost indignantly, eyes flashing. "It's *there*—the scar—exactly like Uncle Ira's!"[37]

Wilma's indignation is just. Why would an intelligent doctor like Dr. Miles Bennell still hold on to such an outmoded model of deception? Bennell's anticipation of the missing scar is a sign of a traditional conception of "identity theft" (he anticipates imperfect imitation as sign of deception)—but what the whole story and Wilma's indignation tell us is that this new form of deception (perfect imitation) is so effective precisely because of the old-fashioned reading of the signs of deception. Dr. Bennell starts with the assumption that if the signs are wrong, then identity must also be problematic. Wilma, however, proceeds the other way around: if identity is wrong, even the right signs are problematic. Uncle Ira's scar is supposed to be the sign of ultimate authenticity. But in Wilma's reading it is precisely authenticity which makes the sign inauthentic: the uncanny moment is an excess of authenticity. The perfectly normal is rather suspicious.

One of the clearest examples of the way this crisis of representation figures in the discourse of Cold War anti-Communism can be found in J. Edgar Hoover's 1962 book *A Study of Communism* (see Figure 1). In its closing chapter, we find a diagram entitled "COMMUNIST FRONT ORGANIZATIONS" (resembling an upside-down genealogical family tree) explaining how the CPUSA exploits other organizations.[38] At the top of the picture we find the CPUSA, from which a line descends into thirteen different categories. Below the little box containing the CPUSA, we read "Main spheres of activity exploited by communist party in its front operations." The thirteen spheres are as follows (from left to right): education; civil rights; veterans; minority groups; youth; women; defense; press, radio, television, and motion pictures; peace movements; foreign born; culture; legislation; and labor. Three main categories can be distinguished in this list: social struggles, government functions, and culture/media. In other words, the three spheres of social existence depicted here include social demands, the institutions that are supposed to represent them, and the channels of communication between the two.

The position of the Communist Party in the picture is precisely that of the ideological "quilting point" which ties together all forms of social antagonisms. The basic assumption of the anti-Communist argument is that the Communists will exploit all forms of social discontent by penetrating organizations or treacherously promising the discontent to cater to their needs. But in reality, so the argument goes, the Communists really want to amplify all forms of social antagonism in order to weaken the unity of the nation. Therefore, the Communist becomes the very figure of antagonism as such. Thus, the diagram provides a reading strategy which is predicated upon the masterful deceit of Communists and allows us to project the ideological figure of the Communist behind all forms of social antagonism.[39] This is why the *exclusion* of the Communist becomes a form of *inclusion*: the act of exclusion establishes the field of politics; but the excluded element threatens to return in the form of a simulacrum.

We can again see that what is unique to the Cold War is not anti-Communist politics, but the fact that anti-Communism could be articulated as the essence of politics as such. If we use the terms provided by Hoover's figure, we can say that the meaning of this articulation is that the box

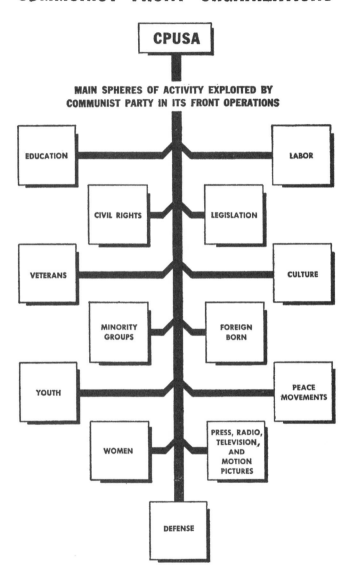

COMMUNIST FRONT ORGANIZATIONS

CPUSA

MAIN SPHERES OF ACTIVITY EXPLOITED BY
COMMUNIST PARTY IN ITS FRONT OPERATIONS

EDUCATION

LABOR

CIVIL RIGHTS

LEGISLATION

VETERANS

CULTURE

MINORITY GROUPS

FOREIGN BORN

YOUTH

PEACE MOVEMENTS

WOMEN

PRESS, RADIO, TELEVISION, AND MOTION PICTURES

DEFENSE

FIGURE 1. "Communist Front Organizations." In *A Study of Communism* by J. Edgar Hoover (New York: Holt, Rinehart and Winston, 1962), 170.

representing the CPUSA could be removed from the series of other political forces and elevated to the level of the element that names the general logic of the series of social struggles. The exclusion of a particular element establishes a field within which, in reference to the very act of exclusion, an articulated totality can emerge. Since the Communists will exploit every social struggle, there is no social struggle without a potential or unknown Communist content. This content, no matter how insignificant it might be, fully contaminates the identity of the given struggle, and reduces it to nothing but a Communist conspiratorial tool. On the other hand, if domestic politics entails a management of society, it requires a regulation of these social struggles. But if the identity of every single social struggle is supposed to be contaminated by Communism, every political act of social management, in turn, has to contain an anti-Communist element.

The logical conclusion is clear: there is no politics unless it is anti-Communist. The identity of both particular social struggles and particular governmental politics is necessarily split by this discourse: beside their particular content (racial, feminist, immigrant, cultural, etc.) social struggles contain a Communist invariable as their universal content; while every act of social management, beside their particular content, contains an anti-Communist universal content. Through the equivalence of the universal contents, this split establishes an internal social frontier that allows the populist discourse of anti-Communism to align two opposing forces, since social struggle equals Communism and legitimate politics equals anti-Communism. But what concerns us the most is that the figure of the Communist, by introducing an excess of representation, threatens the very democratic framework of representation, since the politics of deceit undermines the fundamental process of democracy, representation itself.

So it is important to point out that the diagram is an attempt to represent the agency that makes political representation impossible. In other words, Hoover provides his readers a certain "phenomenology" of political heterogeneity. Although the Communist Party must be excluded from the field of politics, the question behind the diagram is this: How does the excluded Communist (the enemy of the democratic principle of representation) nevertheless still appear within the normal system of representations? This strategy effectively achieves two significant things. On the one hand, it establishes a field of political visibility in the sense that, according to this diagram, what comprises the field of anti-Communist politics is the collection of representable entities that can be infiltrated by the Communist Party. To the degree that politics by definition has to be anti-Communist in the Cold War, the diagram defines the primary terrain of politics itself. By naming the little boxes, it effectively summons into being the very entities whose relations will define politics as a field of visibility. On the other hand, the diagram also establishes the phenomenology of the impossibility of representation in that it displaces a constitutive impossibility to the Communist threat. Hoover shows that the enemy basically saturates the whole field of political representation (or at least has the potential to do so) in a manner that makes it, strictly speaking, impossible to locate in one single spot. The enemy is truly dangerous because it does not appear as such within the field of representation, but disguises itself through the otherwise "normal" mechanisms of American democracy. The absurd logical consequence of this phenomenology of anti-Communist enmity, however, is that it opens up the possibility of the suspicion that the impossibility of representation appears as its very own opposite.[40] The worst enemy of democracy turns out to be democracy itself.

Anti-Communism and the Limits of Representation

The solution offered by anti-Communism to this crisis of representation was to set the proper limits of representation. The proper way of controlling the errant simulacrum was to contain legitimate representation within clearly defined boundaries. The logic of war legitimized restrictions on representation as it declared a state of exception, while the logic of aestheticization moved beyond the naïve political realism of representation and instituted a new kind of realism that moved beyond mere appearances. In spite of their political differences, however, both of these positions were clearly predicated upon the separation of representation from a domain beyond its legitimate limits. As the truth of anti-Communist politics named the totality of legitimate political positions, it was also responsible for setting the constitutive limits of such politics. Therefore, the limitation of representation had to proceed on two separate levels: as a first step, anti-Communism had to establish the very terrain within which politics could take place; and as a second step, within this political terrain the proper limits of political representation had to be drawn. This is exactly what we saw in Hoover's diagram: first it established the field of politics and then defined proper politics as a necessary limitation of representation in order to purge it of its harmful excesses.

Anti-Communist politics had to produce the kind of public knowledge that could legitimize this double move. This is why this kind of propaganda explicitly defined itself as the dissemination of a "necessary knowledge" about the Communist threat. One of the most often recurring motifs of the genre is George F. Kennan's proposition that "There is nothing as dangerous or as terrifying as the unknown."[41] In the introduction to his *Masters of Deceit*, Hoover calls this "a body of knowledge that we *dare not* be without."[42] In more sensational terms, Fred Schwarz opens his book,

You Can Trust the Communists, with the warning: "In the battle against Communism, there is no substitute for accurate, specific knowledge. Ignorance is evil and paralytic."[43] While W. Cleon Skousen charges that the "unbelievable success" of the Communist conspiracy is "the result of two species of ignorance—ignorance concerning the constitutional requirements needed to perpetuate freedom, and secondly, ignorance concerning the history, philosophy and strategy of World Communism."[44]

Hoover's expression, "the knowledge that we dare not be without," however, also displays the inevitable ambiguity of this anti-Communist knowledge, which proved to be a rather serious nuisance for architects of national security in the 1950s. The full sentence in the original clearly designates the limits of this knowledge as well: "Obviously this book does not pretend to disclose a body of material known exclusively to the FBI. What it does express is the hope that all of us may develop a shared body of rudimentary knowledge about communism: a body of knowledge *we dare* not be without."[45] There appears to be an implicit tension here between what is known exclusively by the FBI and the "rudimentary" nature of the public information. This was precisely the question that kept haunting anti-Communist politicians: Just how much knowledge is still beneficial and when does too much knowledge start working against the alleged goals of national security? While ignorance is no doubt evil, knowing too much can also be a serious liability. This complication concerning the right kind and correct amount of information to be made available to the American public is not just a theoretical exercise for the historian, it was a real problem for those involved in the fight against Communism. It is at this point that we touch upon an essential conflict within the so-called Cold War liberal consensus: although democratic politics implies an unconditional openness, the unquestionable imperative of national security might demand secrecy.

Consequently, the propagation of anti-Communist truth could not be equated with a simple production of a "necessary knowledge"—it had to be complemented with the creation of "necessary secrets" (or, as the renowned sociologist Edward Shils put it in 1956, "the necessary minimum of secrecy") and "necessary illusions" (to borrow a phrase from Reinhold Niebuhr, who eventually became the most prominent theologian of the Cold War).[46] In other words, anti-Communist propaganda had to define a certain field of proper knowledge, on the one hand, by reference to what always remains external to this field (the secret) and, on the other hand, what necessarily appears as an excessive element within this field (the illusion). In the following chapter, I will examine in detail the ideological figures used in the construction of these three separate fields.

3 /   The Enemy, the Secret, and the Catastrophe

Inventing the Cold War Enemy

The construction of this necessary anti-Communist knowledge was mostly driven by the ideological figure of the enemy, and it gave rise to what we could call the political theology of American nationalism in the Cold War. We are well accustomed to speaking of the structure of Cold War enmity as a highly moralized "Manichean" discourse that defines political conflict in terms of absolute good and absolute evil. This symmetrical opposition, however, was based on a crucial lack of symmetry. According to this asymmetrical definition of Cold War enmity, the fundamental conflict was not between two rival ideologies, but between an evil ideology and the neutralized universal concept of human nature and a generalized concept of freedom. For anti-Communist liberalism, "ideological politics" represented one of the most odious developments of modernity. Consequently, political opposition to Communism meant the rejection of ideology as such.[1]

The naturalization of anti-Communist politics, however, functioned as the foundation of the theologization of Cold War enmity. This move toward the religious register found an exemplary expression in Whittaker Chambers's sentimental account of his break with Communism. Chambers relates the story of a domestic conversion. As he is contemplating his daughter's delicate body, he deduces the existence of God from the complexity of his creation:

> One thing most ex-Communists could agree upon: they broke
> because they wanted to be free. They do not all mean the same thing

by "free." Freedom is a need of the soul, and nothing else. It is in striving toward God that the soul strives continually after a condition of freedom. *Political freedom, as the Western world has known it, is only a political reading of the Bible. Religion and freedom are indivisible.* . . . Hence every sincere break with Communism is religious experience, though the Communist fail to identify its true nature, though he fail to go to the end of the experience. His break is the political expression of the perpetual need of the soul whose first faint stirring he has felt within him, years, months or days before he breaks. A Communist breaks because he must choose at last between irreconcilable opposites—God or Man, Soul or Mind, Freedom or Communism.[2]

Chambers demonstrates a crucial aspect of early Cold War anti-Communism: for popular anti-Communism, freedom is a religious rather than a political concept. As freedom is transposed to the register of the "soul," it is depoliticized in the sense that it becomes the apolitical foundation of all correct politics.

It appears, then, that the political concept of truth is only the "expression" of religious truth in a specialized language. As a matter of fact, Chamber suggests that the agents of these political actions do not even have to know that they are participating in a "religious experience." Consciousness of the religious content of anti-Communist politics is not necessary for the propagation of its truth. This is why, discussing the "internal nature of Soviet power," George F. Kennan had to explain to his readers that, contrary to Western beliefs, for the Communists truth is a political concept: "This means that truth is not a constant but is actually created, for all intents and purposes, by the Soviet leaders themselves. It may vary from week to week, from month to month. It is nothing absolute and immutable—nothing which flows from objective reality."[3]

This distinction between a religious and a political definition of truth is essential, since anti-Communism fights Communist totalitarianism. As Hoover explains, "Communism wants the *total* man, hence it is *total*itarian."[4] In other words, the fallacy of totalitarianism is the total politicization of man and society. As opposed to totalitarianism, therefore, anti-Communism must find the legitimate boundaries of politicization, so that the totality of man or of society will never be completely politicized. And, partly for historical reasons, this is why the apolitical foundation of anti-Communism must be religion. Since Communism is an atheistic totalitarianism, as long as there is religion, the totalization of politics within society is impossible. The role of religion is precisely to provide an alternative politics, a logic of social organization that is not politics. But the question of legitimacy remains important. What could be the legitimate limits of democratic politics? How can you limit democracy in a democratic fashion? Or at least in a way that does not violate the spirit of democracy?

This theologized definition of political enmity, however, functioned as a source of two separate sources of cultural anxiety: imitation *by* the enemy and the imitation *of* the enemy. One of the central concerns of anti-Communist ideology is the negotiation of the contradiction between the two. In order to maintain ideological consistency, anti-Communism had to renounce not only the enemy but the methods of the enemy as well. A basic problem of anti-Communist politics had long been the fact that Communists use democracy in order to destroy it. As Hoover put it: "The Red Fascists have long followed the practice of making full use of democratic liberties: elections, lawful agitation and propaganda, and free speech, press, and assembly. Their basic premise: Reap every advantage possible. However, if it will help, don't hesitate to use illegal methods, such as underground operations, terrorism, espionage, sabotage, lying, cheating."[5] The problem is that Communists use the freedoms provided by a democratic society in order to reach totalitarian aims. The major method of this Communist pseudo-democratic take-over is the imitation of democratic ideals.

On the other hand, George F. Kennan warned his fellow policymakers of the Cold War in the following terms: "Finally, we must have courage and self-confidence to cling to our own methods and conceptions of human society. After all, the greatest danger that can befall us in coping with this problem of Soviet communism is that we shall allow ourselves to become like those with whom we are coping."[6] At the same time, Clinton Rossiter, discussing "constitutional dictatorship," spoke of American democracy during World War II in the following terms: "At the very moment when the people of the United States were shouting about the differences between democracy and dictatorship, they were admitting in practice the necessity of conforming their own government more closely to the dictatorial pattern! The wartime inadequacies of their constitutional government were remedied in most instances by an unconscious but nonetheless real imitation of the autocratic methods of their enemies."[7]

Rossiter's description calls attention to a significant complication: the conscious vilification of totalitarian politics can coincide with an unintentional but real imitation of the enemy. In a similar manner, while the fear of imitating the enemy was a genuine concern of the early Cold War, a number of later scholars came to see it as an ambiguous wish-fulfillment. In his classic 1963 essay, "The Paranoid Style in American Politics," Richard Hofstadter writes: "This enemy seems to be on many counts a projection of the self: both the ideal and the unacceptable aspects of the self are attributed to him. A fundamental paradox of the paranoid style is the imitation of the enemy."[8] In other words, within the paranoid mode, the imitation of the enemy is no longer a strategy to be avoided—it is actually unavoidable, since it is a structural paradox. Michael Rogin took this line of argument one step further when he argued that the demonology of countersubversion is not a marginal but a central component of American politics: "Countersubversive politics—in its Manichean division of the world; its war on local and partial loyalties; its attachment to secret, hierarchical orders; its invasiveness and fear of boundary invasion; its fascination with violence; and its desire to subordinate political variety to a dominant authority—imitates the subversion it attacks."[9] Thus, on the one hand, imitation by the enemy was defined as a limit of representation. It is a politics that undermines the apolitical presupposition of representative democracy itself and is supposedly the dark source of evil enjoyment. On the other hand, imitation of the enemy was imagined as a necessary limit of democratic politics itself. It was the democratic suspension of democratic politics that also functioned as a source of narcissistic wish-fulfillment. A central complication of early Cold War anti-Communism was precisely the fact that the preservation of the democratic framework by nondemocratic means coincides with the imitation of the totalitarian enemy.

The Russian Communist

As Peter H. Buckingham pointed out, during World War II the American government tried to encourage the public to accept the wartime alliance with Soviet Russia by disseminating a more positive image of this otherwise inimical nation. This strategy led to the coexistence of a general hostility toward domestic Communism and a more positive representation of Soviet Russia.[10] With the onset of the Cold War, however, this positive representation came to an abrupt end.[11] The Russians suddenly became the exact opposites of everything American.

In order to illustrate the way national identity comes to complement ideological enmity, let us briefly examine one of the most important documents of containment: Kennan's so-called "Long Telegram" from Moscow, February 22, 1946.[12] Kennan gives us a brief historical background for the paranoid-authoritarian nature of all Russian leaders. This is essentially the same narrative that will form an integral part of his famous Mr. X article, "The Sources of Soviet Conduct," published in *Foreign Affairs* in 1947. In the latter article, the argument is structured by the basic thesis that Soviet politics has to be understood on the basis of a double determination: one is historical, the other is ideological. This split allows Kennan to separate the Russian people, who are essentially good and "great," from their Soviet

Communist leaders. But Soviet ideology is understood by Kennan to be merely a "highly convenient rationalization" of the "Russian-Asiatic" historical experience.[13] In other words, ideology has a secondary function in relation to national identity, since the ultimate source of the political conflict is Russian *insecurity* as a national trait. In the words of the Long Telegram: "At the bottom of the Kremlin's neurotic view of world affairs is traditional and instinctive Russian sense of insecurity."[14]

As a result of this double determination (both historical and ideological), the Russian leader is depicted by Kennan as being by definition paranoid. This thesis is heavily underlined in the closing paragraph of the second section where everything, all hard facts, are dissolved in the Russians' paranoid political fantasies:

> Finally we have the unsolved mystery as to who, if anyone, in this great land actually receives accurate and unbiased information about outside world. In an atmosphere of Oriental secretiveness and conspiracy which pervades this Government, possibilities for distorting or poisoning sources and currents of information are infinite. The very disrespect of Russians for objective truth—indeed, their disbelief in its existence—leads them to view all stated facts as instruments for furtherance of one ulterior purpose or another. There is good reason to suspect that this Government is actually a conspiracy within a conspiracy; and I for one am reluctant to believe that Stalin himself receives anything like an objective picture of outside world. Here there is ample scope for the type of subtle intrigue at which Russians are past masters.[15]

The crucial point is that Kennan relies on a language that evokes Russian national identity. Thus, the religious foundations of truth in American politics can be opposed to the lack of truth in Russia as a national instinct, and this lack of objective truth is the source of a purely political definition of truth. Ultimately, *Soviet* politics is anchored in *Russian* national identity.

The potentially redemptive split between the Russian people and the Soviet leaders has to be interpreted in the same terms. Kennan insists on the difference and antagonism between the people and the leaders, and considers the split between the two to be one of the ultimate guarantees of the success of containment. But rather than a clear-cut separation of what is evil and what is good in Russian national identity, this division only leaves us with further contradictions: on the one hand, Russian national identity is the historical condition of Soviet politics; on the other hand, it is precisely the split between the Russian and the Soviet that is the basis of a successful anti-Communist politics.

After reading Kennan's telegram, one is tempted to ask: To what extent is the politics of containment dependent on a particular definition of Russian national identity? What is more dangerous to American national security, Russian national identity or Communism? The enemy in Kennan's narrative is explicitly pathologized as a paranoid/authoritarian personality. Since this pathological aberration is inscribed into a larger historical scheme, however, the Communist Russian is simply the contemporary manifestation of what forms the real problem. It seems as if the Russians would be at war with the Western world even without this particular totalitarian ideology, which simply provides them a "comfortable" dogmatic framework. So the real enemy is primarily the pathological national identity and not just the totalitarian ideology that it sustains.

Alan Nadel, who reads containment as a rhetorical and political strategy that attempts to overcome the internal contradictions of American culture by constructing a coherent national narrative, speaks of the "dual nature" of the Cold War enemy. Discussing Kennan's "psychological realism," Nadel writes:

> This unquestioned need to counter the Soviets motivates Kennan's analysis, one that shows this political analysand to be full of contradictions: flexible and intransigent, impetuous but patient; monomaniacal and monolithic but filled with enough hidden rivalries and disagreements to doom it; committed to ideology above pragmatics but also using ideology as a mere excuse for practical actions; part of the long-term political landscape but also likely to collapse with the first transition of power.[16]

What Nadel's analysis brings to light so precisely is the *overdetermination* of the figure of the enemy. Overdetermination, however, does not simply mean that one can keep hurling all imaginable insults at an unlucky scapegoat. As Nadel's words already indicate, the issue is that the "unquestioned need" to determine the enemy inevitably leads to an excess of determinations. Therefore, every attempt to ground this enmity in a discourse external to the actual antagonism (capitalism vs. Communism) produces inconsistencies. In Kennan's text, Russian national identity functions as such a nodal point of overdeterminations, since it becomes the name that, while not exempt from inconsistencies, "contains" all other contradictions by grounding them in an identity.

By way of a quick detour, let me briefly illustrate here the power of the image of the "Russian Communist" with an example taken from the other end of the political spectrum. National identity was equally important not only for the politics of containment but also for the American Communists who worked against it. In his autobiography, Whittaker Chambers narrates the curious fact that for a while people involved in the Washington apparatus of the Communist underground believed that Chambers was one of "them"—that is, that he was a Russian: "I do not remember whether the word Russian was actually used. But, if not, that was the unspoken word that made possible this strange self-deception. Carl [Chambers' underground pseudonym] was one of 'them.'"[17] Chambers argues that there is a necessary self-deception involved in the Communist conspiracy that allows the revolutionary to suffer the banality of dull conspiracy. The alienating nature of conspiracy can only be suffered if one maintains the illusion of authenticity—the conspirator needs to have direct access to the "subject supposed to know."

For example, this is how Chambers writes about Alger Hiss: "A curious kind of snobbery was playing a part in the delusion. Alger Hiss wanted to be one of those who were in direct touch with *the real revolution*, with the Workers' Fatherland. I sensed, too, that he felt more confidence in dealing with a Russian than he would have in dealing with the most trusted American Communist."[18] Let me quote Chambers at length because he gives us a very useful account of how to pass for a Russian:

> Word quickly spread through the underground that Carl was a Russian. . . . I myself quickly began to play the part assigned me. At first, it was amusing as any charade. Soon it became another of the underground nuisances. It was not difficult. The great thing was not to overdo it. I had only to appear, not as a man with an accent, but as a man who is trying to purge his voice of any trace of accent. In part, the illusion was possible because every language implies a special logic of thought. I had only, once in a while, to think out loud like a German, though in unaccented English, to create the effect. An occasional European intonation, perfectly natural to someone who speaks another language, and the trick of never saying Russia, or the Soviet Union, but always saying "home," completed the illusion. But in fact it was scarcely necessary for me to do anything at all. Once the idea had been fixed, it was less anything I did than what they wanted to believe that made the illusion possible. . . . [T]here was almost nothing that the underground Communists in Washington would not gladly do for me as a Russian.[19]

According to this account, revolutionary activity is authenticated by an act of self-deception that projects the figure of the "real revolution" onto the surface of Russian national identity. This self-deception is necessary for conspiratorial politics, since without such an illusion the revolution would appear in its naked reality as mere treason. In fact, the implication is that Chambers broke with Communism precisely because he managed to free himself from such illusions.[20]

As Chambers explains, since this self-deception is a "necessary illusion" for conspiratorial activities, his part in the deception was actually minimal. He simply had to provide the screen for the projection of an illusion. To do so, he did not have to imitate being a Russian, he had to imitate trying not to be a Russian. As the reference to "the trick of never saying Russia" illustrates, the most important element of the deception was actually creating the absent center of authenticity by avoiding all direct reference to Russia. In Chambers's performance, the center of authenticity must be either completely absent or only the traces of its obliteration must remain visible. This absence is necessary for the illusion, since it allows for the reversal of logic in this deception: "it was less anything I did than what they wanted to believe that made the illusion possible." Russian national identity thus becomes the screen of a wish fulfillment.

Discussing the strange world of conspiracy, Chambers adds: "This story will seem perfectly incredible to anyone who has had no experience of the underground and cannot imagine its strange atmosphere and emotions."[21] He seems to suggest here that it might be strange for outsiders to realize the extent to which the reality of conspiracy is sustained by fantasy. Of course, what is missing here is the reverse, a discussion of how the fantasy of conspiracy sustains the reality of anti-Communist ideology: that is, when Chambers appears in public as a Communist defector, he is actually playing a role similar to the one played by "Carl" as the Russian. In both cases, as a Russian Communist and as a patriotic ex-Communist, Chambers found himself in the position of the guarantor of authenticity. As his comments about Hiss demonstrate, the reality of the "revolution" is unbearable without the fantasy of the "real revolution." But the fight against Communism is equally unbearable without the fantasy of "the real conspiracy."

Thus, in both Kennan's and Chambers's case, we see that political enmity has to be propped up by a certain fantasy of national identity that authenticates the political opposition. In the case of the political and ideological conflict between the Soviet Union and the United States, the cause of enmity was displaced from the ideological to the national terrain. In the case of conspiracy, however, the "real revolution" was removed from the here and now (the mundane, unexciting revolution) to an elsewhere signified by Russian national identity. Due to the asymmetrical definition of enmity, the conflict of the Cold War is not ideological but "natural," since ideology is opposed to the apolitical essence of man. National identity naturalizes the ideological and political conflicts, since according to this definition the Russian and the American cannot help but be enemies. At this point, it becomes clear that the purely ideological definition of enmity (Communists against capitalists) was instable, since the figure of the enemy was overdetermined and carried a number of different and contradictory traits.

The Domestic Communist

But if the representation of ideological enmity relies on a nationalist supplement, the figure of the "domestic Communist" comes to indicate an internal complication of this nationalism. For the very existence of the domestic Communist provoked a disturbing question: How is it possible for an American to become un-American? What is it in American identity that makes such a conversion possible? Why isn't an American an anti-Communist by nature? Hoover essentially reduces the figure of the "American Communist" to a contradiction in terms when he writes: "*Communists are not American.* The Communist Party, USA, endeavors, in every possible way, to convince this country that it is American. . . . Communism stands for everything America abhors: slave camps, rigged elections, purges, dictatorship."[22] On a practical level, the basis of this claim is, of course, the fact that every single Communist is supposed to follow the party line set down in Moscow. Therefore, every single Communist is a Soviet agent and not a loyal American citizen. On a more abstract level, however, Hoover also posits an incompatibility between Communist and American ideals which indicates that "being American" is not merely a fact of citizenship but an active participation in a set of shared ideas. Therefore, national identity implies a necessary ideological identification that is independent from the mere fact of citizenship. While in the case of the constitution of the "Russian Communist" political ideology needed a national supplement, this time national identity is in need of an ideological supplement.

In his *I Led Three Lives: Citizen, "Communist", Counterspy* (first published in 1952 and soon turned into a television show that ran between 1953 and 1956), Herbert Philbrick, commenting on his experiences as he is drawn further into the Communist organizations that he is trying to penetrate for the FBI, writes the following:

> But the most difficult task facing me was also the most essential. . . . Where communism is concerned, there is no one who can be trusted. Anyone can be a Communist. Anyone can suddenly appear in a meeting as a Communist party member—close friend, brother, employee or even employer, leading citizen, trusted public servant. Now I could understand the instructions of the party leaders when I first joined: "Your membership will be secret. . . . Don't separate yourself from the masses. . . . Maintain your normal ties and lead a

perfectly normal life." Anyone can do that, I reflected. No one is safe. No one can be trusted. There is no way to distinguish a Communist from a non-Communist.[23]

Philbrick's amazement here is, of course, an explicit expression of the general anxiety concerning the legibility of the enemy. The shocking discovery is that the most trusted people can turn out to be Communists: "close friend, brother, employee or even employer, leading citizen, trusted public servant." Communism infiltrates the private sphere (friends and family) as well as the public sphere (work and politics). The impossibility of "distinguish[ing] a Communist from a non-Communist" rests upon a perfect imitation of a "perfectly normal life." But, since the perfectly normal can always turn out to be abnormal, and the perfectly American may reveal itself to be wholly un-American, we encounter here a limit of American identity itself.

As contemporary sociologists worried, and we could cite here Riesman's *The Lonely Crowd* as a primary example, perfectly normal American life might itself be a performance or simply an "imitation of life."[24] On the basis of Riesman's study, one could conclude that if the norm itself is a performance, as in the case of the "other-directed" personality, this lack of essence marks a limit of the very norm itself. There must be a *necessary* imitation of the norm (the American way of life) which is essential to maintaining the norm itself. This imitation, however, should be distinguished from an evil imitation that is simply infiltration. Nevertheless, in this context imitation itself emerges as the instance that makes American life possible, but it also makes infiltration by the enemy possible. In other words, we encounter here two different displacements of an internal antagonism: while the Russian Communist functions as an external obstacle to the American way of life, the domestic Communist represents a limit that inhibits American identity and threatens it from the inside.

We have already discussed the important role Russian national identity played in Kennan's definition of containment. Let us now briefly examine his views on American national identity as they relate to the very same policies. In spite of his famously optimistic conclusion to his Mr. X. article which celebrated the Cold War as a providential chance for America to prove herself to be worthy of her destiny, Kennan himself had a rather harsh judgment on contemporary America.[25] In one of the chapters of his memoirs, entitled "Re-encounter with America," Kennan describes a few of his trips through the country after 1950.[26] Having lived his whole life in diplomatic isolation from the realities of everyday America, the experience proved to be a disturbing revelation. Kennan describes three separate trips: one was a train ride from Washington D. C. to Mexico City (a trip that he repeatedly refers to as "a trip to Latin America"); the other was a trip to Chicago where he delivered his lectures later collected in *American Diplomacy 1900–1950*; while the third trip took him to Southern California.[27] For Kennan, the three destinations—Latin America, the Middle West, and California—form the basic locales of a symbolic topography of the fate of the United States. While the mid-West is supposedly the source of genuine American character, its failings give way to a certain "Californization" of the American way of life, which eventually threatens to lead to the "Latin Americanization" of American democracy.

Describing his trip to Chicago, Kennan quotes his diary at length and narrates the events of a day when practically at every corner in the city another disappointment ambushed him: "So I shuffled back to the hotel, in the depression born of hunger plus an overpowering sense of lack of confidence in my surroundings; and a small inward voice said, gleefully and melodramatically: 'You have despaired of yourself; now despair of your country!'"[28] The depressing experience, however, is framed by an apologetic ode to his native region:

> I believed then deeply in the Middle West, and I still do—in its essential decency, its moral earnestness, its latent emotional freshness. I viewed it, and view it now, as the heart of the moral strength of the United States. This was precisely why I was so sensitive to its imperfections. Increasingly, under the impressions of this and other visits in midcentury, I came to see this native region as a great slatternly mother, sterile when left to herself, yet immensely fruitful and creative when touched by anything outside herself.[29]

The failures of the moral center of America are exacerbated by the cultural tendencies already clearly at work in California, which Kennan considered to be just like "the rest of America, but sooner and more so."[30] His final judgment is clear: "In this sense, Southern California, together with all that tendency of American life which it typifies, is childhood without the promise of maturity."[31] At the same time, Kennan speaks of a "'latinization' of political life": "Southern California will become politically, as it already is climatically, a Latin American country. And if any democracy survives it will be, as in Latin America, a romantic-Garibaldi type of democracy, founded on the interaction of an emotional populace and a stirring, heroic type of popular leader." Contemplating the prospect of such a cultural transformation, Kennan asks: "Will it not operate to subvert our basic political tradition? And if so, what will happen to our whole urbanized, industrialized society, so vulnerable to regimentation and centralized control?"[32] The unspoken conclusion is that totalitarianism might actually be the direct outcome of the internal development of American identity.

Thus, Kennan's reflections on Russian and American identity both foundered on the same stumbling block: overdetermination. Due to the inherent split in this anti-Communist discourse between national and ideological determinations, the "dual nature" of the enemy had to be complemented by the "dual nature" of America itself. The attempt to derive the truth of anti-Communism from the mere (pre-ideological) fact of national identity repeatedly ran into the necessity of giving an ideological content to this national identity. As a result, while foreign policy demanded an unequivocally and exuberantly positive image of national identity, domestic politics increasingly relied on the rhetoric of crisis that was seriously aggravated by the moral and social failures of American society.[33]

The Third World Communist

Discussions of the category of race in Cold War studies tend to endorse one of two extreme positions. Some argue that the requirements of Cold War foreign policy actually had a positive effect on domestic race relations, as the Cold War accelerated the civil rights movement by providing an international (rather than a strictly domestic) framework that could be used to force the United States government simultaneously to preach and practice democracy.[34] At the same time, others claim the opposite, emphasizing the fact that the Cold War institutionalized an environment hostile to any kind of social change and, therefore, it had a detrimental effect on domestic race relations.[35]

In order to illustrate the logic behind these two positions, I will quote two contemporaneous statements. The first is by Albert Canwell, chairman of the Washington State Legislative Fact-Finding Committee on Un-American Activities, which illustrates how the externalization of racial conflict through its projection onto the Communist threat can stifle social demands: "If someone insists that there is discrimination against Negroes in this country, or that there is inequality of wealth, there is every reason to believe that person is a Communist."[36] In other words, as we have seen in the previous chapter, the interests of African Americans will not be represented, since the Communist enemy has managed to turn the very process of representation into the enemy of democracy (and, therefore, representing those interests would actually mean representing Communist interests).

On the other hand, the logic of the "externalization" of racial conflict found another surface of inscription: the anti-colonial struggles of Third World countries. For example, civil rights activist Charles Hamilton Houston argued that "a national policy of the U. S. which permits the disfranchisement of colored people in the South is just as much an international issue as the question of free elections in Poland or the denial of domestic rights in Franco Spain."[37] In other words, institutional racism within the United States is in direct conflict with the ideology that legitimizes American foreign policy. But Houston's statement shows that the internationalization of the problem of racism can also mobilize the rhetoric of international anti-Communism: the inclusion of race in an international rather than a merely domestic political agenda also made it possible to turn racial reform into a chief necessity of the anti-Communist cause. Thus, while on the domestic scene the problem of racial oppression could be neutralized by anti-Communist politics, on the international scene it had to be one of the prime causes championed by anti-Communism.

My central concern here is that "race" emerges in this context as the category that problematizes the very division of foreign and domestic politics. The question whether race was primarily an issue of domestic or foreign policy was itself turned into a political question. To be more precise, the category of race entered the field of politics in the 1940s not only as a controversial issue, but also as the category in which domestic and foreign policy *justified by the same political ideology* (that is, anti-Communism) actually ended up contradicting each other.[38] The question of racial equality, thus, caused an internal split within anti-Communist discourse: on the one hand, the suppression of the civil rights movement could be perceived by some (especially Southern Democrats) as serving the cause of anti-Communism by maintaining internal order; on the other hand, an increasing number of State Department employees concluded that it was precisely an end to segregation that served the cause of anti-Communism in an international struggle for the hearts and minds of a world whose population was about two-thirds "colored."

At the heart of this contradiction we find the problem of "national sovereignty" in an increasingly "globalized" politics: while the United States waged war in the name of a universalized concept of freedom (whose political equivalent was democracy), this very "universality" came to threaten the particularity of American national identity. On the one hand, in this new global environment domestic and foreign affairs are no longer clearly separable, but the principle of reorganization of their relationship still demands the primacy of the foreign over the domestic. On the other hand, according to the logic of a certain American "exceptionalism," the United States could remain an exception to the very rule it strove to establish as an international order founded on the universal concept of human freedom.[39]

Thus, in the early Cold War context, the civil rights movement was a success to the degree that it could inscribe its goals within a broader anti-Communist framework. This inscription of domestic race relations in an anti-Communist foreign policy, however, was not without its

consequences: the gain on the domestic front was paid for by a loss in foreign policy. In order to critique domestic relations, foreign policy (and its
primacy) had to be affirmed: internal reform was achieved by renouncing
critical attitudes toward American foreign policy. As Penny von Eschen
argued, the internationalization of racial struggle was endemic to African-
American politics long before the Cold War. By the 1940s, an important
link was established between the anti-colonial movements of the world and
the struggles of African Americans. But the successful inscription of the
category of race in anti-Communist foreign policy, as von Eschen claims,
resulted in a "domestication" of anticolonialism.[40] Although anticolonialism was still the official program of the U.S. government, it had to assume
the only legitimate form: it was acceptable anticolonialism only when it
restricted all political choices to the bipolar division of power characteristic of the Cold War.

We have to interpret anti-Communist politics as it relates to the Third
World in this particular context. The orchestrated effort at managing information was so much the more interesting, as it veiled a negative assessment
of the international political situation. Kennan, for example, held a rather
pessimistic view of American prospects in Asia. In a 1948 Policy Planning
Staff document (PPS 23), he wrote: "It is urgently necessary that we recognize our own limitations as a moral and ideological force among Asiatic
peoples."[41] In relation to Asia, Kennan renounced all "idealistic slogans"
and recommended that the United States deal with Asia in "straight power
concepts" and restrict American involvement to military and economic
influence. As Kennan observed, "we have about 50% of the world's wealth
but only 6.3% of its population," a situation that inevitably leads to "envy
and resentment."[42] But what the political realism of containment demands
is precisely the maintenance of this disparity:

> Our real task in the coming period is to devise a pattern of relation-
> ships which will permit us to maintain this position of disparity
> without positive detriment to our national security. To do so, we will
> have to dispense with all sentimentality and day-dreaming; and our
> attention will have to be concentrated everywhere on our immediate
> national objectives. We need not deceive ourselves that we can afford
> today the luxury of altruism and world-benefaction.[43]

What concerns us most in the negative assessment of the fate of Asia is
that, just like the dual determination of the sources of Soviet Communism
(ideological and historical) that anchored enmity in a national identity, the
political prospects of Asia were anchored in an "Asiatic" identity. In NSC
34, for example, we read the following assessment of the fate of China:
"The political alternatives which this vicious cycle will permit for China's

future are chaos or authoritarianism. Democracy cannot take root in so harsh an environment."[44] Due to historical and national traditions, the two imaginable political alternatives in Asia are either absolute lack of order (chaos) or absolute authority (totalitarianism). The third option, democracy, is understood to be impossible to implement: under the present circumstances, it is simply not a realistic option.

But the impossibility of Asian democracy is not only an unfortunate coincidence of conditions. It is actually part of Asian character: "In estimating the degree of political pressure that the USSR may exert from its present position in Asia, it should be remembered that its proteges deal with Asiatic peoples who are traditionally submissive to power when effectively applied and habituated to authoritarian government and the suppression of the individual."[45] In PPS 39/1, his elaboration of the conclusions of NSC 34, Kennan adds: "It must be emphasized that this state of affairs [the instability of Chinese government] stems not only from national traits of long standing but also and predominantly from a pervasive and organic weakness which no sudden reform measures or personal leadership could overcome."[46]

If we connect the two sides of the argument presented here, the following scenario emerges: on the one hand, security implies the concentration of global wealth in U.S. hands; on the other hand, the United States needs to fight Communism on a continent where the rejection of Western influence and democracy has such deep historical roots that it actually became a character trait. Thus, one of the central problems of American policy concerning Asia was to implement a certain post-colonial hegemony: concentrate global power in America in such a way that Third World countries still remain pro-American and anti-Soviet. And this is where the category of "race" gained special significance.

As Christina Klein argued, "The United States thus became the only Western nation that sought to legitimate its world-ordering ambitions by championing the idea (if not always the practice) of racial equality."[47] We should not forget that the official policy of the United States was anticolonial. Decolonization, however, had a number of components: it had to be measured against the Soviet threat, the interests of America's colonizer allies, the independence of colonized nations, and the economic and political interests of the United States. The difficulty of the American position was that the United States found itself between two potential allies and an enemy. On the one hand, as a strategic move, the dual division of the Cold War allowed America to depict Soviet Communism as a form of imperialism and Soviet rule as "slavery," so that America could assume the role of the anticolonial, anti-Communist champion of freedom. But, on the other hand, the rest of the free world—which was to be wooed and transformed by the "American way of life"—was still divided between colonizer and colonized nations. The goal was to invent a vocabulary of international anti-Communism that could simultaneously attract the old European colonial powers and their ex-colonies, and still serve American interests in the long run.

In NSC 48/1, for example, we read the following assessment of Soviet influence: "In any event, colonial nationalist conflict provides a fertile field for subversive communist activities, and it is now clear that southeast Asia is the target of a coordinated offensive directed by the Kremlin."[48] This threat implies that Third World nations must be given their freedom so that they will not consider Western democracy an essentially exploitative system. But the problem with decolonization is that it works against the interests of America's Western allies. Furthermore, decolonization can also serve American economic interests as well. Therefore, the United States has to try to please both colonizers and the colonized in order to serve the demands of security: "The United States should continue to use its influence in Asia toward resolving the colonial-nationalist conflict in such a way as to satisfy the fundamental demands of the nationalist movement while at the same time minimizing the strain on the colonial powers who are our Western allies."[49] Anti-Communist anticolonialism implies the inclusion of Third World nations in an international system of free-market economy in order to keep them in the American geopolitical sphere of influence.

Whereas the Russian Communist was an external and the domestic Communist an internal problem, in the category of race the two fields not only overlapped but actually came to contradict each other. Since pure ideological enmity (Communism vs. capitalism) turned out to be an instable construct due to the overdetermination of the figure of the enemy, it appeared that the definition of enmity based on nationality (American vs. Russian) could potentially sustain a manageable division of outside and inside. But as soon as the category of race was introduced, purely nationalistic enmity was no longer imaginable either. Racial conflict turned out to be the internal antagonism that makes the national definition of enmity inconsistent—if not impossible.

Thus, we can now present the schematic outline of the political theology of anti-Communist nationalism which consists of four components: religion, politics, nationalism, and race. First, truth itself was placed in a religious register. This is how we moved from religion to politics: politics is the mere expression of this religious truth in a particular form. Anti-Communist politics is therefore fundamentally an attempt to limit the total politicization of the social in the name of religion. But, as a next step, we found that the radical opposition of enemies did not provide a consistent discourse, and it had to be supplemented by the discourse of nationalism. As result, political enmity was placed on a "naturalized" national foundation. Finally, however, this national foundation was undermined by the conflict between the rhetoric of universalism and the problem of racism. Race emerged as a category that disturbed these ideologically constructed forms of American nationalisms.

The Joys and Torments of Secrecy: Conspiracy and the Secrets of Democracy

In the early Cold War context, the discourse on secrecy was characterized by an essential split between two basic forms. On the one hand, we have a positive form of secrecy, the secrets of American democracy that are essential to its identity. The most important example of such a secret was the atomic bomb which, while it was an American monopoly, served as the guarantor of American military supremacy. On the other hand, we have the negative form of secrecy exemplified by subversive conspiracies. In the case of the former, we encounter the problem of the democratic distribution of knowledge as the secrets of American democracy must be kept secret from its own citizens as well; in the case of the latter, we come across the ideological fantasy of what is often referred to as a "theft of enjoyment." In other words, the early Cold War discourse on secrecy elaborated the *necessary limitations* on knowledge and enjoyment essential for anti-Communist democracy.

The Cold War represented an important stage in the history of official secrecy, since it sanctioned the full-blown institutionalization of political secrecy. Patrick Moynihan, for example, argues that "Secrecy is a form of regulation. There are many such forms, but a general division can be made between those dealing with domestic affairs and those dealing with foreign affairs. In the first category, it is generally the case that government prescribes what the citizen may do. In the second category, it is generally the case that government prescribes what the citizen may know."[50] Thus, due to the primacy of foreign policy in the early Cold War context, secrecy was removed from the sphere of foreign policy and became a general component of politics. When Moynihan claims that during the Cold War "secrecy had become the norm," he also shows how a supposedly exceptional measure could be turned into a permanent solution.[51]

The reorganization of American democracy around these secrets and the concomitant concern with security, however, raised a number of predictable questions. To put it bluntly, the relation of secrecy to democracy itself became a problem: *Can democracy have secrets at all?* Harold D. Lasswell referred to this complication in his *National Security and Individual*

Freedom (1950) in the following terms: "As the first head of the Atomic Energy Commission said, 'Democracy and secrecy are incompatible.'"[52] Very early on in the Cold War it became apparent that secrecy is in direct opposition to the principle of publicity believed to be one of the foundational pillars of American democracy. Government secrecy, even if it is allegedly serving the common good, withdraws politics from the sphere of public scrutiny. In the words of Herbert S. Marks, such politics might lead to "public administration without public debate."[53]

David E. Lilienthal, chairman of the U.S. Atomic Energy Commission, devoted a whole campaign to this issue. In his article, "Democracy and the Atom" (published in 1948), he argued for a program of public education about all matters atomic, since in the atomic age it is *public knowledge* that can save American democracy from itself: "Unless the American people as a whole do become informed, so that they can chart the course of their own destiny in the atomic age, then democracy in its very essentials is doomed to perish, not by the action of a foreign foe but by default by our own hands."[54] The secret of the atom marks an internal limit of democracy: it is the force that can lead to the internal collapse of American democracy by turning it into a totalitarian system in the name of the security of democracy. The very same instance that is supposed to guarantee the security of democracy might actually lead to its destruction. The apparent contradiction of the politics of security centered on secrecy is clear: American democracy has to be based on a secret in order to be secure, but if the politics of secrecy is in conflict with basic democratic principles, it must be admitted that the very democratic framework of politics can only be secured by an essentially undemocratic politics.[55]

The most important critique of the politics of secrecy coming from a Cold War liberal was Edward A. Shils's *The Torment of Secrecy* (1956). Shils's work is significant because his critique of official secrecy is based on a particular definition of democratic politics. According to Shils, the essence of democratic politics is the necessary delimitation of the field of politics. Democracy can only function properly if the limits separating politics and society are clearly drawn: "Democracy requires the occasional political participation of most of its citizenry some of the time, and a moderate and dim perceptiveness—as if from the corner of the eye—the rest of the time. It could not function if politics and the state of social order were always on everyone's mind."[56] Here we encounter two necessary limits: a temporal and a social. Democracy has to be a part-time concern for only a certain segment of society. In fact, Shils goes further and argues that the essence of pluralistic politics is a "lukewarm 'politicization.'" Politicians "must also be concerned with objects other than political objects and they must look at them from a nonpolitical point of view."[57] In other words, properly democratic politics must move beyond the political and must find room for a certain concern with the nonpolitical. Democracy can only maintain itself as a genuine democracy if depoliticization (which prevents the total politicization of society) is a structural part of its organization.

As a correlative of the politics of depoliticization, the foundational civic virtue of democracy, rather than the "demand for extreme solidarity," is actually indifference—an affective limit on social organization: "Without the willingness to disregard much of what our fellow citizens do—a disregard based on indifference and principle—there could be no freedom."[58] That is, apart from the necessary move beyond politics, rather than an excessive concern with the fate of our neighbors, democracy "requires from its practitioners a spread of interest beyond the range of politics; it also *prohibits emotional intensity*, especially emotional excitement continuing over long stretches of time or running on without intermission."[59] If pluralistic politics is the maintenance of democracy by the containment of emotions in the name of the all-inclusive imperative of moderation, "extremism" is the unjustified introduction of an affective dimension to the field of politics in the form of "base passions."[60] Liberal democracy is predicated upon the prohibition of emotional intensity: democratic passion is a contradiction in terms. To be in a democratic mood means to guard the limits of politics and society (by introducing an apolitical limit to the field of politics) with the moderate passions of a cool-headed liberal. Anti-Communism, if managed with moderate emotional intensity, is liberalism; if reveled in through base passions and enjoyed, it is extremism.

The central point of Shils's argument, however, is that democracy must be based on an equilibrium of publicity, privacy, and secrecy. Moderation means that none of the three should reach a degree of excess over the others: "Privacy is the voluntary withholding of information reinforced by a willing indifference. Secrecy is the compulsory withholding of knowledge, reinforced by the prospect of sanctions for disclosure. Both are the enemies, in principle, of publicity."[61] Thus, one way of imagining the relationship of the three spheres is that privacy and secrecy represent two different limits of publicity. For Shils, privacy is the terrain of the citizen as it willingly withdraws itself from publicity; and secrecy is the terrain of the state as it compulsively withholds information from the public sphere. Privacy should be the "secret" that no one wants to know, whereas secrecy is public information that no one is allowed to know.

Shils's objective is, therefore, to locate at the heart of democracy a structural secrecy without enjoyment. Such a distribution of spheres already shows that it is insufficient to theorize the rise of modern democracy merely in terms of the public and the private spheres. Their supplement is the sphere of secrecy that is a constitutive component of modern political theory and practice:

"The principles of privacy, secrecy and publicity are not harmonious among themselves. The existence of each rests on a self-restrictive tendency in each of the others."[62] In Shils's historical account, modern democracy is actually a reaction against the *arcana imperium* of absolute monarchy. Democracy is the very demand that politics belong to the public sphere rather than to that of aristocratic secrecy. This transformation of the structure of politics, however, is an impossible project: "At least as important, however, in the limitation of the total triumph of the dual pattern of publicity and privacy, was the recognition that the tasks of government and the obligations of society did not require or allow their complete fulfillment."[63] The dual demand for the publicity of politics and the privatization of republican citizenship founders on a structural impossibility: the historical process of democratization (as the move from aristocratic secrecy to democratic publicity) is truly democratic only if it is impossible, if it cannot be fully accomplished. Secrecy is, therefore, unavoidable.

This legitimation of secrecy by Cold War liberals found its mirror image in the necessary renunciation of extremism and conspiracies. In this context, the question of enjoyment surfaced again as a central problem. While Shils speaks of the illegitimate enjoyment of extreme anti-Communist politics, Arthur Schlesinger, discussing the existential appeals of totalitarian systems explains the flight from the burden of freedom in the following way: "Outsiders sometimes wonder how Communists can endure strict party discipline. How foolish a speculation! Members of a totalitarian party *enjoy* the discipline, they revel in the release of individual responsibility, in the affirmation of comradeship in organized mass solidarity."[64] Here Schlesinger recycles the common existentialist theme, popularized in America by Eric Fromm, that "freedom" results in a state of anxiety. Therefore, there is something in our very being that can only be endured by an escape from freedom. The seduction of totalitarian enjoyment is that it offers a means of escape from the responsibilities of freedom and, thus, from democratic anxiety.

Contrary to Schlesinger, however, Whittaker Chambers purges the mystique of conspiracy of all enjoyment with the authority of the ex-Communist:

> For conspiracy is itself dull work. Its mysteries quickly become a
> bore, its secrecy a burden and its involved way of doing things a nui-
> sance. Its object is never to provide excitement, but to avoid it. Thrills
> mean that something has gone wrong. The mysterious character
> of underground work is merely a tedious daily labor to keep thrills
> from happening. I have never known a good conspirator who enjoyed
> conspiracy.[65]

Chambers describes for us the alienated revolutionary: this is what happens to the professional conspirator when the revolution (instead of liberating us from work) is itself reinscribed into the logic of "dull work." Chambers demystifies the supposition of evil enjoyment projected onto the figure of the enemy and redefines conspiracy on the basis of the lack of enjoyment. To be more precise, Chambers not only claims that conspiracy is devoid of thrills because it is work; he goes as far as saying that it is precisely the kind of work whose objective is to do away with enjoyment. If it were enjoyed, it would not be real conspiracy.

Similarly, Hoover describes conspiracy as the most unpleasant experience: "That's why the underground is a nightmare of deceit, fear, and tension, where one has to tell falsehoods, fabricate a background, adopt a new name, and live in fear of being recognized by old friends or acquaintances."[66] In this context, Hoover quotes Harry Gold: "Mom was certain that I was carrying on a series of clandestine love affairs. . . . It was drudgery . . . anyone who had an idea this work was glamorous and exciting was very wrong indeed—nothing could have been more dreary."[67] While Mom believes the son's clandestine escapades to be a sequence of promiscuous adventures full of enjoyment, for the son subversion is the exact opposite: no smut, only dreary work and mere drudgery. The joys of conspiracy are mere illusions that are substituted by the image of alienating labor: to conspire here primarily means to work hard to avoid all thrills.

But when FBI plant Herbert Philbrick discusses the "professional revolutionary," he uses enjoyment to exonerate himself as the counterintelligence agent merely posing as a conspirator: "[the Communist] will work long hours, pass days or even months away from family, alienate his friends, betray non-Communists who trust him, even go to jail. Whereas the Communist seems to find *some enjoyment* from all of this, I found none."[68] That is, in a situation where the distinctions between performance and reality seem to be rather blurry, determination in the last instance belongs to enjoyment. For example, expressing his anxieties concerning his role, Philbrick writes:

> This was the beginning of what I ultimately recognized as a manufactured schizophrenia. I was sinking so deep that it was no longer possible for me to "play" the role of a spy. I could no longer simply make believe that I was a Marxist. Like an experienced actor, who must sublimate himself to his part and immerse himself in the playwright's creation, whenever I walked into the stage setting of a cell meeting, I had to *be* a young Communist. The costume alone was not enough. No disguise would have been adequate.[69]

If disguise is no longer adequate, the counterintelligence agent has to *be* a Communist even if he is really an anti-Communist. As we can see, Philbrick's only way of distinguishing his performance from a complete identification with the enemy is by reference to enjoyment: although the two identities are really difficult to separate, what distinguishes the real Communist from the undercover anti-Communist is that the latter does not enjoy performing his role. Thus, in Philbrick's case, in direct opposition to Chambers, the evil pleasures of conspiracy still need to be maintained.

Thus the question remains, who enjoys politics according to anti-Communist propaganda? As we have seen, Shils identified the self-serving enjoyment of secrecy with extremist anti-Communism. According to the same logic, proper anti-Communism is devoid of all base passions. Even Chambers, discussing his anti-Communist duty to his country, expresses the same attitude toward the joys of anti-Communism: "I cannot ever inform against anyone without feeling something die within me. I inform without pleasure because it is necessary."[70] As it appears, for Chambers there was no joy either in conspiracy or informing. Conspiracy is not a thrill but dull work, while anti-Communism is not a joy but a necessity or a duty. Similarly, Hoover advises his readers about proper anti-Communist action in the following manner: "*Wage the fight in a democratic manner.* Emotion should never replace reason as a weapon. To pursue extralegal methods is simply to injure your case. Fight hard, but fight according to the rules."[71] As Hoover right away places "emotion" on the same level as the renounced "extralegal methods," it is clear that emotion cannot be a democratic weapon. Properly democratic politics is understood to be devoid of enjoyment, as if the latter marked the political limit of the former.

As we can see, therefore, the anti-Communist discourse on secrecy is defined by necessary restrictions on knowledge and enjoyment: certain things must remain secrets, but the protection of secrets should not be the source of excessive enjoyment. To be more precise, within the field of knowledge, anti-Communism imposes a double imperative: on the one hand, it is essential for democracy that its citizens know certain things in order to be able to participate in this democracy; on the other hand, the democratic framework itself can only be maintained through the restriction of knowledge with reference to vital secrets. Similarly, in the case of enjoyment we encounter a double movement: it is important to depict totalitarianism as a state of suffering and, simultaneously, explain its seductive force as the enjoyment yielded by the escape from existential anxiety. And as a symmetrical counterpart of this double determination of totalitarian joy and suffering, anti-Communism itself has to be defined as a duty rather than a source of enjoyment. Anti-Communist duty could be interpreted as the disavowed enjoyment of anti-Communist politics. And maybe this is where we encounter the ultimate horizon of anti-Communist politics, the point where anti-democratic exclusion in the name of democracy coincides with the disavowed pleasures of anti-Communist duty in the discourse on secrecy. Hence the reserved poise of the Cold War liberal: he acknowledges and accepts the necessary limitations on democracy, but refuses to enjoy them.

Preparing for Catastrophe: Civil Defense and Its Vicissitudes

Beside secrecy, the atomic bomb introduced another motive to politics: the real possibility of absolute catastrophe. In the immediate aftermath of the war, two basic solutions were offered to this predicament. The first was the internationalist position that argued for the necessity of "outlawing" war in the age of atomic weapons through the institution of a global authority. This position represented a certain "universalistic" stance that tried to neutralize the most threatening political antagonisms by displacing them to a global level. The second solution, which eventually won out over the other, was the "particularistic" position that proposed the strengthening of national sovereignty in the name of spreading a global pax Americana. Thus, in order to avoid the blurring of essential distinctions within the national framework, the mobilization of the home front under the heading of civilian defense was primarily concerned with the establishment of proper lines of demarcations and necessary limits. Accordingly, the main concern of anti-Communist propaganda was to convince Americans that a nuclear war with Soviet Union was imminent but survivable.

The history of Cold War civil defense reflects the same developments that we have been discussing so far. To a large extent, the institution of a nationwide civil defense program was dependent on the domestication of psychological warfare methods. Its primary function was to achieve a certain militarization of American society. The American civilian population had to reorganize its life according to standards of survival in case of nuclear warfare. "Preparedness" demanded that every family become a vigilant tactical unit ready to be mobilized in case of war. As a consequence, the American way of life had to be organized around a necessary fiction or an illusion. Although it never actually took place, nuclear catastrophe had to be represented constantly. In order to be prepared for it, life had to be lived as if the catastrophe had already happened, as if life were already survival of what might come in the future. In the words of Norman Cousins: "total destruction . . . must be dramatized."[72] Just as in the case of secrecy, the problem of publicity led to a discussion of the necessary limits of public knowledge about atomic war and the proper affective response to this knowledge.

During the period we are concerned with here (1945–1963), there were two major waves of nuclear fear in America. The first was a reaction to the birth of the atomic age and was set off by the bombs dropped over Hiroshima and Nagasaki. It saw the loss of American atomic monopoly in 1949 and settled down to a troublesome coexistence. The second wave hit the country during the mid-1950s as a reaction to the hydrogen bomb. This time, the nuclear test ban debate focused the nation's attention on the problem of radioactive fallout. This period reached its peak with the Cuban missile crisis, after which, beginning with 1963, the question of the atom suddenly dropped out of sight for a while.[73]

The first stage of the atomic age was riddled by guilt caused by the American use of weapons of mass destruction to end a glorious war. The most immediate cultural debate was primarily concerned with the ethical implications of such an act and the prospects for the future in the new age. Hiroshima loomed large in the nation's consciousness and left the majority of the population with guilt over the recent past and anxiety about the immediate future. This period saw the rise and fall of the short-lived but influential world government movement, the so-called scientists' movement, and an attempt to bring nuclear power under international control. The early reactions to the power of the atom were so despairing, so apocalyptic in magnitude, that the government soon realized that it had to intervene to counteract atomic hysteria—partly fueled by the fear tactic exploited by activist scientists. This intervention assumed the form of a consciously devised propaganda effort to promote the peaceful use and the positive side of the atom. By the end of the forties, public interest in the dangers of the atomic age quickly dropped. As early as 1946, responding to the general disappointment among the American public about the Bikini tests, Norman Cousins was speaking of the "standardization of catastrophe."[74] It is characteristic of this kind of positive propaganda that, as Paul Boyer observed, the promotion of a more positive thinking coincides with the recognition by government officials that such positive effects lay much further in the distant future than had previously been believed.[75] Boyer calls this propaganda tactic "secrecy and soft soap": secrecy about the government's nuclear programs and the dissemination of a positive image of the uses of atomic power.[76]

The second wave of atomic fear was mainly concerned with fallout. The roots of the controversy concerning radioactivity and its effects go back to the very origins of the atomic age. Nevertheless, it was primarily the 1954 BRAVO test—and the unfortunate fate of the Japanese fishing boat *Lucky Dragon*, which received a fair amount of radioactive ash—that called the world's attention to the dangers of fallout. What proved to be rather confusing for the general public, however, was that government secrecy was this time accompanied by an admitted lack of scientific knowledge about the effects of radioactivity. This combination of official secrecy about what is known and the public admission of the lack of essential knowledge helped raise the issue of fallout as a crucial political question. It was in this climate that the nuclear test ban debate became a pressing issue for the second half of the fifties, as it gained some momentum during the 1956 election when Adlai Stevenson attempted to make the test ban into an important part of his campaign against Eisenhower. For proponents of the ban, it was not merely World War III that meant catastrophe. As they argued, the preparation for nuclear war in the form of nuclear testing was already producing such an excess of radiation that the annihilation of the human race was already underway as an invisible and slow process. A common response of their opponents was that it was in the best interests of national security to continue testing, since the vague threat of the long-term effects of radiation did not compare with the threat of an actual nuclear war with the USSR.

What became immediately obvious in this debate, however, was that fallout is a worldwide rather than just a national concern of the nuclear powers. Like the issue of race, world opinion again became a point of contention for national politics. In a 1957 article of the *Bulletin of the Atomic Scientist*, Eugene Rabinowitch wrote: "Whether this danger is great or small, the most important thing is that it is *universal* and *compulsory*."[77] Similarly, a *New Republic* editorial of the same year spoke of "the age of 'radiation without representation.'"[78] As the reference to the revolutionary slogan makes it clear, the political conflict created by the problem of radiation was that secret decisions can affect the whole population of the country or even the whole globe, whose opinion is not reflected in those decisions.

In this context, it is not surprising that one of the most salient features of postwar American culture was the historical consciousness of having entered a new age. Therefore, most of the early responses that considered the political impact of the bomb assumed a virulently revolutionary rhetoric.[79] As early as August 7, 1945, the *New York Times* argued in an editorial that "Civilization and humanity can now survive only if there is a revolution in mankind's political thinking."[80] Similarly, Harold D. Lasswell spoke of "the world revolution of our time" and claimed that "Ours is an epoch of changes profound enough to be called revolutionary and of sufficient scope to cover the globe."[81] While the list of examples could run much longer, we should simply note here that the rhetoric of revolutionary change is combined with a certain thought of universality (indicated by the expressions "human race" and "global scope"), as if global politics itself had reached a new phase of its history with the atomic age. As opposed to a mere "abstract" universality, to many the essence of this revolution appears to have been that technological development produced a "real" universality in the form of the global interconnectedness of the human race: the universal threat of global annihilation can make humanity politically one. To be more precise, the choice was quite often presented in absolute terms. In the words of Philip Wylie, this new "universality" meant either "doom or deliverance."[82]

The discussion of the universalization of politics in this global revolution automatically led to the general concern with the end of national sovereignty. In this respect, one of the most influential documents of the era is Norman Cousins's manifesto calling for world government, *Modern Man Is Obsolete* (1945). Without going into detail concerning Cousins's argument and the response it provoked, I want to highlight here the position of national sovereignty in his text. As Cousins bluntly states, we "will have to recognize the flat truth that the greatest obsolescence of all in the Atomic Age is national sovereignty."[83] He adds that humanity has already proven to be a "world warrior" in the twentieth century; the new task is to become "world citizens." This move involves a "transformation or adjustment from national to world man."[84] Therefore, "common security" has to be balanced off against "common cataclysm" by setting up a world sovereignty that does not amount to the establishment of a dictatorial world state, as it leaves room for national jurisdiction and only concerns itself with global foreign policy.[85] When Cousins briefly discusses the feasibility of such a project, he claims that although "strictly speaking, no precise guide to the present is to be found anywhere," the failure of Greek democracy should be contrasted with the success of American democracy.[86] In other words, even for Cousins's internationalism, the model of world government is the American federal government as it regulates the states. Thus, although it is never stated explicitly by Cousins, ultimately we could conclude that the global end of national sovereignty had to be modeled on American national sovereignty.

As Boyer argued, "The limited evidence available suggests that in this period when the shock of Hiroshima and the fear of atomic war were most intense, the idea [of world government] won at least passive support from a third to a half of the American people."[87] In spite of this relatively wide support, the movement proved to be rather ephemeral, since there was an essential conflict (if not an outright contradiction) at the heart of the American people's support for the world government movement. On the one hand, the world government movement was partly predicated upon the critique of nationalism that gained popularity during World War II. On the other hand, as Boyer adds, "when specifics were offered as to aspects of national sovereignty that might actually have to be surrendered, [pollsters] noted, support for world government dropped sharply."[88] Not surprisingly, this meant that Americans were ready to criticize nationalism but only if it did not involve surrendering their own national sovereignty. The seeming contradiction of atomic universality was its foundation in a critique of nationalism in the name of American national sovereignty.

Thus, early on in the history of the atomic age it was settled that global anti-Communism had to serve the interests of American national sovereignty. The universal concept of freedom had to be anchored in American national sovereignty. Consequently, as the politics of national security came to be defined by the policy of "deterrence" on the international level, on the domestic front security meant the installation of a national civil defense program based on what administrators called "national morale" and "national will." According to Guy Oakes, this civil defense program was predicated upon four premises: first, survival is possible; second, if it is possible, it is based on personal responsibility (that is, it is modeled on "self-help" skills); third, this self-help, however, is only workable if it is fortified by self-control (what Oakes discusses under the heading of "emotion management"); and finally, it had to be demonstrated that this kind of civil defense is basically a form of American traditionalism, that it is a revival of American virtues from the past.[89] Oakes's conclusion, however, is that civil defense "was a *necessary illusion*: indispensable to the moral underpinning of national security, but ultimately irrelevant to survival under atomic attack."[90]

Oakes's analysis allows us to speak of the complications of anti-Communist propaganda in terms of two contradictions: one concerns the relationship of knowledge and affect in politics, the other the relationship of the norm and the crisis. First, the official assumption was that without publicly available information, the fear of the unknown will grasp the souls of the nation with "nuclear terror." Accordingly, the role of civil defense would be to enlighten the public. But, as Oakes argues, the conclusion appeared to be that civil defense "would magnify public fears by confirming that they had a sound basis in reality."[91] As a result, the fundamental dilemma of civil defense emerged in rather clear terms: "In the absence of civil defense, the public would be gripped by nuclear terror. But once civil defense had done its work, the public would be even more terrified."[92]

The paradox of nuclear crisis management followed the same logic. In order to deal with crisis, one must normalize it. In other words, life must be restructured as if it were already the survival of crisis. But the ultimate result of such normalization is that the distinction between the crisis and the norm disappears:

The collapse of the distinction between crisis and normality is a definitive feature of the Cold War conception of nuclear reality. It means that when the nuclear emergency occurs, nothing extraordinary or unexpected can happen. A nuclear attack is not a horrible and barely conceivable anomaly, but a problem, immensely challenging, of course, although still amenable to solution by means of standard methods and strategies indigenous to American culture.[93]

Thus, the ideological fantasy at the root of civil defense mobilization was the conviction that the norm can be maintained in crisis if the distinctions between the two are collapsed. But the fact appeared to be that in order to be effective at all, civil defense already needs as a given what it actually aims to restore. Thus, Oakes concludes his book with the following judgment: "Paradoxically, if civil defense was necessary, then it was impossible. If it was possible, then it was not necessary."[94]

Just like the category of race, therefore, atomic catastrophe introduced a new kind of universality to politics. This universality turned Cold War politics into a truly global politics. The problem, however, was that according to the political theology of Cold War anti-Communism, national sovereignty was a necessary limit on this universality. As a result, anti-Communist nationalism had to maintain its affective foundation by reference to a set of "necessary illusions": it had to constantly dramatize a global catastrophe that never actually happened, and it had to maintain the illusion that it is possible to survive such a catastrophe. The ultimate consequence of the official propagation of this institutionalized illusion, however, was the collapse of the distinction between crisis and norm. The necessary illusions of anti-Communist politics became justifications of a permanent crisis.

Cold War Anti-Communism and the Paradoxes of Security

Taken to its extreme, the paradox of security demands sacrifices of the very thing it sets out to secure. Thus, the logic of security implies that we make sacrifices of the very thing we want to protect as we supplant it by another object without being able to guarantee its absolute security. Simply put, security changes the very thing it tries to secure: its essence is not mere conservation but the unavoidable transformation of an identity. So the identity that the politics of security claims to protect is not the same as the identity produced by this politics.

This is where we encountered some of the constitutive paradoxes of the propagation of anti-Communist truth. First, in the case of the representation of the enemy, we have seen that this overdetermined ideological figure marked the internal limits of democratic representation by introducing the logic of the simulacrum to the sphere of politics. Second, in the case of secrecy, we found that democracy depends on structural secrecy that withdraws some of its vital conditions from the sphere of public representation. Finally, in the case of catastrophe, we found that the public representation of a necessary illusion organized the everyday reality of a permanent crisis. Yet the basic contradiction of civil defense turned out to be that it institutionalized and normalized the very crisis that it allegedly prepared for. While in the different figures of the Communist we encountered figures of the representation of the unrepresentable antagonism that constitutes radical enmity, in the figure of the secret we found the unrepresentable conditions of democracy itself (and if certain secrets are necessary to maintain security—that is, the very democratic framework of democratic politics— this figure also functions as a nodal point of the disavowed enjoyment of a foundational exclusion). In the case of catastrophe, we encountered the other side of the same argument: the end of the nation, the end of democracy, and the end of the world all function as the inverse images of the very condition of democracy. The catastrophe, in this sense, is the reverse image of the secret: a confrontation with the very condition of democracy as a condition of impossibility.

Thus, what is common to all three of the ideological figures examined here (enemy, secret, catastrophe) is that they all participated in the same political project: they legitimated the expansion of the logic of the exception in the name of security. In this sense, they were the key figures of the postwar transformation of American political life. The "enemy" justified the expansion of a politics that increasingly relied on nondemocratic measures in the name of democracy. The "secret" allowed the withdrawal of executive power from the sphere of pubic deliberation. And the "catastrophe" institutionalized the rhetoric of "permanent crisis" that legitimated the militarization of civilian life. As the exception became the norm, war was turned into the standard mode of politics; secrecy became the standard terrain of sovereign power; and crisis became the standard of civilian life.

4 /   Anti-Communist Aesthetic Ideology

The Aesthetics of the Vital Center

Let us now turn to the problem of "art" as it appeared in anti-Communist politics. We must start here by acknowledging the fact that anti-Communist aesthetic ideology was born at the intersection of the politics of anti-Communism and the aesthetics of high modernism. When it comes to a definition of art, at the heart of this aesthetic ideology we find one single proposition: according to its very essence, art is anti-Communistic. And this is where some of the complications can be clearly articulated as internal contradictions of this discourse: while art as such is anti-Communistic, not everything that is anti-Communistic is actually art. The problem of this aesthetic ideology is to articulate the implications of the irreversibility of this statement.

Its task is to find a definition of art that will reconcile two seemingly paradoxical statements: on the one hand, it asserts that art is not political; nevertheless, it also claims that art is anti-Communistic. The first statement ("art is not political") reflects the consensual agreement of the 1950s that art cannot be reduced to a political message—that is, art is not "propaganda." This distinction between art and propaganda was the politicized version of the foundational division of modernist aesthetics between high art and mass culture. Both propaganda and mass culture had to be excluded from their respective fields in order to create the proper terrains of political truth and high art. The second proposition, "art is anti-Communistic," is an equivalent of the first: since art is not political (it is actually decidedly apolitical to the degree of being antipolitical), it has to renounce any Communist message, because a Communist message is always political. The problem of Communism, thus, enters the field of aesthetics in a slightly displaced form: it is not directly Communism that is a threat, but reducing art to mass culture through a populist political message. Due to this displacement, "politics" as such becomes a threat to art. The inherent difficulty of this position is to explain how it is possible that the relation of art and politics can be simultaneously an opposition (since art is apolitical) and an essential agreement (since apolitical art is anti-Communistic).

Thus, we can provide a more emphatic formulation of the foundational paradox: while art as such is anti-Communistic, "anti-Communist art" is a contradiction in terms. Although the "the politics of apolitical art" can be easily translated into an anti-Communist message, it is somewhat troubling that the symmetrical conclusion has to be true as well: the renunciation of all political content should also imply the rejection of anti-Communist politics. How is it possible that the simultaneous suspension of Communist and anti-Communist politics within the aesthetic field should still serve the politics of anti-Communism? The answer is self-evident: by depoliticizing (i.e. "naturalizing") the anti-Communist position. Accordingly, the function of art is defined as the revelation of an apolitical freedom. Thus, the ideological work of anti-Communist aesthetic ideology consists of the neutralization of the anti-Communist position as nonpolitical and merely "artistic."

But at this meeting point of anti-Communist politics and modernist aesthetics we encounter yet another significant complication: namely, that political realism and the aesthetics of antirealism do not merely coincide historically—they form an essential alliance. While the politics of the vital center is a politics of realism (in Arthur Schlesinger's words, a critique of the political "sentimentalism" of the fellow-traveling left), its aesthetics is the renunciation of all forms of artistic realism.[1]

In order to unpack the implications of this duality, let us now briefly return to our discussion of Schlesinger's *The Vital Center* and Trilling's *The Liberal Imagination* in Chapter 2. The two authors start from opposing positions but arrive at identical conclusions. While Schlesinger's primary objective is to define the political coordinates of the politics of the center, Trilling defines this liberal center on the basis of an analogy with literary complexity. It is more than just a coincidence that Trilling's book singles out three opponents in order to formulate a properly anti-Communistic aesthetics: a literary adversary (Theodore Dreiser and naturalism), a critical adversary (V. L. Parrington's *Main Currents in American Thought*), and a political adversary (ideological politics and Stalinism). For Trilling, the common element in authentic art, criticism, and politics is a certain kind of "complexity" which, therefore, emerges as a simultaneously aesthetic, critical, and political category.

One of the central categories of Trilling's redefinition of liberalism is "reality." As the argument goes, political realism demands that the aesthetics of realism become more realistic than naturalism by abandoning mere mimetic representations of empirical reality. We could say that Trilling redefines traditional "American metaphysics" in accordance with what Dolan called "Cold War metaphysics."[2] In the opening essay of *The Liberal Imagination*, entitled "Reality in America," Trilling writes: "In the American metaphysic, reality is always material reality, hard, resistant, unformed, impenetrable, and unpleasant. And that mind is alone felt to be trustworthy which most resembles this reality by most nearly reproducing the sensations it affords."[3] This is why later on in his book Trilling extols Henry James's "imagination of disaster" and calls for a "moral realism" that moves beyond the crude opposition of reality and mind, and leads to a "perception of the dangers of the moral life."[4] This catastrophic moral realism is the aesthetic principle which defines the (apolitical) source of liberal politics. The move beyond aesthetic realism serves the purposes of political realism.

If we examine the role art plays in Schlesinger's definition of anti-Communist politics, we find a similar scenario. When Schlesinger "politicizes the aesthetic" and defines the kind of art that can effectively resist totalitarian oppression, he calls for an ambiguous complexity that transcends in artistic merit the products of state-sponsored social realism. But when he turns to politics, he calls for the exact opposite, an honest realism of facts. This is how Schlesinger defines the ultimate goals of his politics: "The new radicalism seeks to fight for honesty and clarity in a turbulent and stricken society, to restore a serious sense of the value of facts, of the integrity of reason, of devotion to truth."[5]

In accordance with the general descriptions of his times, in Schlesinger's text Soviet strategy is defined by a split between reality and appearance. But Schlesinger describes the Soviet attitude toward art in the following manner: "The totalitarian man requires apathy and unquestioning obedience. He fears creative independence and spontaneity. He mistrusts complexity as a device for slipping something over on the régime; he mistrusts incomprehensibility as a shield which might protect activities the bureaucracy cannot control." In other words, art is by definition impossible under totalitarianism, and thus "Soviet art" is yet another contradiction in terms. For example, the problem with Picasso and Stravinsky is that "they reflect and incite anxieties which are incompatible with the monolithic character of the 'Soviet person.' Their intricacy and ambiguity, moreover, make them hard for officialdom to control."[6] Schlesinger dismisses Communist art in the following terms: "The conclusion is clear. Let artists turn their back on Europe. Let them eschew mystery, deny anxiety and avoid complexity. Let them create only compositions which officials can hum, paintings which their wives can decipher, poems which the Party leaders can understand."[7]

While the proper form of art is complexity, incomprehensibility, and ambiguity, its content is the anxiety of democratic freedom. In other words, art is only possible in a free society. But if it is only possible in a free society, it is essentially an expression of the (social, political, and existential) conditions of its very own production. On the one hand, Soviets have simplistic theories of art (so that even officials can hum their melodies) but unreadable political strategies (no one can interpret the strategies of the CPUSA). On the other hand, Americans have complex theories of art celebrating incomprehensibility, but their honest and clear politics is based on a realistic conception of facts, reason, and truth. This alignment of the aesthetics of antirealism with the politics of realism, however, was not just a superficial contradiction. My point is not to argue that this opposition could discredit Cold War liberalism. Rather, in what follows, I would like to show that the definition of political representation in anti-Communist discourse was based (in a fundamental and not merely accidental sense) on a particular definition of aesthetic representation.

Anti-Communist Modernism

In order to explain its ties with anti-Communist politics, I want to highlight here two aspects of modernism: on the one hand, its constitutive exclusion of mass culture (what Andreas Huyssen called the "Great Divide") and, on the other, its principle of self-transcendence (which, following Fredric Jameson, we could call the "modernist Sublime").[8] While the first move established the *external* limits of modernism as it divided the field of the aesthetic between art and non-art, the second move instituted an *internal* limit in the form of the principle of its self-transcendence. In early Cold War cultural discourse, the terrain within which the sublime moment of modernist art could appear was first produced by the radical exclusion of mass culture (that is, the sphere of culture that cannot or does not aspire for the same sublime transcendence). Once this terrain was established, the moment of sublimity was politicized as the moment of universal freedom and the inherent anti-Communism of pure art.

We witness here the parallel construction of the two fields, anti-Communist politics and modernist aesthetics, through two separate exclusions that were nevertheless articulated as equivalent. As we have seen earlier, anti-Communist politics was based on the definition of the proper field of representation established through the primary exclusion of a heterogeneous element from the field of politics (Communist totalitarianism) as it threatened the very symbolic framework within which democratic politics could take place (that is, it threatened the principle of political representation as such). At the same time, modernist aesthetics was understood to be based on the exclusion of mass culture from the field of real art. This exclusion defined the proper field of aesthetic representation in excess of mere mimetic representation (hence the necessary move toward nonrepresentational, nonobjective art). Culture was, thus, divided into two spheres: "mass culture," which is not more than mere culture, and "high art" which according to its own logic strives toward a transcendence of culture.

The two exclusions (the political and the aesthetic) follow the same logic: in order to maintain the purity of politics and the purity of art, something must be excluded. Both exclusions are legitimized by the inner logic of the field they institute. That is, one of them is political and, therefore, it belongs to the very essence of politics as such to exclude the heterogeneous element (since it is not really political but a criminal conspiracy); the other is aesthetic and, therefore, the exclusion of mass culture can be legitimized in purely aesthetic terms (without necessary reference to external fields) since only that which is not really art anyway will be excluded. The elements that are not really political and those that are not really aesthetic have to be excluded, although the fields of politics and art are only constituted by these very exclusions. In early Cold War cultural discourse, we find that these two exclusions are aligned and declared to be equivalent, since the high art/mass culture divide is politicized according to the freedom/totalitarianism opposition.

Let us now examine in more concrete historical terms how the aesthetics of modernism meets anti-Communist politics. As the aesthetic and political distance separating Bertold Brecht from Ezra Pound also demonstrates, it would be a mistake to assume that modernism could be reduced to the realization of a unified political program. Right away, it should be clear that we have to approach modernism as a potential surface for contesting political inscriptions. In this regard, it is a rather telling historical fact that the dual division of political culture along the lines of Communism/anti-Communism was projected onto the modernist art/mass culture divide in all possible variations. Whereas Senator George Dondero of Michigan argued that modernism is merely a Communist conspiracy, Clement Greenberg sought to define it as the very essence of Americanism. On the other hand, while the Gathings Committee tried to define mass culture as a Communist conspiracy, representatives of the pulp industry argued that it was the most important means of the democratization of American culture.[9] As a result, we can easily find examples of all possible political judgments: modernism could be judged Communistic as well as anti-Communistic, just as mass culture could be judged in the same opposing terms. What emerges in the postwar period is the final consensus according to which modernism had to be institutionalized as clearly anti-Communistic.

Jane de Hart Mathews has argued that the identification of modern art with Communist conspiracy proceeded through three stages. First, we witness an "opposition to social commentary in predominantly representational art."[10] In this case, the object of criticism was clearly located on the level of content, fully within the traditional field of representation. As a second step, we see a shift toward a growing concern with the political affiliation of the artists. This new orientation, however, removed the target of anti-Communist critique from the field of aesthetics. If a painter, for example, is proven to be a Communist, no matter what and how he paints, he should not be able to exhibit his works. Finally, "the objection to modern art as Communist conspiracy . . . involved a yet more 'sophisticated' thought process, for the assumption was that rejection of traditional ways of seeing and space inherent in vanguard style of painting implied rejection of traditional world views."[11]

As we can see, the anti-Communist political critique of art moved from the criticism of content to the person of the artist and then returned to the aesthetic field by politicizing the form of representation. Since modern art emphasized the problem of representation by moving beyond objective content, "form" as such became the central issue. It was no longer the potential Communist content that counted the most, but the subversion of the traditional field of artistic representation, which could serve Communistic interests. As Mathews's language suggests, the fact that art can question "traditional ways of seeing and space" by moving beyond classic forms of representation was interpreted as the undesirable political moment of art.

Although the attack on modern art was one of the most dominant cultural trends of the late forties, ultimately it was the exact opposite tendency that came to dominate public discussions of American art. At some point, in spite of the fierce opposition, the redefinition of the field of representation had to be accepted and even celebrated as the inherently American tendency of art history. Although scholars disagree about the exact moment of the victory of modern art in America, it is clear that by the second half of the fifties (especially after McCarthy's demise) it was no longer acceptable in mainstream discussions to equate modern art with Communism.[12] The most important thing for us, however, is not so much the exact historical moment of this redefinition but the logic behind it.

At the risk of simplifying matters, we could say that this argument had four important logical steps. First, following the same movements that were so clearly formulated in Schlesinger's work, art as such had to be redefined as both politically and aesthetically the art of the center: in order to be authentic art, it had to go beyond both political and aesthetic extremes. Second, as an attempt to establish a genuinely American artistic tradition, the center had to be redefined as the authentic expression of Americanism. Third, this American national tradition had to be reinterpreted as the representative of universal values. Finally, the universal content of American art had to be equated with the modernist sublime, the self-transcendence of the aesthetic field of representation toward universal freedom. Again, we can see that the move beyond representation is the political moment within art, but instead of being a (Communist) threat to the established order, it was now redefined as the universality of human freedom.

These four logical steps can be easily traced in the cultural discussions of the late forties. Let us first consider the constitution of the "center" in aesthetic terms. We must point out that it is not always easy to speak of this topology of aesthetic values without direct reference to political categories. The same way the politics of the center had to be situated between the extremisms of the left and the right, art had to occupy the center located midway between extreme aesthetic positions, but the available aesthetic positions were often directly related to the political left/right opposition. To put it briefly, the general formulation of the available extremes offered the following choices: on the one side, we find American nationalism, realism, emphasis on content, and the political right; on the other side, we have European internationalism, abstraction, the primacy of form, and the political left. While a more detailed analysis of the era would have to uncover quite a number of different linkages between these categories, the liberal politics of the center, as it became the dominant political discourse of the fifties, was necessarily dependent on this twofold distribution of aesthetic categories.

One of the clearest formulations of this centrist aesthetics can be found in George Biddle's article "The Artist on the Horns of a Dilemma" published in the *New York Times Magazine*.[13] Biddle formulates the fundamental dilemma of the American artist as a false choice between "Modernism without content or Traditionalism without form."[14] He argues that both aesthetic and social components are endemic to art, but excessive concern with only one of them is going to damage the final product: "As long as a painter is preoccupied with esthetic values, his work may lack vitality, but there is a conscious effort to maintain the esthetic standard. If, however, a social creed or the pressure of business contact is his immediate concern, his esthetic standard may rapidly deteriorate."[15] This is why it is important to point out that Biddle's objective is not to provide an apology of modernism. As a first step, for example, he distinguishes "modernist" from "modern" art and claims that the former is "a style and school like any other," prone to the same academic tendencies that characterize institutionalized art in general. Consequently, no absolute aesthetic or political value can be attached to modern art: "We must, however, guard against the fallacy that the exponents of Modern art are today either liberal or modern."[16]

Biddle's warning shows that in its institutionalized form modern art does not necessarily represent "progressive" values either in politics or in aesthetics. But for Biddle the choice between "fashionable Modernism" and "deadening realism" is a false choice, since it is the center that counts: "This is the dilemma which confronts the artist and pubic today; or, more accurately, these are the twin reefs, the Scylla and Charybdis, which he must avoid in that narrow channel between functioning vulgarity and sterile estheticism. He will need courage and discipline to create a vital expression in the grand manner. Whether his chosen style is Traditional or Modernist, is vastly unimportant." Therefore, the conclusion is "that all creative artists today of any worth or stature must show in their work evidence of the influence of both traditions."[17] Although Biddle's text predates Schlesinger's book, we find here an explicit definition of the aesthetics of the vital center: "a vital expression in the grand manner" is only possible if the artist simultaneously avoids "the Scylla and Charybdis" of aesthetic extremes by using both traditions.

In a series of articles published in the late 1940s on the pages of the *New York Times*, Howard Devree spoke up for modern art in similar terms. In "Straws in the Wind," Devree argued that the exhaustion of the modern movement in Europe created a unique opportunity for American art, but the simultaneous attacks on surrealism and regionalism in America had to be balanced in order for this chance to realize itself.[18] Rehearsing a few common formulas, Devree continues by claiming that nationalist regionalism ("hard and photographic") and international modernism ("the sterile surface patterns of nonobjectivism") represented the two extremes that a genuinely American tradition must avoid. In Devree's case, however, the aesthetic extremes were clearly marked by political orientations, and the aesthetics and the politics of the vital center fully coincided. As Devree warns in the standard language of his times, "the outworn formulas of academicism on the right and the stereotypes of the new academicism of the left" must be avoided. His conclusion is that although "there is an essentially abstract basis for all art," the American artist of the future will have to produce art that is "the deeply felt expression of a time, a place and the spirit of an era that looks forward."[19] In other words, he moves beyond realism by saying that art as such has an abstract basis, but at the same time he tries to anchor this abstraction in the particular conditions of its production. The result is either a new kind of realism or a new kind of abstraction. But perhaps the best way to describe this redefinition of art is to discover in it a rearticulation of the relation of realism and abstraction: abstraction gains a certain realistic power.

In "The Old That Leads to New," as a continuation of his argument from the previous week, Devree writes about the necessary compromise between the indiscriminate conservative critiques of modern art and the excesses of modernism.[20] The rhetoric of the center is indeed hard to miss: "Between these two extremes lies the answer. Toward an equilibrium the modern movement has been struggling, against the harsh and frequently ignorant reactionary criticism on one side and against the excesses generated in the heat of progress among some of its own misguided followers on the other hand."[21] He repeatedly asks for a "true balance between reactionary formulas on one side and excesses on the other." Again, Devree's conclusion is that true art must transcend the realist paradigm: "We have learned much of the abstract basis of all art and that the finding of that basis means a constant search for the essence and the underlying truth instead of being content with mere resemblance and surface reality."[22]

In what could be hailed as the aesthetic version of Henry R. Luce's "The American Century," Clement Greenberg announced in 1948 the historical triumph of American art in the following terms: "the conclusion forces itself, much to our own surprise, that the main premises of Western art have at last migrated to the United States, along with the center of gravity of industrial production and political power."[23] Although for Greenberg this relocation of the center of the art world into New York also meant the victory of modern art in general, quite a few of his contemporaries disagreed and relentlessly insisted on the necessity of defining the American tradition in representationalist terms. Mathews, discussing the traditional definitions of American art of the 1930s and 1940s, writes: "A majority of Americans, literal-minded in their taste, continued to assume that American art must be representational."[24]

Lionel Trilling provided a forceful expression of the same thesis in relation to literature in his attack on V. L. Parrington. As Trilling charges, Parrington's aesthetics can be expressed by the simple formula: "Fig. 1, Reality; Fig. 2, Artist; Fig. 1', Work of Art."[25] The aesthetics of this simple mimesis was directly linked to a certain political ideal of democracy which is supposedly equally realistic: "It does not occur to Parrington that there is any other relation possible between the artist and reality than this passage of reality through the transparent artist; he meets evidence of imagination and creativeness with a settled hostility the expression of which suggests that he regards them as the natural enemies of democracy."[26] This underlying assumption that the move beyond realistic representation is the natural enemy of democracy also suggests that the relations of aesthetic and political notions of representation are intricately intertwined.[27]

Thus, proponents of modernism had to make the case that rather than being a threat to democracy, modern art was actually the fullest expression of the very freedom that is the foundation of democracy. Nevertheless, this move did not mean that the specifically American nature of art had to be renounced. Quite the contrary, the point was to redefine the meaning of America in such a way that the move beyond representation was no longer an embarrassing European development imitated by half-talented Americans. Consequently, the meaning of America could no longer be reduced to what merely "appeared" to be American. Rather, it had to be defined as that which is American according to its universal essence. The solution to the problem was that American national identity had to be equated with universal freedom, and the function of art had to be defined as the expression of this human freedom.

Probably one of the most explicit contemporary expressions of the rearticulation of American art as universal art can be found in Edward Alden Jewell's article "When is Art American?"[28] In the background of this article, we find the attempt to redefine nationalism as a form of universalism. Jewell argued for an internal transcendence of the nationalist paradigm: rather than an end in itself, the national content of art had to be redefined as the necessary means for the communication of universal messages. This rearticulation, however, also makes it clear that the move from national to international art is not enough:

> This brings me once again to a distinction of pressing relevance
> to the whole problem of "native" expression in art: the distinc-
> tion between art that is "international" (too often merely a fac-
> ile hodge-podge of undigested derivations) and art that is "univer-
> sal." . . . "International," like "national," has always a kind of political
> connotation. It refers to politically separated groups rather than to
> humanity; whereas "universal" art roots of [sic] individual experi-
> ence and for that reason may have a profound appeal for individuals
> everywhere.[29]

According to general usage, "national" art in America denoted the regionalist art of the thirties, while "international" art essentially meant the cosmopolitan cultural hegemony of Parisian modernism. The invention of universal art made it possible to simultaneously return to national roots and transcend both the national and the international paradigms. It is an essential part of Jewell's argument that the move beyond the international is not a simple negation of national particularity. Rather, the particularity of the national experience had to be reinterpreted as the carrier of the universal human experience:

> But does this mean that universal art may not also be distinctively American art? By no means. Art to be American in the only sense worth talking about is the creative expression of the individual, the individual creating art out of his own experience, the individual who acknowledges first of all the citizenship of selfhood. This true objective is within, not without. And following that objective the artist, if he be American, will without deliberate attempt, create American art—American art not superficially so, but in the deepest, universal, sense.[30]

The universal appeal of "distinctly American art," however, was not as self-evident as Jewell's words might suggest. Although middle-class hostility toward modernism had a long history by the middle of the twentieth century, we can safely claim that two basic paradigms of these attacks were the moral and the political rejection of modern art.[31] The problem with the historical avant-garde was that it combined political and aesthetic radicalism and completely rejected bourgeois standards. As many commentators of the modernist movement observed, however, one of the paradoxes of the institutionalization of modernism in the 1950s was that it came to represent both politically and culturally the exact opposite of what appears to have been its historical mission.[32] In the early Cold War context, the moral critique of the cultural effects of modernism prepared the ground for the political attack, which was an attempt to appropriate the anti-modernist attitude of the middle class for anti-Communist purposes. For example, Alice B. Louchheim, surveying the debate about modernism in 1948, complained in the *New York Times* of the tendency to reject modernism based on "abstract moral judgments": "the ethical approach leads from general assumptions to lofty conclusions and seems, en route, to have overlooked the paintings in question." Louchheim concluded that "Even if one admits a connection between esthetics and ethics, I think the fallacy of this year's moral attacks lies in the fact that ethical judgments have obscured the best of the works of art of our time."[33]

The inherent contradictions of the political appropriation of these ethical judgments, however, were immediately apparent to contemporary audiences, since the equation of modernism with Communism seemed to imitate the evil it attacked in a rather obvious and paradoxical manner. In "Modernism under Fire," Devree considered the contradictions of the political arguments brought against modern art in the following terms: "Modern art, which has withstood charges that it is distorted, unintelligible, unreal, specious, ugly, et cetera, has in recent months been faced with a new and most fantastic charge of all—that it is Communist . . . somehow possessed of the devil and, through the extensions of esthetic frontiers, dangerous to American culture and realism, to say the least."[34] The article clearly demonstrates the standard argument brought forth in defense of modernism against anti-Communist attacks. Speaking of a "fog of contradictions," Devree points out that it is absurd to call modern art Soviet propaganda when the USSR only endorses socialist realism. As a matter of fact, Devree claims that "it is the sturdy individualism, the refusal of modernism to become propaganda or to cater to the anecdotal and the illustrative that have led to its suppression under totalitarian governments."[35] Emily Genauer tried to expose the very same contradiction at the heart of the anti-Communist critique of modern art when she spoke of George A. Dondero, senator from Michigan, in the following terms: "It is a paradox, and a frightening one, to behold an elected representative of the people naively and inadvertently following the Moscow line about art, and demanding that the communist techniques of constraint be applied to American artists and critics."[36]

In the course of her article, Genauer quotes one of her interviews with the senator, who said that:

> Modern art is communistic because it is distorted and ugly, because it does not glorify our beautiful country, our cheerful and smiling people, and our great material progress. Art which does not portray our beautiful country in plain, simple terms that everyone can understand breeds dissatisfaction. It is therefore opposed to our government, and those who create and promote it are our enemies.[37]

William Hauptman summarized Dondero's charges in the following terms: "modern artists who advocate freedom to experiment in a nontraditional style were charlatans because 1) they really could not draw; 2) they were insane; 3) they were involved in a plot to make the bourgeoisie nervous; and 3) they were committed to degrade their art for the purpose of communist propaganda."[38] We encounter here the same problem that Trilling identified in his reading of Parrington: if art is not immediately accessible, it is automatically understood to be undemocratic. Of course, what Dondero adds to this "anti-elitist" formula is that such an art also must be clearly antidemocratic, in which case it must serve the interests of Communism. Naturally, Dondero was aware of the complications that liberal critics like Devree, Genauer, and Barr expounded as the fundamental contradiction of his position. But, as Mathews explained, there was an easy solution: "To be sure, socialist realism prevailed in Russia itself. But the art of the Revolution had been cleverly retained for subversion abroad."[39] According to this argument, at the heart of aesthetic antirealism, we find communist political realism at its most devilish extreme.

Ultimately, this anti-Communist attack on modernism threatened to lead to a general rejection of modernism by both Communists and anti-Communists. Writing in the *South Atlantic Quarterly*, R. B. Beaman formulated in the clearest manner the paradoxical situation of modern art caught between two deadly enemies:

> Today the cubist witch, like that dread lady of old Salem, feeds bountifully again on fear of the unknown. The weird cacophonies and twisted watches of the modern arts harbor God knows what threat to law and order, probably communism itself—almost certainly communism. Let ignorance of actual Communist art direct this fear long enough and all modernism will be banned from the colleges and outlawed, together with the Communist party, from the face of America. One pictures Mr. Rockefeller, active sponsor of the Museum of Modern Art, seated on a log beside Mr. Prokofiev, both staring in utmost perplexity at the cubist witch, the one trying to imagine how he ever became confused with communism and the other equally amazed to discover that he is a "decadent bourgeois."[40]

As Devree pointed out in "Modernism under Fire": "the cubist witch is called bourgeois art in Russia and Communist art in America."[41] Alfred Frankfurter of *Art News* formulated the double reversal inherent in this situation in the following terms: "Only a great, generous, muddling democracy like ours could afford the simultaneous paradox of a congressman who tries to attack Communism by demanding the very rules which Communists enforce wherever they are in power, and a handful of artists who enroll idealistically in movements sympathetic to Soviet Russia while they go on painting pictures that would land them in jail under a Communist government."[42] It was this reversed mixture of aesthetic and political categories that the liberal discourse of anti-Communism had to straighten out by redefining the terms in a clear opposition.

Politics and the Novel

As we move from these popular discussions of the politics of modernism in the arts to the field of literature, we need to trace the emergence of the same logical arguments. It is customary to speak of literary criticism in the 1950s in terms of an institutionalized compromise between the New Critics and the New York intellectuals.[43] What concerns us the most is that the opposition of the two critical camps reproduced the basic terms of the cultural politics of the vital center. On the one hand, New Criticism had its roots in antimodern Agrarian regionalism which displayed politically conservative, even right-leaning tendencies. After the war, this conservative regionalism had to be redefined as international, formalist, modernism. On the other hand, the New York intellectuals started out in the thirties as Communists. By the second half of the thirties, they became Trotskyites, then Cold War liberals, and in the sixties cultural conservatives.[44] On the level of their literary priorities, it was clear that the New Critics were primarily concerned with poetry, while the New York intellectuals were predominantly preoccupied with novels. But in spite of their continuing disagreements, the New Critics and the New York intellectuals agreed on two crucial points: they both asserted the relative autonomy of art in relation to politics, and they both held that this autonomy defined the social function of art. In other words, literature was always beyond politics, but by moving beyond politics it fulfilled an essentially political task.

The most striking fact of the early postwar period is that the whole genre of the novel occupied a precarious position. It was not until the late forties that critics started to worry about the discrepancies between the critical arsenal accumulated to tackle the intricacies of poetry and the almost complete lack of a standardized critical language to deal with the novel.[45] There was an urgent need to invent or reinvent the critical language of the novel which, of course, also meant that the novel itself had to be reinvented. This critical neglect of the novel was usually explained as a suspicion of popular entertainment and social commentary. The two major methods of redefining the novel beyond simplistic realism were, on the one hand, the relegation of the merely realistic to the field of mass culture and, on the other, the construction of the category of the "romance" as a nonrealistic novel.

Let us now briefly examine the way some of the most illustrious New Critics and New York intellectuals attempted to redefine the novel in relation to the anti-Communist consensus of their times. The most sustained contemporary effort at isolating the purely aesthetic component of literature can be found in René Wellek and Austin Warren's *The Theory of Literature* (1949). But we need to ask the following question now: What is the relationship of this argument to anti-Communist politics? Surveying the smoldering ruins of European criticism, Wellek and Warren conclude their work with the same diagnosis that formed the basis of both the political and cultural reinventions of America's global position. In short, they diagnose the transference of the center of power from Europe to America: "One cannot yet anticipate the way in which European literary scholarship will be reconstituted. But it seems probable that, in any case, leadership has passed to the United States."[46] In more concrete terms, they specify their meaning by speaking of America's historical chance to become the land of authentic literary criticism: "Here there is a chance . . . to reconstitute literary scholarship on more critical lines: to give merely antiquarian learning its proper subsidiary position, to break down nationalistic and linguistic provincialism, to bring scholarship into active relations with contemporary literature, to give scholarship theoretical and critical awareness."[47] The methodological shortcomings of European criticism ("antiquarianism") are linked with historical shortcomings (an inability to engage contemporary literature) and the political failure of nationalistic paradigms.

Of course, what the very same text also bears witness to in an oblique way is that this reinvention of American criticism did not necessarily reflect traditional American values. It is an intriguing historical fact that Wellek and Warren conclude their work with the following disclaimer: "It has been objected to such a program as ours that it asks for a reform of *homo Americanus*, that it ignores his preoccupation with the job, his ideal of efficiency, his belief in teaching anybody and everybody, his inborn positivism. This objection we do not grant. While we all hope for a change in man, and in the American specifically, the scheme proposed is not Utopian nor does it contradict fundamental American traditions."[48] On the very last page of the book, they formulate their position in even more evocative language: "A turn toward the study of theory and criticism is neither 'idealistic' nor un-American."[49] This suggestion, that literary theory in general could be perceived as "un-American," reflects the troubled move from national to global politics, as we have outlined it in previous sections. The scholarly study of literature was redefined by Wellek and Warren as a global and universal study of literariness rather than the investigation of the realistic representations of the "American Scene." But, as we can see, this overcoming of the nationalist paradigm had to take place in the name of American traditions.

A striking feature of *Theory of Literature* is that it aims to define the properly aesthetic component of literature by reference to the particular and universal aspects of art. The problem of universality is elaborated by Wellek and Warren on the level of the scholarly study of literature as well as that of the onto-phenomenology of the literary work of art. In the first case, the authors claim that the proper object of study is the "nature" of literature. The "function" of literature can be derived from its "nature," and the "evaluation" of literature is based on the relation of its essence and function. They claim that the scientific model of establishing universal laws is just as mistaken as the exclusive attention paid to the particularity of a given piece of art. Rather, one could say that the proper object of inquiry is the "concrete universality" of the aesthetic as it manifests itself in a particular work of art. It is precisely the articulation of this structure that renders their work exemplary.

It is now clear how the nationalist paradigm of literary analysis is to be transcended. The argument presented in the chapter entitled "General, Comparative, and National Literature" attempts to articulate the universal problem of literature in relation to national particularity.[50] The authors argue that comparative literature cannot be reduced to a comparison of two or more national literatures. They claim that comparative literature has to move beyond this international paradigm toward a genuinely universal study of literature "by identifying 'comparative literature' with the study of literature in its totality, with 'world literature,' with 'general' or 'universal' literature."[51] Just as the stratified aesthetic object has to be studied in its totality as a work, the meaning of literature also needs to be extended to include all of its global manifestations. But the question of nationality is not dismissed by the move toward the global. Quite to the contrary, its position is reformulated as "central": "Indeed, it is just the problem of 'nationality' and of the distinct contributions of the individual nations to this general literary process which should be realized as central."[52] The dialectical conclusion is that the "Universal and national literatures implicate each other."[53]

When Wellek and Warren turn to a discussion of the novel, they start by acknowledging the inferior status of novel criticism.[54] They continue to enumerate the general reasons for this state of affairs and warn against two extremes: on the one hand, the novel should not be perceived as mere escapism, but neither should it be reduced to a historical document. They blame the Platonic suspicion of imitation as mere deception for this continuing suspicion of the genre and add that "the earnest writer of novels . . . knows well that fiction is less strange and more representative than truth."[55] They argue that "realism" is a mere artistic tool rather than the exclusive terrain of novelistic discourse. Therefore, the criticism of the novel should not be concerned with a choice between reality and illusion, but with the totality of the world created by the given piece of fiction.

The political significance of the autonomy of the aesthetic can be explained according to the same logic. Here autonomy means that the aesthetic field has its own law: "Its prime and chief function is fidelity to its own nature."[56] Wellek and Warren are careful not to reduce their position to a simple negation of the political and philosophical relevance of literature. For example, discussing propaganda they reject extreme positions which either claim that art cannot be propaganda at all or that all art is propaganda.[57] In their definition, propaganda is a persuasive purveyor of truth rather than its aesthetic discovery. If we take "propaganda" in its broader meaning, we could maybe call artists "responsible propagandists": "The view of life which the responsible artists articulates perceptually is not, like most views which have popular success as 'propaganda,' simple;

and an adequately complex vision of life cannot, by hypnotic suggestion, move to premature or naïve action."[58] In fact, art and propaganda designate two distinct ways of relating to truth: in the case of propaganda truth is already given, it only has to be communicated; in the case of art, the truth needs to be discovered through the aesthetic experience. That is, ideological components can appear within a work of art, but they can only function as components of a structured whole whose artistic value cannot be judged on the basis of a single element.

In his attempt to restore the centrality of the "literary idea," in contrast to Wellek and Warren, Lionel Trilling criticized the idea of "pure art" and argued that this purity is a mere critical fantasy: "Say what we will as critics and teachers trying to defend the province of art from the dogged tendency of our time to ideologize all things into grayness, say what we will about the 'purely' literary, the purely aesthetic values, we as readers know that we demand of our literature some of the virtues which define a successful work of systematic thought."[59] Since in the final analysis Trilling might be much closer to his opponents than he believes, we could say that he is trying to find here a different way to formulate the inherent political relevance of literature. One of the clearest signs of Trilling's opposition to New Critical methodology was his attempt to redefine the novel as the most important genre of the period.[60] The most direct formulation of the central position of the novel occurs in the famous concluding lines of the essay "Manners, Morals, and the Novel": "For our time the most effective agent of the moral imagination has been the novel of the last two hundred years."[61] Trilling's essay reflects a sense of crisis and impending catastrophe as it points toward the novel as the guiding light in this dark age. The cultural and political function of the novel is to prevent the corruption of liberalism by moving beyond mere realism (championed by totalitarian systems) to the kind of moral realism that always reminds us of the corruptibility of human nature and questions all forms of politics conducted in the name of moral righteousness. But in order to fulfill this function, the novel must move beyond the classic forms of realism.

Since Trilling has always been sensitive to the constitutive paradoxes of liberal democracy, it is no surprise that he considers the politics of modernism precisely from this perspective. In "The Meaning of a Literary Idea," he suggests that the move beyond realism in high modernism does not necessarily guarantee political liberalism: "For it is in general true that the modern European literature to which we can have an active, reciprocal relationship, which is the right relationship to have, has been written by men who are indifferent to, or even hostile to, the tradition of democratic liberalism as we know it. Yeats and Eliot, Proust and Joyce, Lawrence and Gide—these men do not seem to confirm us in the social and political ideals which we hold."[62] Conversely, Trilling also questions the value of contemporary American fiction precisely in these terms: to the degree that authors choose to be explicitly liberal and democratic, they might turn out to be good American citizens, but they are likely to produce uninteresting literature. The relationship between good literature and liberal democracy cannot be reduced to a mechanical reproduction of the democratic ideals in a fictitious terrain.

But the best formulation of the paradoxical nature of the "politics of the novel" comes from another New York intellectual. In *Politics and the Novel* (1957), Irving Howe analyzes the contradictory nature of the category "political novel" and argues that the paradoxical political task of the novel is precisely to transcend politics. After rehearsing some of the difficulties inherent in precise generic definitions, Howe defines the "political novel" as constituted by an internal tension between experience (always concrete, stemming from life, and operating on the level of emotions) and ideology (constituted by abstract political ideas): "The conflict is inescapable: the novel tries to confront experience in its immediacy and closeness, while ideology is by its nature general and inclusive."[63] Later on, Howe uses even stronger language to express this internal tension: "Because it exposes the impersonal claims of ideology to the pressures of private emotion, the political novel must always be in a state of internal warfare, always on the verge of becoming something other than itself."[64] This internal warfare between concrete experience and abstract ideology pushes the political novel beyond itself, toward a transcendence that can no longer be called political: "The political novel turns characteristically to an apolitical temptation."[65]

It is precisely by "becoming something other than itself" that the novel gives way to the romance here. The most significant expression of the romance thesis is to be found in Richard Chase's book *The American Novel and Its Tradition* (1957). This book is important for us because it identifies the move beyond classic forms of realism as the essence of a genuinely American literary tradition. In other words, we see here a very clear formulation of the thesis that the move beyond realism is simultaneously a move toward universal truths and the expression of a genuinely American tradition. Whereas the English novel displays a tendency toward "absorbing all extremes, all maladjustments and contradictions into a normative view of life" and it is primarily an "an imperial enterprise, an appropriation of reality with the high purpose of bringing order to disorder," American novels "explore" the radical contradictions of their culture and "discover a putative unity in disunity" and "rest at last among irreconcilables."[66] This amalgamation of fiction and reality, in turn, ensures that the romance gives fiction "a universal human significance" while still maintaining "local significance."[67] Therefore, the romance is capable of penetrating truth otherwise inaccessible to traditional novels: "The inner facts of political life have been better grasped by romance-melodramas . . . than strictly realistic fiction."[68] By moving beyond politics toward the realm of universal morality, the romance is actually more realistic politically than the novel, because it is capable of investigating the moral foundations of politics.[69]

Thus, we can see now how the four logical steps behind the anti-Communist appropriation of modernism (defined in the previous section) can be applied to the field of literature as well. First literature had to be aligned with the politics and aesthetics of the center. In terms of available critical discourses, this center was defined as the common ground between New Critics (on the right) and New York intellectuals (on the left). Second, this center had to be occupied by a genuinely American literary tradition. The establishment and institutionalization of the field of American studies served precisely this purpose. Third, this American national tradition had to be interpreted as the expression of universal aesthetic and moral values. And finally, the universal content of American literature had to be equated with the modernist sublime. In this particular case, the self-transcendence of novelistic discourse through the romance pointed toward the poetry of a sublime anxiety. What is at stake in this aesthetic moment is again freedom and the anxiety produced by contradictory cultural determinations that are specific to a given culture.

Anti-Communist Popular Fiction

Bernard Rosenberg opened his 1957 anthology of essays devoted to mass culture with the observation that the political left, right, and center have clearly defined aesthetic views on mass culture:

> The political lines that have crystallized are approximately these: radicals (Dwight Macdonald, Clement Greenberg, Irving Howe) who, like the arch-conservatives (Ortega y Gasset, T. S. Eliot, Bernard Iddings Bell), although for opposite reasons, are repelled by what they commonly regard as vulgar and exploitative, and the liberals (Gilbert Seldes, David Riesman, Max Lerner) who take a predictable position in the middle. The parallel between left, right, and center in politics and in the "popular arts" is virtually perfect.[70]

In fact, Leslie Fiedler's essay from the same anthology, "The Middle against Both Ends," suggests that this liberal center entertained an undemocratic attitude towards mass culture: "We live in the midst of a strange two-front class war: the readers of the slicks battling the subscribers to the 'little reviews' and the consumers of pulps; the sentimental-egalitarian conscience against the ironical-aristocratic sensibility on the one hand and the brutal populist mentality on the other. The joke, of course, is that it is the 'democratic' center which calls for the suppression of its rivals; while the élite advocate a condescending tolerance, and the vulgar ask only to be let alone."[71]

These points clearly demonstrate that we are dealing with political as well as aesthetic definitions of the center. While the field of politics was divided among leftist radicals, right-leaning arch-conservatives, and centrist liberals, the field of culture was divided among highbrow, middlebrow, and lowbrow artifacts. From the perspective of the sentimental democratism of middle-brow culture, the two fields can be clearly aligned on the basis of the coincidence of the two centers: middlebrow aesthetics and the politics of the center should be identical. In case of the middlebrow, the political opposition to extremism was reflected in the simultaneous rejection of modernism and mass culture. Quite often, anti-Communist cultural imaginary conceived of the relationship of the two fields in the following way: highbrow modernism = leftist extremism, middlebrow sentimentalism = liberalism, mass culture = right wing extremism.[72] From the perspective of modernist liberalism, however, the problem with this formula was that the middlebrow had absolutely no aesthetic legitimacy. For them, the politics of the liberal center had to be aligned with modernism.

The symmetrical juxtaposition of the external political crisis (international Communism) and the internal cultural crisis (mass culture) led to a general suspicion of simulation. The problem of "simulation" appeared in both fields as the return of the excluded element that threatens the principle of representation: as we have seen, the excluded Communist represented the apolitical (criminal) agency which through deceit and imitation undermined the very practice of democratic representation; at the same time, high art was threatened by the mere imitation of art. Communism and mass culture emerged as the internal subversions of the fields of politics and aesthetics through deceitful imitation. While Communism was the simulacrum of politics that tried to do away with democracy, mass culture was the simulacrum of culture threatening the very existence of real art.

Historically speaking, however, we have to insist on the point that the twofold division of cultural production between highbrow and lowbrow is not sufficient. Already in one of the earliest contributions to the highbrow-lowbrow debate, Van Wyck Brooks's *America's Coming of Age* (1915), we find a conscious program to establish three separate positions. Brooks defines the split between highbrow (which he identifies with theory, culture, and the feminine) and lowbrow (practice, business, and the masculine) as constitutive of American identity: "Human nature itself in

America exists on two irreconcilable planes, the plane of stark theory and the plane of stark business."[73] He argues that one of the reasons why there is always something "wanting" in American literary works is that this split erected an insurmountable barrier between social and personal genius.[74] Celebrating Walt Whitman as the center of the middlebrow canon, however, he suggests that things could be otherwise.

But Brooks argues for a successful synthesis of the two extremes in a genuinely American middlebrow culture. He speaks of "the rudiments of a middle tradition" which is "just as fundamentally American as either flag waving or money grabbing."[75] He calls this middle ground "the focal center in the consciousness of [a nation's] own character."[76] Brooks displays a conscious effort to formulate the basic premises of a cultural politics of the center that should represent the essence of national character. In Brooks's case, by the 1940s, this plea for a "focal center" turned into an uncompromising nationalistic attack on literary modernism in the name of middle-class values. In On Literature Today (a lecture delivered at Hunter College in 1940), Brooks makes it clear that highbrow modernism is simply the enemy of the American spirit.[77] Brooks works with a familiar set of oppositions: on the one side, we find modernism that stands for negativity, ugliness, chaos, international values, urban hatred of the countryside, formalism, and the "death-drive." On the other side, we have "primary" literature, which is positive, concerns itself with the beauty of life and the goodness of human beings, and remains provincial in the good sense.

Although Dwight Macdonald's famous attack on the so-called "Brooks-MacLeish Thesis" (as Archibald MacLeish held similar views about contemporary literature) rejects the content of this critique, ultimately he reaffirms its ideological form by fully canonizing the threefold division of culture. Macdonald's most famous formulation of his theory of mass culture can be found in "Masscult and Midcult."[78] This article, clearly written out of a sense of cultural crisis, defines the threat posed by Masscult as the false and deceitful universality of democratic equality. But the important point for us is that the logic of the simulacrum emerges in the form of the Midcult as a result of the radical exclusion of Masscult from the terrain of art.

As a first step, Macdonald establishes the fact that Masscult is not art. The historical opposition between high art and mass culture is explained not as the difference between successful and failed art, but as the difference between art and its negation. That is, the distinction is not internal to the field of art: "Masscult is bad in a new way: it doesn't even have the theoretical possibility of being good. . . . It is not just unsuccessful art. It is non-art. It is even anti-art."[79] But the dialectical synthesis of art and its negation is not the happy marriage of extremes, but the total destruction of art through its empty simulacra:

> A whole middle culture has come into existence and it threatens to absorb both its parents. This intermediate form—let us call it Midcult—has the essential qualities of Masscult—the formula, the built-in reaction, the lack of any standard except popularity—but it decently covers them with a cultural figleaf. In Masscult the trick is plain—to please the crowd by any means. But Midcult has it both ways: it pretends to respect the standards of High Culture while in fact it waters them down and vulgarizes them.[80]

As we can see, Macdonald's cultural discourse was split between essence and appearance in the same way as the political metaphysics of the Cold War. As Macdonald put it: "The special threat of Midcult is that it exploits the discoveries of the avant-garde."[81] Midcult pretends to be avant-garde art and infiltrates the cultural field of high art in order to subvert this field from within and substitute the negation of art for genuine high art. And this attack on art cannot even be isolated anymore as a local problem since it is happening everywhere. In Macdonald's more evocative words: "A tepid ooze of Midcult is spreading everywhere."[82]

The specificity of the threat posed by Midcult can thus be explained by reference to two familiar categories: on the one hand, it is a mere simulacrum and, on the other, it stands for a false universality. Macdonald uses rather suggestive language and repeatedly points out that Midcult only *pretends* to be art. It is characterized by a certain ambiguity and deceit as it undermines the field of aesthetic value from within. Midcult is the mode of appearance of non-art or anti-art within the field of art: "The enemy outside the walls is easy to distinguish. It is its ambiguity that makes Midcult alarming. For it presents itself as part of High Culture. Not that coterie stuff, not those snobbish inbred so-called intellectuals who are only talking to themselves. Rather the great vital mainstream, wide and clear though perhaps not so deep."[83] The populist rhetoric of the middlebrow appropriates certain elements of highbrow only to drag it down to a democratic common denominator: "Midcult is not, as might appear at first, a raising of the level of Masscult. It is rather a corruption of High Culture which has the enormous advantage over Masscult that while also in fact 'totally subjected to the spectator,' in Malraux's phrase, it is able to pass itself off as the real thing."[84]

This subversion of art happens in the name of central and universal human values: "Technically, they are advanced enough to impress the midbrows without worrying them. In content, they are 'central' and 'universal,' in that line of hollowly portentous art which the French call *pompier* after the glittering, golden beplumed helmets of their firemen."[85] Macdonald quotes Thornton Wilder as a quintessential middlebrow to illustrate his point: "'There is something way down deep that's eternal about every human being.' The last sentence is an eleven-word summary, in form and content, of Midcult."[86] As Macdonald makes clear, "The Midcult mind aspires toward Universality above all," but this universality of human essence is disqualified by its lack of artistic form.[87]

If we revisit Clement Greenberg's classic 1939 essay "Avant-Garde and Kitsch" from this perspective, it is striking to what extent he also relies on the language of the simulacrum. This is more than just mere rhetoric, since the very logic of the exclusion of kitsch is justified in these terms: "Kitsch, using for raw material the debased and academicized simulacra of genuine culture, welcomes and cultivates this insensibility. . . . Kitsch is vicarious experience and faked sensations. Kitsch changes according to style, but remains always the same."[88] In other words, kitsch is the persistence of the same harmful essence throughout all possible stylistic manifestations that are mere simulacra of genuine culture.

In order to establish the field of pure art, what needs to be excluded from the field of the aesthetic is non-art masquerading as genuine art. Greenberg's language even suggests a deliberate victimization of the "dupes" of mass culture: "Traps are laid even in those areas, so to speak, that are the preserves of genuine culture."[89] Later he adds: "Kitsch is deceptive. It has many levels, and some of them are high enough to be dangerous to the naïve seeker of true light."[90] In a familiar turn of the argument, we find out that kitsch (just as the external political enemy) is building a global empire of anti-aesthetic deception: "Nor has it shown any regard for geographical and national-cultural boundaries. Another mass product of Western industrialism, it has gone on a triumphal tour of the world, crowding out and defacing native cultures in one colonial country after the other, so that it is now by way of becoming a universal culture, the first universal culture ever beheld."[91]

But beside the aesthetic reason (the fact that it is a mere simulacrum of art), there is also a political justification for the attack on kitsch. This time, the problem is that it has disturbing ties with totalitarianism: "The encouragement of kitsch is merely another of the inexpensive ways in which totalitarian regimes seek to ingratiate themselves with their subjects."[92] While the exclusion of kitsch can be justified on purely aesthetic grounds (since it is non-art), the political argument further reinforces the necessity of this exclusion. The exclusion of kitsch from the field of aesthetics is linked to the exclusion of totalitarianism from the field of politics. The political argument functions as the ultimate justification of the aesthetic judgment on kitsch.

The status of anti-Communist literature has to be understood in this context. The anti-Communist canon was constructed on the basis of a threefold division of cultural products: at the top of the hierarchy, we find anti-Communist modernism; at the bottom, we find anti-Communist popular culture. Between these two extremes, the grand classics of anti-Communism occupy a dubious cultural position. Due to its overtly political nature, anti-Communist literature was always on the verge of being propaganda, so its artistic status was always rather precarious.

Nevertheless, there did exist a tolerated middle ground in the fifties between high modernism and mere propaganda. The absolute center of this anti-Communist literary canon was George Orwell's *1984*. The second place went to Arthur Koestler, with such works as *Darkness at Noon* (1940), *The Yogi and The Commissar* (1945), and *The Age of Longing* (1951). Koestler was closely followed by authors such as Ignazio Silone, Alberto Moravia, and André Malraux. As we can see, the literary canon of anti-Communism in America was mostly composed of European authors who were themselves disillusioned ex-Communists. It is, in fact, really difficult to find positive estimates of American anti-Communist novels at all. In this context, the most often discussed American works are Lionel Trilling's *The Middle of the Journey* (1947) and Irwin Shaw's *The Troubled Air* (1951). The criticism concerned with anti-Communist fiction was clearly troubled by the difficult articulation of aesthetic and political judgments. Basically every discussion of these texts foundered on the same conclusion: "sound in intellectual conception but deplorably weak as a novel."[93]

Below the level of these works, we find anti-Communist popular fiction, which otherwise remained almost completely invisible in the works of these critics. Nevertheless, it is easy to see what is ideologically wrong with anti-Communist popular fiction from the perspective of these aesthetic considerations. The most direct contemporary example of the general argument against anti-Communist fiction can be found in Charles I. Glicksberg's 1954 article entitled "Anti-Communism in Fiction." Although the article is mostly a set of plot summaries, it nevertheless displays the most common arguments of this line of criticism. The text opens with the rather telling comparison of anti-Communist fiction with the proletarian novels of the 1930s. While anti-Communist and proletarian novels have different ideological orientations, the reasons for their failure are the same: by emphasizing political commitment they deny the essence of art. The political judgment on art has to be derived from the judgment whether it is true to its universal essence or not. To the degree that anti-Communist fiction fails to be art, it fails in its political mission as well.

After surveying the works of Koestler, Silone, and Orwell (the generally accepted although always criticized anti-Communist canon), Glicksberg considers the lesser authors in the following terms:

> Other writers of fiction have attempted to grapple with the theme of Communism, but the work they have produced is generally feeble in invention, undistinguished in character, lacking in imaginative depth and dramatic tension. . . . Though these novelists are undoubtedly moved by a profound urge to make the truth prevail and by a genuine desire to uphold those values that make room for freedom, the fiction they concoct about Communism is neither fantasy nor parable but a laboriously constructed fairy tale, abstract and lifeless. . . . The trouble with most anti-Communist fiction is that it is too violently biased in temper; its satire lacks the edge of irony; everything connected with Communism is reduced to a black and white pattern.[94]

We can see that Glicksberg expresses sympathy with the political sources of this kind of fiction, but he dismisses these authors on basic aesthetic grounds. There appears to be a problem with their conception of "reality": it is simplistic and, therefore, propagandistic. They start with the truth of freedom, but they fail to transpose it successfully into the field of the aesthetic. Instead of an "imaginative realization" of this truth, we receive a fairy tale which is neither properly imaginary nor properly realistic.

Glicksberg further explains these objections in the conclusion of the article when he writes:

> The contemporary literary debate over Communism reaches to the roots of human conscience and is concerned over ultimate values. The writer who projects this debate in fiction must avoid presenting a study in black and white, counterpoising evil against virtue, Satan against God. . . . The supreme error lies in perverting literature to serve propagandistic purposes. The anti-Communist writer of fiction neglects the problem of form, of objectivity, of psychological truth, while he proclaims his faith and seeks to confound the enemy. Thus, in concentrating on ways and means of combating the evil of Communism, the novelist runs the risk of compromising his integrity, his vision of truth. Fighting fire with fire, poison with poison, he loses sight of his goal and gradually abandons his position as artist.[95]

All of the obligatory clichés of liberal criticism are put on display here. The opposition of art and propaganda is rendered in explicit terms. On the side of art we have irony, form, objectivity, psychological truth; on the side of propaganda, we find violent temper, simplification, and demonization of the enemy. The unsymmetrical definition of Cold War enmity surfaces in this last paragraph, which renounces the imitation of the enemy as a legitimate method of fighting totalitarianism. Anti-Communist fiction as propaganda is "fighting fire with fire, poison with poison," when the most important weapon in the cultural Cold War is the universality of pure art, which reveals "the truth about the condition of man, his cosmic destiny, his tragic predicament."[96] By misconstruing its aesthetics, anti-Communist fiction assumes totalitarian methods.

Based on Glicksberg's critique, the question that I would like to raise in the following three chapters is the following: What does it mean to understand anti-Communist fiction as a *field of representation*? In the cultural topology of anti-Communist liberalism, the name "anti-Communist fiction" designates a hardly visible terrain of cultural production whose existence is, of course, acknowledged, but it is located beyond the "great divide." Being beyond this great divide, anti-Communist fiction is reduced to a certain kind of cultural immanence without the sublime self-transcendence of art.

As we can see in Glicksberg's analysis, anti-Communist fiction is often defined by critics as the aesthetic corruption of a political truth. In other words, anti-Communist fiction can be defined as a fictional field of representation within which the political truth of its own institution can only emerge in a distorted form. Even if it is politically correct, anti-Communist fiction is by definition aesthetically unacceptable. The basic failure of this kind of fiction is precisely that it fails to translate its political truth into an aesthetic method: it cannot successfully aestheticize its politics. This split between political truth and its aesthetic perversion is explained as a false conception of reality that makes it impossible to render extra-aesthetic reality in an adequately complex form. In other words, this kind of fiction fails to connect the politics of realism with the aesthetics of anti-realism in a sufficiently sophisticated manner.

Mostly, anti-Communist fiction appears to remain on the level of a literary "Donderoism" and imagines that the same democratic principles apply in politics and aesthetics. While anti-Communist modernism separates this politics and aesthetics on the level of representation only to reunite them as ideological equivalents, anti-Communist popular fiction attempts to make an aesthetic method out of its politics (without necessarily succeeding in this mission). And it is on this level that the connections between anti-Communist politics and anti-Communist fiction can be articulated. To the degree that this kind of fiction professes that political and aesthetic representation follow the same logic, the anti-Communist ideology that provides the consistency of its world is simultaneously a political and an aesthetic ideology. These novels defined a certain field of fictional visibility the same way anti-Communist political ideology defined politics as a field of representation. What needs to be examined in more detail are the limits of representation as they are articulated in this kind of fiction.

Thus, what has to be explained is the way these works account for the emergence of the field of representation (as a field of fiction) within which they can appear as authentic representations of reality. The key to this problem is that there is always a privileged sublime object that marks a limit of representation; but by marking this limit, this object also accounts for the possibility of the emergence of the whole field. Without the original figure of the catastrophe, there could be no nuclear holocaust fiction, but the catastrophe itself represents that which can never be fully represented even in these works. Without the figure of the stolen secret, there could be no spy novels, but the secrets of democracy must remain secret forever and their content can never be fully exposed within the field of fiction either. And without the unreadable enemy, there could be no political novels, but neither can the principle of political unreadability be fully eradicated in these novels. As we can see, these objects, as figures of ideological investments, become the conditions of whole genres. Of course, the kind of politics a particular novel will advocate within the field opened up by its original figure cannot be logically deduced from the figure itself, but we can be sure that whatever this politics might be, it will have to be articulated in relation to this figure.

PART II

ANTI-COMMUNIST FICTION

5 /   One World: Nuclear Holocausts

The Idea of World Politics

The minimal historical precondition of the type of literature that we are concerned with here is the invention of a particular notion of the "world." It is not enough to say that atomic holocaust fiction is only possible in an "atomic age" in which speculation about atomic matters assumes a certain realistic relevance and practical urgency. Neither is it enough to declare, if we recall the simple fact that atomic holocaust fiction actually predates the atomic age by half a century, that a certain degree of technological development was necessary to render the human destruction of the world by atomic energy a plausible fiction. Concentrating exclusively on the technical means of destruction might obscure the fact that the object of this destruction itself had to be created in the first place. Rather than simply asking the question "How is the world destroyed?", we also have to ask: "What is it that is destroyed when the world comes to an end?"

Consequently, we have to assume that in order for this type of literature to emerge, a particular set of transformations had to take place within the history of the concept of the world as the ultimate horizon of human existence. Foremost among these changes is the break that rendered this world "modern." Every definition of the "world" as a totality oscillates between two extremes. On the one hand, the world is a totality of *meaning*; on the other hand, the world is the *empirical* substance of the infinite universe. The "modern world," thus, starts with a double discovery that rearticulates the relationship of these two extremes. Humankind "discovered" its world, through an act of circumnavigation, and found it to be of a particular shape: a globe. At the same time, the very meaning of this totality seems to have fallen from its heavenly throne, and the idea of the world assumed a "worldly" (that is, "secular") form. The physical infinity of the universe, however, made the human world infinitely smaller. The globe eventually became simultaneously the terrain of infinite possibilities as well as an inexorable limit: the globe now meant the empirical limit of human action. The world is only so big, and we know exactly what world conquest would mean. But this radical empirical limit at the same time opened up the possibility of the infinite multiplication of meaning. In modernity, then, the globe became the empirical limit that rendered possible the plurality of the worlds of meaning.[1]

The infinite multiplication of meaning, however, does not mean a lack of meaning. We could recall here Martin Heidegger's famous formulation according to which, in the age of modern metaphysics, it is no longer the world who is watching us; it is now the subject who is watching the world.[2] For Heidegger, this reversal implies a relation of representation, which defines the world as a "picture." But if the world is not a representation of something else, but a representation according to its essence, it becomes possible to conceive of this world as a representation which is, on the one hand, simply one representation among many others and, on the other hand, the representation of the totality of representations. This logic also allows us to think of the idea of the world as something that has the capacity to appear as one particular represented object in the field of representation at the same time as it defines the basic characteristics of this field of representation. In other words, for modernity, the idea of the world comes to denote a totality of representation which is itself necessarily represented.[3]

But what is the meaning of "catastrophe" for a world like this? Of course, we should remember that the birth of modernity is registered in our history books as the more or less beneficent outcome of a series of "traumas": the political, social, scientific, technological, and philosophical revolutions that gave birth to this world turned out to be so many wounds on our collective egos. The traumatic inception of modernity shows us two important things. On the one hand, the world of infinite meanings can only emerge as an intrinsically threatened totality. Catastrophe, in this sense, is the figure of the infinite displacement of meaning. Since no singular world can be the World anymore, the birth and subsequent destruction of the worlds is the norm of existence. On the other hand, the ultimate catastrophe is the birth of the modern itself. Taken to its absurd logical conclusion, the modern simultaneously names the realization of the new as well as the principle of its self-cancellation. For the modern world, catastrophe is not merely the act of an angry God that brings its creation to a conclusion, but the permanent crisis of its very own existence.

Borrowing Joseph Schumpeter's famous definition, we could say that catastrophe is the "creative destruction" that is the very essence of the modern.[4] The most compelling image of this new historical experience, of course, comes from Walter Benjamin. From the perspective of the "angel of history," progress *is* catastrophe: "This is how one pictures the angel of history. His face is turned toward the past. Where we perceive a chain of events, he sees one single catastrophe which keeps piling wreckage and hurls it in front of his feet."[5] The crucial point for us is the split of perspectives: the very same thing that appears to be the "chain of events" (the reality of history) from the immanent perspective of historical subjects is actually, from the transcendent perspective of the angel of history, "one single catastrophe." This is the catastrophic content of the modern: the metaphysics of the modern is based on a split between form and content in such a way that the form of history (its mode of appearance to human beings) has one single content, catastrophe (and not even "catastrophes" in the plural). Regardless of the concrete form that the realization of "the modern" assumes in a historical situation, the actual content of this realization is the creative destruction of the old in such a way that the new simply becomes an occasion for its very own self-overcoming.

Thus, if we assume that modernism and mass culture were two basic cultural formations of modernity, the question we have to raise here concerns their relation to the catastrophic content of the modern. The parallel historical emergence of modernism and mass culture is already a well-documented development and I only want to add two things to the customary accounts: the appearance of a particular genre (atomic holocaust fiction) and its relation to anti-Communist politics. Discussions of the history of atomic holocaust fiction usually work with a consistent set of periods: first, they examine its origins in the first half of the nineteenth century; then they discuss the late nineteenth-century developments before World War I (1870–1914); this is usually followed by the interwar years as a separate period; finally, the post-Hiroshima years form an independent unit that comes to an end sometime during the sixties.[6] We can see that atomic holocaust fiction emerges as an independent genre exactly at the same time as modernism emerges as the main mode of cultural production. We can also see that in this scheme the early Cold War years form a discreet period dominated by American authors.[7] Therefore, historically speaking, the institutionalization of American modernism and the Americanization of atomic holocaust fiction coincide. This is why we start with the assumption that the juxtaposition of modernism and atomic holocaust fiction in a discussion of the American 1950s should yield important insights into the role of catastrophe in anti-Communist ideology.

In order to illustrate the way this relationship is usually conceived, we could cite here Susan Sontag's "The Imagination of Disaster" (1965). Sontag's article on the sci-fi movies of the 1950s is a critical classic that interprets these movies as allegories of the unthinkable. In a typical turn of the argument, however, she considers mass culture to be an "inadequate response" to the metaphysical condition of human finitude magnified by the real possibility of collective (instead of merely individual) annihilation.[8] As allegorical representations of the mass trauma of the atomic age, these movies provided their contemporary audiences a protective shield against the two basic threats of the age: "unremitting banality and inconceivable terror."[9] Thus the "fantasy" fulfilled a double purpose: it saved the ordinary citizens of consumer capitalism from dehumanizing banality by transporting them to exotic, alien worlds; at the same time, it protected its audience from the unbearable horrors of the atomic age by normalizing them. In these stories, the normal is made extraordinary, while the extraordinary is normalized.

For Sontag, the essential problem with these movies is a moral failure, since they disavow an "unthinkable" event.[10] At the same time, this moral failure is also an artistic failure: "The interest of these films . . . consists in this intersection between a naïve and largely debased commercial art product and the most profound dilemmas of the contemporary situation."[11] As we can see, a crucial distinction emerges from Sontag's reading that will be essential for us. The point is not simply that mass culture is debased commercial art, but that it is the wrong kind of art about the right kind of material. Sontag's argument, therefore, allows us to juxtapose modernism and mass culture (atomic holocaust fiction) as different artistic treatments of the very same historical material, which, nevertheless, is declared to be "unthinkable."

This concern with the unthinkable leads us to the fundamental paradox of atomic holocaust fiction: in its extreme forms, the genre invites us to imagine its own impossibility. Whatever other task it may perform, the genre is in essence the formalization of the very impossibility of fiction, of a world without imagination, a world without subjects. The most extreme representatives of the genre simply narrate a sequence of events that obliterate the very conditions of narration. No matter what kind of a solution the particular work might offer in face of this imminent threat, the narrative drive is always toward self-annihilation. As explorations of the cultural conditions of narration, these fictions are caught in a double bind: the imagination of the event that renders narration impossible opens up and makes possible the fictional field in which these novels can narrate their stories. We are dealing with a genre which is only made possible by the possibility of imagining its total destruction. This is why William

J. Scheick calls these works (borrowing a term from Stanley Fish) "self-consuming artifacts."[12]

As we can see, in this case narration as such is threatened by what makes it possible, as if the ultimate catastrophe of this kind of fiction were the catastrophic confrontation with its very own conditions. This complication accounts for the constitutive self-reflexive component of the genre which reached its artistic peak in Orwell's *1984*. The foundation of this self-reflexive dimension is that, beside the represented elements, the very principle of representation has to be accounted for. Therefore, it follows from its foundational paradox that in nuclear holocaust fiction the "event" that constitutes the genre as such always has to be located on the level of the symbolic framework. The story is not simply internal to this framework (the field of representation); it is *about* this framework as well. In a typical case, this framework is threatened by something or someone and the story usually examines the nature of this threat, the possible consequences of the collapse of the framework, and the measures necessary for the reconstitution or reformulation of this framework. This is why we could say that it is the very idea of the "world" which is politicized in this kind of fiction.

One of the most important consequences of the paradox of atomic holocaust fiction concerns the very status of the "voice" that discloses to us an unthinkable "event." It is customary to speak of the atomic holocaust fiction of the immediate postwar era in terms of the reality of the atomic menace. During this period, atomic holocaust fiction was supposedly invested with certain "realistic" values.[13] But the important point is that it is misleading to speak of realism here. Rather, we must insist that the anti-Communist atomic holocaust fiction of the fifties is defined by a structural move toward the documentary. I speak of a structural move because, on the most fundamental level, this move toward the documentary manifests itself as a mutation of the function of the narratorial voice and not always as a conscious and explicit imitation of the generic traditions of the documentary.

If the narrative space of atomic holocaust fiction is opened up by the real possibility of the utter destruction of narration, the question we must never forget to pose is this: How is it possible that a voice emerges that can tell the story of its own demise? As Pascal Bonitzer's definition of realism and documentary shows, what is at stake in this discussion is the so-called "voice-off." For Bonitzer, there are two basic paradigms of this voice-off: the homogenous narratorial space of realistic fiction (Bonitzer's example is the detective film and *Kiss Me Deadly*) and the heterogeneous space of the documentary voice-off:

> The conventional realist homogeneity of narrative space calls up identification by means of the image, and thus all which intervenes

from offscreen immediately causes questioning (at least of an anterior identification by means of the play of the shot/reverse shot, reframings, etc.). At the inverse of such narrative space, in the divided, heterogeneous space of documentary, the voice-off forbids questioning about its enunciator, its place, and its time. The commentary, in informing the image, and the image, in allowing itself to be invested by the commentary, censor such questions.[14]

I will distinguish here atomic holocaust fiction and the spy thriller precisely in these terms. Whereas the first establishes the possibility of the heterogeneous "voice-off" of documentary as its very own possibility, the second investigates the limits of the image but (as I will try to show later) it also establishes the possibility of an alternative (heterogeneous) perspective. That is, atomic holocaust fiction, when it falls under the sway of the documentary, strives to establish the heterogeneity of the narratorial voice in such a way that it "lets the event speak": it disguises its act of mediation as the self-disclosure of the world.

Highlighting the structural significance of the documentary voice allows us to question the common practice of the overhasty allegorization of popular narratives. Allegoresis is, of course, possible, but only if it performs a double task: it has to establish the principle of representation that allows a particular world to appear in such a way that certain figurative substitutions become possible and necessary in order to maintain the consistency of this world. Gary K. Wolf, for example, attempts to displace the allegorical readings of atomic holocaust fiction in similar terms: "To narrowly allegorize any of these novels . . . would of course be dangerously reductive, but to ignore such potential meanings altogether would be reductive in an entirely different way. . . . Perhaps, after all, the profoundest question we can ask of such novels is that simple question of Hernando's in Bradbury's 'The Highway': 'What do they mean, "the world"?'"[15] The question "What does a particular figure stand for?" has to be preceded by another question: "How is 'the world' defined by the text?"

The shift from the realistic to the documentary reading, however, does not mean the complete denial of the allegorical dimension. Rather, it claims that the space of allegorical substitutions is made possible by a documentary voice on the level of the "primary aesthetics" of the disclosure of a world. In fact, this is the point where we can return to the question of the catastrophic content of the modern in relation to mass culture and modernism. On the most basic level, mass culture and modernism could be understood as two basic paradigms of dealing with the constitutive limits of representation: while mass culture thematizes the limits of representation and, therefore, discusses them on the level of content, modernism turns the inherent limitations of representation into a formal principle. For the same reasons, we could call the catastrophe story an "allegorical" critique of representation, since it "narrates" the inherent limit of representation. In other words, it always gives a narrative form to something which is alien to narration. At the same time, modernism turns catastrophe into a formal principle in the sense that no matter how trivial its contents might be (let us recall, for example, Leopold Bloom's bowel movements), the very principle of formalizing this content already performs the impossibility of representation. In opposition to mass culture, we could speak of a "performative" critique of representation. What is common to both, however, is their mutual concern with the catastrophic content of the modern.

Modernism and Catastrophe

But we need to be more specific about the consequences of this opposition of mass culture and modernism in terms of the split between form and content. As we have seen, if modernism conveys the traumatic experience of modernity, according to traditional accounts, mass culture offers it for mere voyeuristic enjoyment.[16] To put it differently, whereas modernism maintains an indirect tie with the historical experience of catastrophe, mass culture reduces it to entertainment and thereby renders the catastrophic kernel of the age inaccessible. According to the ideology we are examining here, while modernism represents catastrophe as the sublime self-transcendence of art, all mass culture has to offer is the simulacrum of catastrophe. More precisely, in the case of modernism the universal content of formal innovation is catastrophe. To the degree that modernism tends toward the elimination of content, it *always speaks about catastrophe* (which now appears as the very figure of the disappearance of content). On the other hand, in the case of mass culture, catastrophe is linked to the tendency toward the elimination of the problem of form. To the degree that catastrophe is reduced to nothing but mere content, mass culture *never really speaks about catastrophe* even if it appears to do so.

To illustrate these points, it is enough to cite two classic statements made by modernist writers about the atomic bomb. The most striking aspect of Gertrude Stein's short statement "Reflections on the Atomic Bomb" (1946) is her categorical dismissal of the atomic bomb as a legitimate topic for literature: "I never could take any interest in the atomic bomb."[17] Although this comment might suggest that catastrophe is not a concern for modernism after all, Stein's point is that the atomic bomb is the exact opposite of literature. The bomb is not just an extra-literary object but the logical negation of literature: wherever it appears, we can no longer speak of literature. To the degree that the atomic bomb is the exact opposite of modernism, it is specifically atomic holocaust fiction and not mass culture in general that gains "symptomatic" significance: "I like to read detective and mystery stories. I never get enough of them but whenever one of them is or was about death rays and atomic bombs I never could read them."[18] While mass culture retains a modicum of legitimacy for Stein as an infinite form of entertainment, it loses all such legitimacy once the atomic bomb appears in it. Thus, what the atomic bomb renders visible is that the opposite of modernism is atomic holocaust fiction.

In his 1951 autobiography, William Carlos Williams criticized Eliot in the following terms: "Then out of the blue *The Dial* brought out *The Waste Land* and all our hilarity ended. It wiped out our world as if an atom bomb had been dropped upon it and our brave sallies into the unknown were turned to dust."[19] For Williams, however, "the essence of a new art form" (that Eliot's poem rendered impossible) was "locality which should give it fruit."[20] This comment primarily demonstrates a conflict internal to modernist poetics itself, of course, as it suggests a potential difference between catastrophic and "regenerative" modernisms. But for Williams, Eliot was the atomic bomb of modernism, since *The Waste Land* imagines history in terms of a post-apocalyptic scenario. Eliot's modernism was, then, a failure to the degree that it simply anticipated the atomic bomb in the midst of a general cultural crisis.

Whereas Stein defined the atomic bomb as the exact opposite of modernism, Williams defined it as the very content of a wrongheaded modernism. These two positions are more than incidental to a definition of modernism, and they confront us with the following formula: atomic holocaust fiction is simultaneously the exact opposite and the hidden content of modernism. While in the case of modernism formal fragmentation corresponds to a displaced catastrophic content, in atomic holocaust fiction we find the opposite tendency: a reductive formalization of an experience that modernism tried to communicate at the limit of its historical possibilities. Atomic holocaust fiction is, therefore, simply a literal rendering of the ideological content of catastrophic modernism. We can speak of an "ideological content" here in the sense that it is precisely the narrative of the trauma of modernity that provides the consistency of the modernist fragmentation of form. Modernist fragmentation is rendered consistent by a narrative that remains external to its field. What appears to be a mere dissolution of meaning in works of modernism is actually an expression of an epochal consciousness. But if the exclusion of mass culture is constitutive of modernism, the excluded element is likely to carry contradictory determinations. It has to be renounced not only because it is the opposite of modernism, but precisely because modernism recognizes itself in it in a displaced form.

We can revisit Frank Kermode's *The Sense of an Ending* (1966) from the perspective of this thesis precisely because Kermode's book is one of the most enduring readings of the modernist apocalypse produced in a Cold War setting.[21] Kermode's arguments can be summarized in four steps. First, he locates the constitutive apocalyptic component of experience on the level of form. He defines catastrophe as a *formal principle* that is radically separated from the problem of content. The basis of this argument is the ontological presupposition that contingent human experience is always necessarily formalized. It is this act of unavoidable formalization that inscribes an ending (and, thereby, also catastrophe) into human experience. Regardless of their actual content, the subject's world-constituting acts of formalization will always contain a catastrophic component.

Next, Kermode inserts this structural catastrophe in a historical scheme. In fact, the central thesis of Kermode's book is that modern apocalypse is no longer imminent but *immanent*. This change implies a shift from the concrete historical prediction of the apocalyptic event to the diagnosis of a permanent crisis. The immanence of the end implies that it is no longer external to the world; it is no longer a "transcendental" event designating the end of history but the mode of existence of history itself. In this regard, modernity is the age in which the structural catastrophe is realized as the permanent crisis of existence. In fact, we could take this as Kermode's definition of the modern: "the age of perpetual transition in technological and artistic matters is understandably an age of perpetual crisis in morals and politics."[22] Modernity is, therefore, the moment when "transition" itself becomes an age: modernity is not a transition between two ages but transition as an epoch.

Third, Kermode defines the relationship of the structural catastrophe and the historical epoch of modernity as inherently *figurative*. He warns his audience that although "there is a powerful eschatological element in modern thought," it would be a mistake to assume that "nuclear bombs are more real and make one experience more authentic crisis-feeling than armies in the sky."[23] Kermode's critique of nuclear apocalypticism argues that nuclear holocaust is a historical articulation of a structural component of the imagination: "And of course we have it now, the sense of an ending. It has not diminished, and is as endemic to what we call modernism as apocalyptic utopianism is to political revolution."[24] The apocalyptic essence of modernism, however, is not to be taken literally: "Yeats is certainly an apocalyptic poet, but he does not take it literally, and this, I think, is characteristic of the attitude not only of modern poets but of the modern literary public to the apocalyptic elements."[25]

Finally, Kermode uses this theory to formulate a critique of the politics of modernism. When Kermode speaks of a "general critical failure in early modernism," he means that Fascism was precisely the attempt to realize in the world (and in that sense "literalize") the catastrophic content of modernist poetry.[26] Modernism was right to use apocalyptic fictions to rejuvenate poetic language. But it was absolutely wrong to reduce these fictions to myths that tried to change the world to conform to these fictions.[27] The literalization of the catastrophic content of the modern is, thus, simultaneously an aesthetic and a political failure.

During the 1950s, a similar set of convictions organized the liberal anti-Communist definition of modernist catastrophe. Once again, the exemplary case is Lionel Trilling. In *The Liberal Imagination*, Henry James's "imagination of disaster" has emerged as the center of the American literary canon. On the level of political content, this imagination refers us to Trilling's concept of "moral realism." According to Trilling, liberalism remains politically correct to the degree that it successfully aestheticizes its position and uses this aestheticization for a perpetual self-critique: it must protect itself from the false utopianism of the fellow-traveling left. Liberalism *is* the imagination of disaster to the degree that it maintains a sense of perpetual crisis. On the level of aesthetic form, however, the liberal imagination of disaster also means the rejection of realism in defense of a particular kind of modernist aesthetics. The function of the figure of the catastrophe is precisely to bring together the politics of moral realism with the aesthetics of antirealism.

Pondering the history of James's reception, Trilling wonders why the works of the 1880s, which in the 1950s appear to be the most appealing pieces of the oeuvre, were so obviously disliked by James's contemporaries. The answer, of course, is to be found in the catastrophic content of modernism:

> It is just this prescience, of course, that explains the resistance of James's contemporaries. What James saw he saw truly, but it was not what the readers of this time were themselves equipped to see. That we now are able to share this vision required the passage of six decades and the events which brought them to climax. Henry James in the eighties understood what we have painfully learned from our grim glossary of wars and concentration camps, after having seen the state and human nature laid open to our horrified inspection. "But I have the imagination of disaster—and see life as ferocious and sinister" . . . But nowadays we know that such an imagination is one of the keys to truth.[28]

Only a historical delay can bring out the significance of James's modernism. In fact, it appears that the real content of James's art was actually the

Holocaust. It is as if James wanted to imagine the Holocaust in advance as the necessary outcome of modernity.

For Trilling, however, this imagination is not without its own dangerous excesses. He argues that James's real power lies in the combination of "disaster" and "love": "James had the imagination of disaster and that is why he is immediately relevant to us; but together with the imagination of disaster he had what the imagination of disaster often destroys and in our time is daily destroying, the imagination of love."[29] Trilling is never far from the conclusion that one of the major problems of his age is precisely this excessive obsession with disaster. Although disaster can save us from the corruption of liberalism, it can also be corrupted by mass culture. Since the latter is obsessed with visions of "losses of civilization, personality, humanness," it "sinks our spirits not merely because they are terrible and possible but because they have become so obvious and cliché that they seem to close for us the possibility of thought and imagination."[30] This rejection of both the lack and the excess of the imagination of disaster shows that Trilling considered naïve utopianism to be as harmful as clichéd apocalypticism.[31]

This critique forms the basis of Trilling's theory of modernism and mass culture. He conceives this relationship in terms of an ideological reversal: mass culture appears to be doing something, but in reality it is doing the exact opposite (moral indignation hides obscene pleasure). Let us consider the following passage:

> But Ortega was right in observing of modern art that it expressed a dislike of holding in the mind the human fact and the human condition, that is shows "a real loathing of living forms and living beings," a disgust with the "rounded and soft forms of living bodies" . . . the day seems to have gone when the artist who dealt in representation could catch our interest almost by the mere listing of the ordinary details of human existence. . . . This seems to be supported by evidence from those arts for which a conscious exaltation of humanistic values is stock-in-trade—I mean advertising and our middling novels, which, almost in the degree that they celebrate the human, falsify and abstract it; in the very business of expressing adoration of the rounded and soft forms of living bodies they expose the disgust which they really feel.[32]

The argument here is structured by two important oppositions: on the one hand, Trilling sets modernism against representational art (more precisely, against realism as "the mere listing of the ordinary details of human existence"); on the other hand, he opposes art to mass culture (advertising and middling novels). While the ideological content of modernism is a certain critique of classic humanism, mass culture is propelled by a false image of humanism, which actually hides the same disgust that forms the core of modernism. In the case of mass culture, it seems, the realism of cruelty hides pleasure, while the celebration of humanistic values hides secret revulsion. Whatever its content might appear to be, according to Trilling, mass culture actually hides contrary ideological values. Thus, while the same historical experience forms the basis of both modernism and mass culture (the disintegration of humanist values), they represent two different reactions. Mass culture is defined here as the disavowed form of the same ideological content that animates modernism.

As we can see, what is common to Trilling's and Kermode's readings of modernism is that they both redefined catastrophe as a structural moment of the human imagination and experience. We could say that catastrophe is elevated in the discourse of modernism to a "metaphysical concept" which has specific modern forms of appearance. But it has also been suggested that *both* modernism and mass culture can fail to capture the essence of catastrophe. In this regard, it is striking that Kermode's critique reverses the terms of the liberal critique of anti-Communist culture as we discussed it in the previous chapter: while anti-Communist popular culture was deemed to be an inadequate translation of an otherwise correct politics into a faulty aesthetics, modernism emerges here as the inadequate translation of an aesthetic innovation into a politics.

The anti-Communist imagination of catastrophe was caught between these two extremes. One the one hand, as Trilling's misgivings also made it clear, the disturbing politics of aesthetic modernism suggested a totalitarian imposition of aesthetic values on everyday life (Nazism and its aestheticization of politics); on the other hand, the direct politicization of art reduced the latter to propaganda (or Communist socialist realism). This is why the imagination of disaster supposedly guarded against both extremes: it tried to produce an aesthetics that was the very suspension of the imposition on the world (it prevented the naïve transposition of aesthetic values into politics); and it did so in such a way that disaster itself could not be turned into a direct political program. The political value of true art was that it maintained an allegorical (and never literal) connection with the metaphysical core of history.

Necessary Illusions

As Paul Brians observed, the "popular" literature devoted to atomic holocausts produced few truly popular works.[33] During the period we are concerned with, strictly speaking, the culture of atomic fear produced only two important best sellers: John Hersey's *Hiroshima* (1946) and Nevil Shute's *On the Beach* (1957).[34] The historical distance separating these two pieces clearly indicates the crucial differences between the two: Hersey belongs to the first wave of atomic fear primarily concerned with the destructive force of the atomic bomb; Shute, however, belongs to the age of the H-bomb and is mostly concerned with radioactive fallout. But we also have to point out that while Hersey's *New Yorker* article was a response to a historical event that really did happen, Shute's novel was about an atomic war that never took place. What is common to the two, however, is that they both redefine the limits separating facts from fiction: *Hiroshima* starts from a factual account and moves toward a performance of the insufficiency of mere factual accounts; *On the Beach*, on the other hand, is mere fiction that attempts to dramatize the fundamental necessity of organizing reality around necessary fictions. The juxtaposition of these two works allows us to raise the problem of the documentary voice in popular literature of the atomic holocaust.

If we consider its contemporary reception, it appears that one of the most striking features of Hersey's article was its style. To be more precise, the most striking feature of the text was a certain discrepancy between the simplicity of its style and the magnitude of its subject matter. For example, in Ruth Benedict's review for *The Nation*, we read: "the calmness of the narrative throws into relief the nightmare magnitude of the destructive power the brains of men have brought into being. There is no preaching in this book."[35] Hersey explained himself in the following terms: "The flat style was deliberate, and I still think I was right to adopt it. A high literary manner, or a show of passion, would have brought *me* into the story as a mediator; I wanted to avoid such mediation, so the reader's experience would be as direct as possible."[36] The central question, therefore, concerned the proper way of formalizing an exceptional historical content.

In a brief overview of the contemporary reception of Hersey's *Hiroshima*, Michael J. Yavenditti called attention to a curious interaction of moral and political responses. Although the text provoked a predictable moral response by soliciting sympathy for the victims of atomic warfare, on the political level it did not encourage a condemnation of government policies.[37] Arguably, it was precisely this seemingly contradictory response that did incite two of the most ardent critiques of Hersey's text, those of Dwight Macdonald and Mary McCarthy. Macdonald's famous dismissal of the work is based on his radical critique of mass culture.[38] The review proceeds by way of a set of clear divisions. As a first step, Macdonald opposes the middlebrow sentimentality of the *New Yorker* to true art. Then, within the field of art, he distinguishes naturalism from modernism. According to Macdonald, in Hersey's text, middlebrow sentimentality masquerades as naturalism. But precisely because it is a mere simulacrum of art, this sentimentalism can only be "de-natured naturalism"—naturalism without nature. The failure of this naturalism is opposed to the "real" naturalism of Dreiser and Farrell. But Hersey's artistic failure (his inability to find the unifying element that could create a whole) is primarily put in relief by the achievements of Hemingway. If Dreiser had written this report on Hiroshima, it would have been at least good naturalism; but Hemingway could have created a true modernist work. The only adequate representation of the horrors of atomic warfare, both aesthetically and morally, is modernism.

In her response to Macdonald's review, Mary McCarthy took this conclusion one step further by charging Hersey with an additional political failure. For her, Hersey's false representation of an unrepresentable event in the journalistic register is an inherent political failure. As McCarthy explained, the fundamental problem with the reception of Hersey's *Hiroshima* was that everyone (including Macdonald himself) assumed that the political point of the text was to present an argument against atomic warfare. But McCarthy wanted to show that the politics of the text is the exact opposite: "The point is that the *New Yorker* cannot be against the atom bomb, no matter how hard it tries, just as it could not, even in this moral 'emergency,' eliminate the cigarette and perfume advertising that accompanied Mr. Hersey's text."[39] Therefore, Hersey's piece is simply an "insipid falsification of the truth of atomic warfare."[40] This falsification consist of a representation of the unrepresentable: "To treat it journalistically, in terms of measurable destruction, is, in a sense, to deny its existence.... Up to August 31 of this year, no one dared think of Hiroshima—it appeared to us all as a kind of hole in human history. Mr. Hersey has filled that hole with busy little Japanese Methodists; he has made it familiar and safe, in the final sense, boring."[41] McCarthy's message is clear: by reducing an unrepresentable event to the field of representation and "minimizing" the atom bomb "as though it belonged to the familiar order of catastrophes," the very medium in which Hersey's text appears predetermines its politics. The only correct option, offered by real art, is to maintain the unrepresentability of the hole in history through a move beyond this representational framework.

Although these discussions are not directly involved in an evaluation of the politics of anti-Communism, Macdonald and McCarthy effectively perform the same redefinition of the politics of modernism that we discussed in the previous chapter. Modernism is aesthetically, morally, and politically correct because, by moving beyond mere realistic representation, it provides the only viable way of rendering the unrepresentable. These two authors displace the political dimension of the text from its content to the method of representation. Regardless of what may appear within the field of representation, the very institution of this field already predetermines its political force. As a matter of fact, if we follow McCarthy's analysis, we have to conclude that these two levels can be in direct opposition to each other. While the represented content seeks to establish moral sympathy with the victims, the method of representation and the medium of distribution already restrict the political efficacy of the text in such a way that the moral message and political truth are fundamentally at odds with each other.

The paradox of atomic holocaust fiction dwells precisely in this attempt to construct the authority of the narratorial voice by reporting an event that undermines all narrative authority. While Macdonald and McCarthy faulted Hersey for reducing the un-narratable to the field of narration, we have to add an extra dimension here. The question is not simply narrating something that remains always external to the field of narration, but narrating that which makes narration as such impossible: in other words, this event is not simply external to narration but marks its limit. Thus what emerges in the pages of *Hiroshima* is that style guarantees the authenticity of the representation: it is the *quality* of the voice which discloses this catastrophe that renders the representation of the world authentic. As the unity of style gives form to an un-narratable event, the documentary realism of the individual narratives is guaranteed by the fictional unity of authorial voice. But the unity of this style precedes the actual narration itself in the sense that the possibility of this kind of realism is heterogeneous to the narrated events. In the end, narration is made possible by the necessary fiction of narratability. We are up against a politics of realism that has to prove the necessity of illusions.

The central thesis of *On the Beach* is precisely this: certain illusions are necessary. In fact, one of the major objectives of the narrative is to invest seemingly foolish illusions with an ethical bonus. This celebration of necessary illusions, however, leads to a strange mirroring interaction of fact and fiction. In the fictional world of the novel, it is the illusion of normalcy that is revealed to be absolutely necessary in a post-holocaust world; in the pre-holocaust world of the readers (which is supposedly a world of normalcy), however, it is the illusion of catastrophe (the breakdown of normalcy) that is declared to be necessary. This is why we can say that the ultimate point of the novel is to construct a fictional world within which certain illusions can unequivocally emerge as *really* necessary. Both the illusions of absolute normalcy and absolute catastrophe are necessary. The central illusion that holds together the world of the novel has as its content the values represented by the stereotypical white middle-class family. Even if the middle-class nuclear family is only an illusion, according to the novel, it is an ethical imperative to live life as if it were real. In order to reveal the necessity of this illusion of normalcy, however, we need a fictional device that can project the absolute destruction of the world held together by this illusion of middle-class normalcy. In other words, what the illusion of nuclear holocaust reveals is the necessity of the illusion of normalcy.

The story opens after the entire Northern Hemisphere has been destroyed in a nuclear war and Australia remained the only inhabitable continent. In the background of the story, the fallout from the North is slowly devouring the rest of the world, and the novel ends with the utter extinction of life on the face of Earth. The war was probably provoked by Albania and started with an Israeli-Arab war, which turned into a Russian-NATO war, which in turn led to a Russian-Chinese war. Set in this post-holocaust world of melancholy decay, the story is composed of two major subplots (the romantic and the military), both of which remain unfulfilled: love remains Platonic; and the final mission of the U.S. Navy reveals what we already knew, that survival is impossible. After Mary and Peter Holmes (a lieutenant commander of the Australian Navy) befriend Commander Dwight Towers (the man in charge of what is left of the U.S. Navy), the novel narrates the budding romance between Moira Davidson (a friend of the Holmes's) and the American captain. The curious thing about this romance, however, is that it remains unfulfilled simply because Towers used to be married before the war. Although his family is killed in the war, he chooses to live life as if nothing had happened and rejects Moira's advances. At the same time, the novel also narrates the last desperate efforts of the survivors to recover life in America. The last mission of the American submarine *Scorpion* is to investigate a mysterious radio signal coming from the Seattle area. At the end of the dangerous journey deep into the heavily contaminated Northern Hemisphere, however, the survivors find that the mission was in vain. Instead of survivors, they merely find that the wind is moving an overturned Coke bottle, which is hitting a radio transmitter.

The central argument of the text is that both an excess and a lack of illusions are harmful. While a complete lack of illusion is likely to lead to self-destructive behavior and sheer chaos, an excess of illusions leads to self-deception and the complete denial of reality. The reason why Captain Towers can emerge as the ethical center of the novel is that he uncompromisingly chooses to hold on to an illusion while he knows very well that it is merely an illusion. In this respect, the would-be lovers of the story represent two different ways of self-delusion: Moira Davidson lives in "the world of romance, of make-believe and double brandies."[42] Her alcoholism is mere self-destructive escape from reality. But Dwight Towers represents a different form of self-delusion: his delusion is not romantic but realistic, in the sense that it allows him to face the reality of complete annihilation with dignity. Indeed, much of the story is preoccupied with the education of Moira, who needs to be "reformed" and needs to learn the difference between the two forms of illusion in order to be able to accept the truth of Towers's illusion: rather than seduce Towers, she needs to accept the reality of the illusion that organizes his life.

The novel contains quite a few self-reflective elements in which the constitutive paradox of atomic holocaust fiction surfaces. The most important point, however, is that the impossibility involved in this paradox becomes the ground of an ethical principle: in the course of the novel, "can't" becomes "shouldn't." Thus, the limited nature of human imagination is not a deplorable obstacle, but rather a defense against the horrors of reality. Therefore, as the novel suggests, that which is beyond imagination should remain unimagined. As a matter of fact, the importance of the necessary illusions surfaces here: they make up for the inherent limitations of imagination by filling in the hole created by the unimaginable with illusions that make the smooth functioning of the community possible. For example, this is how Moira first contemplates Dwight Towers's obsession with his family:

> She had known for some time that his wife and family were very real to him, more real by far than the half-life in a far corner of the world that had been forced upon him since the war. The devastation of the Northern Hemisphere was not real to him, as it was not real to her. He had seen nothing of the destruction of the war, as she had not; in thinking of his wife and of his home it was impossible for him to visualize them in any other circumstances than those in which he had left them. He had little imagination, and that formed a solid core for his contentment in Australia.[43]

Earlier in the novel, Moira complained to Towers that she has never been outside Australia and has only seen the rest of the world in movies. In a self-reflexive moment of the novel, she tries to imagine the movie one would make of the devastation that took place in the Northern Hemisphere. Towers answers that such a movie would not be possible to make: "A cameraman couldn't live, as far as I can see. I guess nobody will ever know what the Northern Hemisphere looks like now, excepting God." After a brief pause, he adds: "I think that's a good thing. . . . I suppose it's lack of imagination. I don't want to have any more imagination."[44]

This reflection on the limits of imagination and the impossibility of documenting the unimaginable becomes a practical problem when the American submarine goes on an exploratory cruise to investigate heavily contaminated areas. Although the soldiers must write a report of their journey, they conclude that there is nothing to be reported: they have to write a report that reports nothing. Contemplating the lack of information in the report, Towers tells his follow soldiers the same thing that he told Moira: "Nobody will ever really know what a hot place looks like. And that goes for the whole of the Northern Hemisphere. . . . I think that's right. . . . There's some things that a person shouldn't want to go and see."[45] Nevertheless, this insistence on the limitation of what one should try to imagine is not a complete renunciation of reality. As a matter of fact, immediately after this statement, the discussion among the soldiers leads to the problem of historiography. Once again, the novel tries to investigate its very own presuppositions. When Peter Holmes asks if anyone is "writing any kind of history about these times," John Osborne responds that he is not aware of any such efforts, but "there does not seem to be much point in writing stuff that nobody will read."[46] Towers, however, responds that "There should be something written, all the same. . . . Even if it's only going to be read in the next few months."[47] We can see that we are dealing with a double ethical imperative: on the one hand, that which is beyond imagination should remain unrepresented; on the other hand, that which is within the established field of representation should be represented even if it cannot be rendered "as a coherent story."[48] Although an authentic documentary is impossible, it is nevertheless an ethical necessity.

In the most explicitly self-reflective episode of the novel, Moira and Captain Towers visit the National Gallery to see an exhibition of post-holocaust religious paintings:

> They were all oil paintings, mostly in a modernistic style. They walked around the gallery set aside for the forty paintings in the exhibition, the girl interested, the naval officer frankly uncomprehending. Neither of them had much to say about the green Crucifixions or the pink Nativities; the five or six paintings dealing with religious aspects of the war stirred them to controversy. They paused before the prizewinner, the sorrowing Christ on a back-ground of the destruction of a great city.[49]

Their reactions to the painting, however, are quite different. While Moira likes the painting because it has "good composition and good colouring," Captain Towers hates it "like hell."[50] His first explanation for this strong reaction is that the subject of the painting is "phony." Simply put, Towers expects a certain amount of realism. He points out that "No pilot in his senses would he flying as low as that with thermonuclear bombs going off around," and adds that if this city is supposed to be New York City, then the painter got his buildings mixed up. When Moira points out that the subject of the painting is not necessarily a particular city, Towers concludes that "It couldn't have looked like that. . . . Too dramatic."[51] The lack of realism is finally explained by Towers as an excess of "dramatic" effects. He is disturbed by the painting because it is a false form of realism that substitutes dramatic excess for authentic representation in order to convey a propagandistic (in this case, religious) message. This specification is important because Towers does find his own aesthetic ideal in Renoir: "They went and found the French art, and he stood for some time before a painting of a river and a tree-shaded street beside it, with white houses and shops, very French and very colorful. 'That's the kind of picture I like.'"[52] Once again, the illusion of absolute normalcy is declared to be more important than the unavoidably inauthentic representation of the unimaginable. This conclusion sums up the aesthetics as well as the political message of the whole novel.

Just as in the case of Hersey's *Hiroshima*, the general assumption appears to have been that the novel is against atomic war. Such was at least the assumption of the Eisenhower administration, which was stirred to action by Stanley Kramer's film version of *On the Beach*. Spencer R. Weart, for example, writes: "Eisenhower's cabinet discussed confidential actions they might take to undermine the movie, and the State Department and the AEC [Atomic Energy Commission] distributed comments. According to government view, voiced in public through various mouths, *On the Beach* was seriously in error."[53] But the pattern of reception again seems to resemble that of *Hiroshima*: "Audiences came away from *On the Beach* and similar works not with questions about military policy but with a sense of inevitable tragedy."[54] The erroneous assumption about the politics of the story (that it was a critique of government politics) founders on the fact that, through domesticating and romanticizing the end of the world (whereby it completely excluded any representation of actual warfare), it simultaneously asserted the necessity of the illusion of normalcy and the inevitability of catastrophe. Rather than an attack on the ideological foundations of Cold War anti-Communism, *On the Beach* provided the clearest formulation of such an ideology: while it appears to be against atomic war, it actually reinforces the ideological foundations of anti-Communism.

When Worlds Collide: Philip Wylie and the End of the Nation

Let us now examine in more detail how the concept of the "world" functions in the works of one of the most well-known anti-Communist authors of catastrophic fiction. In a typical reading of Philip Wylie's oeuvre, he is usually cited as an eccentric Jungian anti-Communist obsessed with civil defense who also happens to be the father of the term "momism."

Michael Rogin, for example, uses Wylie as an introduction to his reading of Cold War cinema because Wylie "merges" "Communism, mothers, and scientific catastrophe."[55] At one point in the argument, Rogin summarizes Wylie's position in the following terms: "He advocated continued military preparedness after the war and warned that Americans (softened by moms) were not taking seriously the Communist threat. (He also blamed mom for McCarthyism)."[56] But we have to ask the question: if Americans do not take the Communist threat seriously, why is there such a thing as McCarthyism at all? Rogin's otherwise inspiring reading manifests here one of its decisive shortcomings: it concentrates only on Wylie's anti-Communism and refuses to engage in a more comprehensive manner Wylie's critique of McCarthyism.[57]

In accordance with the rhetoric of the anti-Communist liberalism of the fifties, what Wylie renounces is extremism. In this case, "Mom" would not be a figure for Communism but the figure of excess that leads to extremism. Accordingly, for Wylie, lack and excess of anti-Communism are equally detrimental. We have to acknowledge the fact that politically Wylie was closer to the liberal consensus of the "vital center" than Rogin would be willing to admit.[58] One of the major points where Wylie diverges from this politics of the center, however, is his decidedly middlebrow aesthetics, which simultaneously renounces high modernism and mass culture. *Generation of Vipers* (1942) clearly demonstrates this position. In fact, as Wylie himself points out in a footnote, his political centrism is even more authentic than that of the disillusioned fellow-travelers, since he has been opposed to Communism "from the very days when so many of my literary colleagues—the liberals and liberal-intellectuals—were not so opposed."[59]

But the important point is that Wylie already defines the task of democracy in opposition to extremism both on the left and the right.[60] The golden middle between these two extremes is the terrain of Americanism, but the problem is that Americans gave up the true spirit of self-criticism and substituted for it a hypocritical dogmatism of self-deception. This is why Wylie devoted his whole life to trying to cut through the veil of this peculiarly American form of deception. The program outlined by Wylie is not unlike Trilling's notion of the liberal imagination of disaster. But, unlike Trilling, Wylie literalizes the catastrophic content of modernism through the figure of atomic holocaust in the name of anti-Communist political realism.

This is why Wiley's critics even today tend to be right for the wrong reasons. For example, when we consider the problem of "momism," we must keep it in mind that it is essentially a conceptual tool for a liberal critique of gender roles rather than a conservative attack on women. Of course, we have to break down Wylie's argument into two steps. First, momism is introduced as a tool for criticizing a society that only allows two possible social roles for women: that of "Cinderella" (the young girl being trained to marry her Prince) and "Mom" (the married woman). This critique argues that the socially constructed role of "Mom" became the focal point of an ideology, and as a result, the characterology of "mom" provides us a key to what is wrong with a society that does not allow women to assume other roles. In a second step, however, Wylie's argument moves beyond the liberal critique of society to uncover its "metaphysical" foundations. Wylie presupposes a natural order behind the social construction: men and women participate in natural power relations. In Wylie's arguments, liberal political impulses are often short-circuited by metaphysical presuppositions. This mistake, however, is not only Wylie's individual deviation from the essence of liberalism, but rather a general formula that describes much of what we call today "Cold War liberalism."

In one of the early chapters of *Generation of Vipers*, entitled "Subjective Feudalism," Wylie imagines how a future historian would describe the barbaric twentieth century. This hypothetical historian is emblematic of Wylie's narrative techniques in two senses: on the level of content, he proposes a dual critique of dangerous extremes; on the level of form, he displaces the narratorial instance to a hypothetical future. Our historian dismisses modern art in the already all too familiar terms of middlebrow moral revolt: "Under the pretense of being 'abstract' or 'advanced,' artists without ability of any sort covered canvases with daubs, mists, swirls, spirals, cubes and half-envisioned objects which had, admittedly, no significance."[61] At the same time, the hypothetical historian of the twentieth century writes the following about mass culture: "Other forms of entertainment, including periodicals of the most banal sort, motion pictures, serial 'strips' which appeared in the newspapers, and continued dramas on the daily radio, dwelt incessantly with such infantile themes as the sudden and unexpected accession to wealth, the selection of an obviously ill-educated and untrained female for a wife by a figure of worldly prominence, the finding of treasure, and—also inevitably—upon murder, torture, horror, monsters, bastardy, seduction, and other crimes."[62]

The fact, however, that this middlebrow critique of modernity is based on the displacement of the narratorial voice into a hypothetical future shows us something essential about Wylie's catastrophe fiction. We could say that the same hypothetical historian narrates every single one of his catastrophe novels. This proposition partially solves the mystery posed by the narratorial voice in Wylie's fiction, which otherwise remains impossible to locate in the world that it discloses. Catastrophe, thus, is the figure that irrevocably separates the present of reading from the future of narration. A strange illusion indeed: the story is not an "already narrated" history; it "will be narrated" only in the future as the history of the present. For Wylie, the catastrophic content of the modern can only be rendered visible from the perspective of the future. This narratorial position reveals that the catastrophe is located between the disunity of our present world and its future unity. The voice is our only guarantee that the world "will have been" one.

We can clearly outline this problematic in Wylie's earliest truly successful literary venture, *When Worlds Collide* (1933, coauthored with Edwin Balmer).[63] The novel shows that the motive of the "collision of worlds" is one of the central organizing forces of Wylie's fiction. First, some sort of an ideological distortion (in Wylie's language, "an illusion") disturbs the natural balance of forces. As a result, the world is split into two. Second, the institutionalization of the artificial split between the two worlds leads to some kind of catastrophe. Finally, the novels reveal the essence of the original mistake and restore the natural unity of the world. In other words, the central ideological presupposition of Wylie's fiction is the assumption that the world is "one" even if its unity comes about as a harmony of contending forces.

When Worlds Collide, a classic of its genre, narrates the end of the world through natural catastrophe. The Earth is destroyed by a pair of planets torn from their own solar system by unknown cosmic forces, but a well-organized group of scientists manages to construct a spaceship (often compared to Noah's ark) with which they escape Earth in time to restart life on one of the guest planets.[64] The natural catastrophe, however, brings out a social conflict. That is, the novel attempts to naturalize a social catastrophe. On the ideological level, the two worlds of the novel represent class antagonism. In this sense, the bourgeois "fear of the masses" is the most obvious structuring force of the text, which advocates an elitist but pragmatic rationalism against the brutal savagery of the vulgar masses. In this sense, the utopic unity of the world in the novel is that of the enlightened elite who managed to reconstitute society without the barbaric rabble: a pure modernity without the masses.

What is striking about the text, however, is that narratorial authority remains unquestionable. It appears as if the voice were completely immune to the threats represented in the novel. We have the impression that even if the world ended, this voice would be still droning on in a lifeless universe. The fact that the narratorial voice is immune to catastrophe indicates that in this world the total threat is balanced by the total stability of the voice. In fact, we encounter here a common component of Wylie's catastrophe fiction: absolute catastrophe is the necessary device used to establish absolute narratorial authority. Unlike in the case of modernism, the general framework of representation is not in any way affected by the represented object, the catastrophe.

The authority of the voice establishes two major transformations in the novel. On the one hand, there is a necessary shift from historical time to geological time; on the other hand, the logic of social organization has to shift from the nation to the human race.[65] In both cases, as we can see, the post-historical and the post-national are imagined to be the domains of natural unities without artificial divisions. The ultimate unity of the world is defined here as the eternity of the human race. The temporality of the post-catastrophic nation is post-historical in the sense that it must be measured by a natural eternity. The post-historical reorganization of the community is achieved in the name of a new universality, that of the "human race," which transcends the nation. But this post-catastrophic universality is still modeled on the United States. At one point in the text, the heroes of survival receive a medal from their leader, Dr. Hendron, who describes the meaning of the medals in the following manner: "These medals bear on one side the motto of the United States of America, which I think we might still adopt as our own. Out of the many nationalities represented before, we intend to create a single race. Therefore the medals bear the inscription, 'E pluribus unum.'"[66] The catastrophe destroys the nation as such, while salvation allows for the recreation of human civilization beyond the confines of nationhood. The rebirth of civilization is based on the disappearance of the nation in America and the projection of post-national Americanness onto a cosmic time.

Thus, the threat at the heart of the novel is the catastrophe of the modern: traditional social structures can no longer contain the effects of modernity. This, however, is not a full indictment of modernization, because the latter simultaneously produces catastrophe (the masses) and deliverance (the modern elite). In other words, the novel needs to justify an internal split within modernity. The text simultaneously manifests and justifies a social division, which is the necessary social exclusion that will save modern civilization from itself: modernity must divide itself in order to restore its unity on a higher level. But this division also bears the burden of having to account for the formal constitution of the novel as well. Since the voice of the narrator is the voice of the post-catastrophic modern elite, the unity of the world, after all, is the stylistic unity of middlebrow form. As we can see, the condition of the narrative voice is the very same social exclusion that the book renders visible. It is in this sense that the voice simultaneously manifests a split in the world and embodies the unity of this world in the present as an absent presence.

Wylie's catastrophe novels from the fifties represent variations on the same set of themes. In spite of all their differences, the organizing principle of all of his works is the restoration of the unity of the world. *When Worlds Collide* (1933) and *After Worlds Collide* (1936) established in the most straightforward manner the religious universalism of anti-Communist Americanism through an attempt to overcome the social division separating the vulgar masses from the educated elite. *Disappearance* (1951), however, introduced the problem of gender roles and sex as a form of internal disruption of this scheme and strove to establish the unity of a world falsely split into two. *Tomorrow!* (1954) argued for the nationalization and militarization of anti-Communism in the name of a catastrophic realism, which clearly defined the true enemy to be a national enemy. Finally, *Triumph* (1963) introduced the problem of race as the very stumbling block of the free world that will inevitably lead to its utter demise. Thus we could say that although the basic scheme of American anti-Communism was already clearly formulated in Wylie's fiction in the thirties, during the fifties Wylie sought to examine in his atomic holocaust fiction the obstacles that prevented the accomplishment of this scheme.[67]

Disappearance is a fictionalized continuation of the arguments put forth in *Generation of Vipers*. It examines the effects of modernization on gender roles and sexuality within the context of the Cold War. On the first page of the novel, we learn that "on the afternoon of the second Tuesday of February at four minutes and fifty-two seconds past four o'clock, Eastern Standard Time," all the women of the Earth disappeared from the world of men, while in an alternative universe, all the men disappeared from the world of women.[68] The most obvious objective of the novel is to link a critique of American attitudes towards sex (and the cultural codification of "gender roles") to a critique of the official rhetoric of the Cold War.

The idea of the "world" is, thus, introduced here as a subjective category. It names the way representatives of the two genders are socialized. But the political program of the novel is the restoration of the unity of the "human" world without false divisions. This unity, however, does not amount to the complete lack of divisions. Rather, natural and social divisions have to be harmonized. As Wylie suggests, the minimal condition of the necessary social change that will save the world from catastrophe is that the external differences between the sexes become "internalized" (that is, differences need to be recognized as internal to the sexual function). In a Jungian fashion, the balance is to be achieved by acknowledging the male part of sexuality in women and the female part in men. The unity of the world is not the complete extermination of divisions, but the restoration of a natural balance through the internalization of differences.

Wylie's ultimate conclusion appears to be that the solution to the problems posed by the inadequacies of Cold War politics lies in a more realistic approach to human sexuality. A realistic attitude to sex would imply a critique of sexual secrecy that, in turn, could form the basis of a critique of political secrecy. Furthermore, the latter could be used to demystify the politics of security, which could lead to a politics of freedom that respects civil liberties. In Wylie's case, the political realism of the "vital center" is based on "sexual realism." And the novel is replete with philosophical references to the center: "In some almost but not quite comprehensible fashion, Nature seemed to manufacture her every composition from the single thesis of a center surrounded by balancing parts."[69] Thus, from the perspective of the liberal anti-Communist center, one of the major achievements of *Disappearance* appears to be the fact that it laid its politics on "metaphysical" foundations. The novel is essentially an attempt to define the natural metaphysics of the liberal center: beyond the world of social illusions, we find a natural order of things that politics should try to realize. The vital center is not only politicized by Wylie. What is even more significant is that it is naturalized, as the middlebrow aesthetics of balanced opposites is elevated to an ontological principle.

Wylie continued his engagement of Cold War politics in his propagandistic civil defense novel *Tomorrow!* (1954).[70] But whereas *Disappearance* was mostly a self-conscious allegory of a divided world, *Tomorrow!* is based on a programmatic move toward realism. The novel narrates the story of two adjacent Midwestern cities, Green Prairie and River City, as they suffer a devastating Soviet atomic attack. The crucial difference between the two cities is that while Green Prairie has a well-organized civil defense program, the inhabitants of River City believe that civil defense is "a waste of money, a squandering of public energy, a meddlesome civil intrusion into military spheres and, all in all, just one more Washington-spawned interference with the rights of common man."[71] Needless to say, River City is amply punished for this poor judgment. Although both cities sustain considerable damage, Green Prairie manages to mitigate the devastation and puts itself in a very good position to start reconstruction after the war is won by the United States. Wylie's message is clear: civil defense works, and it is essential to the survival of the nation.

This political realism, then, is sustained by the aesthetic realism of nuclear catastrophe. The ultimate purpose of the text is to provide a hyper-realistic description of atomic war. This intention finds its immediate fulfillment in the meticulous cataloguing of the horrors of atomic warfare (at one point, for example, we see a pregnant woman trying to push her dead baby back into her stomach which was opened by a large wound).[72] But what renders the text unique among atomic holocaust novels is that the actual atomic explosion is narrated by the omniscient narrator from the perspective of a character who is instantaneously vaporized.[73] This realism promises us a full exposure to the catastrophe, which is now without its mysteries and becomes fully knowable. If catastrophe is representable, atomic war is survivable.

The narratorial voice of realism, however, is once again that of the future. The final elimination of the obstacles to freedom leads to a uto-pistic rejuvenation of America. In fact, on the last pages of the novel, one of the central characters speculates about the meaning of the war for the future of America in the following terms: "Then the Bomb would be no catastrophe at all, but benefit. 'End of an era,' they would say, 'Good thing, too.'"[74] The national enemy establishes the principle of the reconstitution of American national identity beyond any kind of antagonism. The basis of Wylie's catastrophic nationalism is the belief that the total threat to the nation is an external threat and its elimination will lead the utopic recon-stitution of the community.

It is precisely this utopistic reconstitution of the nation that is ren-dered impossible in Wylie's 1963 novel *Triumph*. To a large extent, this novel picks up the same types of arguments that were addressed in *Tomor-row!*, but in comparison with Wylie's earlier novels, *Triumph* introduces two new themes: the utter uselessness of civil defense programs in case of an all-out thermonuclear war and the centrality of racial conflict to the problem of survival. The novel narrates the story of the last fourteen American survivors of an atomic war with the Soviet Union, who spend over two years in millionaire Vance Farr's private super-shelter before they are rescued by the Australian army. The world that ends in this novel is the "white man's world." Wylie suggests that the catastrophic politics of anti-Communism has to be primarily a racial politics. In *Triumph* racism emerges as the internal contradiction of the free world (and its world poli-tics) and the illusion at the heart of this self-deception is the very source of the total catastrophe.

As in *Tomorrow!*, in this novel the primary threat to the United States is the Soviet Union. But what is most striking about *Triumph* is not so much the graphic depiction of atomic warfare as the insanely excessive atomic overkill that the Russians are capable of. Thus, as the novel seems to suggest, the failure of contemporary anti-Communism was precisely the kind of utopianism that animated the last pages of *Tomorrow!* This time, Wylie argues that the only realism that can be derived from the thought of the end of the world is that there is no such thing as an American victory in case of an atomic war with Russia. Triumph (the total eradication of Communism) might still be possible, but this triumph cannot lead to the reconstitution of an American utopia. In fact, America needs to be sacri-ficed in order for this new kind of (post-American) utopia to come about.

The organizing principle of *Triumph* is still the double program of political and aesthetic realism, but the direct confrontation with the catas-trophe is no longer possible. In fact, the novel suggests that documentary mediation is necessary even for the "witnesses," those who survived the catastrophe. Since almost the entirety of the book takes place underground, we no longer see the actual attack or its effects on the world. Rather, the characters only register the seismic vibrations of catastrophe. In fact, the characters' only exposure to the atomic attack comes in the form of a documentary broadcasted from Costa Rica. These "photographic and taped records of the American Holocaust" are necessary for the survivors, who otherwise would have almost no relation to the catastrophe that is their immediate environment.[75] Although they inhabit the very heart of catastrophe, their only way of knowing it is through an external mediating agent.

At the end of the novel, when the Australian army finally rescues the survivors, we find out that there is a new world order in the making on the Southern hemisphere: "International government, of course. . . . Meaning—men are to become free and equal, from now on. Without race differences."[76] This utopic ending is doubtless similar to the closing of *When Worlds Collide*, in that both novels end with the establishment of a new human universality beyond the total catastrophe. But while in the earlier novel the idea of America was salvaged in this universal rearticulation (as if preserved in a dialectical move of history to a post-historical stage), in the case of *Triumph* the realist politics of anti-Communism allows for only one kind of utopia: a utopia without America. The last sentences of the novel register the complete (even symbolic) annihilation of the nation: "They would leave the United States of America forever. And when they had gone, the place would have no name."[77] This seems to suggest that the voice of the narrator is no longer coming from an American world. In this sense, *Triumph* is a post-American novel.

As a conclusion, we can return to the question of what it means that Hersey, Shute, and Wylie were all writing documentaries. The self-effacement of the narrator in *Hiroshima* and the omniscience of the narrator of *On the Beach* are two sides of the same coin. In *Hiroshima*, the full exposure to the event without any mediation is rendered possible by a narratorial voice which nevertheless presents itself as if it were nonexistent. This voice is never connected to a speaking body that would actually appear in the field of narration (that is, the narrator is not a character in *Hiroshima*). The disconnection between the disclosed world and the narratorial act of disclosure, however, is actually taken to the next level as the very narratorial act is denied by the disclosed world. In order to establish its authority, the narrator transposes the act of disclosure to the event itself: "let the event speak!" Although the narratorial voice is our only means of access to this world, it is not one element in this world and, therefore, it also signifies an absence in the world. The self-effacing, disembodied voice claims that it is the self-disclosing world that is speaking, and in the very same act of reversal, against its own intentions, it pokes a hole in this world, which is no longer complete, as it needs this disappearing voice to render its self-disclosure possible in the first place.

On the Beach demonstrates a similar set of problems. Here we find that a fictional text moves toward the real and (never being able to complete this journey) redefines itself as a documentary. The problem at the heart of this redefinition concerns the very status of fiction: for if atomic holocaust fiction is about a real event that destroys the very possibilities of fiction, imagining this event in advance is the only possible way to document this real, historical eventuality. During the fifties, atomic holocaust fiction is not "just" fiction, since it touches upon the real possibility of atomic warfare; but it is neither simply real, as the event it aims to capture has not yet taken place. This is why it assumes a special role among the available cultural fictions: it is the special form of fiction which is invested with the value of being real (and not just being "realistic"). The only way to mediate the experience of atomic warfare in a realistic way is to write its history in advance and present this history according to the formal demands of documentary. But the most elementary formal convention of documentary is the separation of the voice and the image. In the novel, therefore, the third person narrator is not part of the fictional world, the same way as Hersey's narratorial voice in not an element of the narrated world. They both inhabit a heterogeneous space and efface themselves on behalf of the world they show us. But, through this reversal, the voice also signifies the central lack of this world: it actually lacks the guarantee of its narratability, which ultimately remains forever external to it (as the event destroys the very conditions of narration).

Wylie's fiction displays the same documentary tendency, since the narratorial position in all of his catastrophe novels can be located in a heterogeneous "space-off." But in his case, due to the utopistic structure of his fiction, the final outcome of the story always restores the conditions of narration. Unlike On the Beach, which ends with the utter impossibility of narration, Wylie's novels end with the triumph of narration over the void of absolute nothingness. His novels always run the full circle and end where they began—the establishment of the possibility of the very narratorial act that has just completed disclosing a world to us. We could say that his fiction is utopistic in a double sense: the disclosed world is constructed by a utopistic voice that lacks a concrete place of enunciation; yet, this voice is imbued by the utopistic wisdom of a more perfect world beyond catastrophe. Although it is disembodied, the narrative voice is nevertheless logically possible. Its documentary authority derives precisely from the fullness of this post-catastrophic utopia: rather than a dystopic disintegration of narratorial authority, these texts establish the principles of a new kind of knowledge beyond the void of nothingness. Since order is reestablished on a higher level, the voice which remains external to the narrated field is nevertheless not the traumatized impersonality of a confused survivor. This voice is the pure voice of utopia.

"Utopia," however, has to be understood in a double sense. It is simultaneously the ideal location of fulfilled identity and a "non-place." In other words, it simultaneously names the autonomy of the world and the heteronomy of the voice. Wylie's fiction demonstrated that the unity of the world has no other existence than the unity of the voice. But since the voice cannot be fully located in the world, the unity of the world is dependent on this excessive element. The voice constitutes the unity of the world by introducing a nonworldly component to it. As a result, the condition of the world is the possibility of the voice: a cause which is simultaneously external and internal to the world.

The best way to describe this relation would be to conclude that the voice *embodies* the unity of the world within the world itself, even if the point of enunciation must always remain heteronomous to the world: it is the space-off of documentary. It is through this embodiment that the voice becomes a nonworldly object. Thus, the voice is the agent of representation but not in the sense that it "talks about" the world as if it were unified. Of course, on the level of the statement, the voice does speak of the objects of a given world as it strives to establish hierarchical relations between them. But the representation of the fact that these objects are the elements of the same world cannot be located on the same level as the objects themselves. This unity is simply performed by the voice. The voice embodies the unity of the world by presenting its absent fullness. Therefore, while the constitutive inconsistency of the world is phenomenalized through the figure of the catastrophe, its impossible unity is embodied by the voice.

6 / Two Worlds: Stolen Secrets

The Politics of Secrecy

Whereas nuclear holocaust fiction introduced the idea of the "world" into anti-Communist fiction and strove to establish the unity of this world, spy thrillers split the world into two and claimed that it was always at least two worlds. This split simultaneously accounts for the obstacles that prevent the world of anti-Communism from becoming one unified entity and, at the same time, places the internal division of the world under the law of necessity. Hence the paradoxical proposition that we will examine in more detail in this chapter: in order to become one, the world must be divided.

We could, then, say that the unity of the world depends on a configuration of external and internal limits. The external limit corresponds to the global enmity characteristic of the geopolitical situation. The globe failed to become "one world" in the sense of an ideological unity due to the political opposition of East and West, the Communist world and the free world. The world will be one ideologically, once the enemy is eliminated on a global scale.

But the internal limit of the world introduces a more difficult complication. While it might appear to be a self-evident proposition that an enemy bent on world domination can prevent the free world from achieving its fullness (in the sense of realizing itself eihter as an autonomous totality or as a global order), the claim that the free world must be inherently divided in order to prevail over this enemy is likely to appear as a contradiction. The problem is that if the free world is inherently divided, then freedom is founded on exclusion. The particular exclusion that we are concerned with in this chapter, however, is not the exclusion of different minorities from the ostensibly free domain of democratic politics, but a more comprehensive exclusion which excludes the totality of democratic citizenry from directly participating in anti-Communist politics. This exclusion establishes the necessary limits of democratic politics and establishes a domain where democratic principles no longer necessarily apply.

The product of this more fundamental exclusion is the world of political secrecy. While the interaction of privacy and publicity defines what we could call "the normal world" of everyday experience, secrecy completely separates itself from these fields and institutes its own world. We can speak of this terrain of politics as a "world" in the sense that through its institutionalized mechanisms secrecy creates its own totality with its autonomous laws. One of the major gambits of anti-Communist politics was the establishment of this field as a necessary supplement of democratic politics: in order to secure the framework of democracy, executive power had to retreat into a clandestine zone where nondemocratic acts can be perpetrated in the name of democracy.

As a result, one of the most important tasks of American anti-Communist spy fiction was to legitimize this reduplication of worlds within democracy. The genre could be interpreted as a cultural reaction to one of the most decisive developments of modernity: the parallel historical emergence of absolute surveillance and the simultaneous withdrawal of executive power to the domain of secrecy.[1] It participates in a form of "world politics" similar to the one we identified in the case of atomic holocaust fiction. Accordingly, secret agent fiction had to demonstrate a basic fact of anti-Communism: that politics as such is simultaneously global and clandestine.[2] The function of spy fiction (as a field of representation) was to reveal the dividing line separating the normal world of democratic publicity from the secret world of espionage and to establish the relationship of these two domains as a necessary supplementarity. Just as in the case of atomic holocaust fiction, where the ideological figure of the catastrophe allowed the establishment of a field of representation within which a system of relations could be revealed to be necessary for the survival of the free world, a privileged figure appears in spy fiction as well: the secret. The necessary premise of the genre is that there is a secret vital to a given order of things, and the threat posed to this or by this secret allows the establishment of a fictional field within which a story can unfold.

The necessary reduplication of worlds is such a prominent feature of the genre that it has long been a central motif of criticism.[3] One of the clearest formulations of the two-worlds thesis was provided by John G. Cawelti and Bruce A. Rosenberg, who argue that a "cycle of clandestinity" structures the history of the genre. The cycle consists of three phases. First, "an individual or group conceives a purpose which appears to require actions beyond the bounds of law or morality accepted by other members of their society."[4] Spy fiction always takes us beyond the limits of what is considered to be legitimate political action. In the second phase, however, once the threshold of legitimacy is crossed, a secret group is formed, which immediately leads to the creation of a secret world: "This group constitutes a clandestine world defined by the secrets they share."[5] The important point about this clandestine world is that it "exists side by side with the ordinary world in the mind of the spy. Participants in clandestinity believe that their secret world is more real than the ordinary world and that it is exempt from the rules that govern those who are not part of the clandestine world."[6] This duplicity leads to the characteristically "schizophrenic" structure of the genre, as these characters have to inhabit both worlds simultaneously.[7] The final phase of the cycle marks the turning in on itself of the secret world (a conspiracy within a conspiracy) as the "clandestine group begins to feel isolated not only from ordinary society, but from other members of the group."[8] According to Cawelti and Rosenberg, the predicament of this final phase is embodied by the double agent betrayed by his or her own organization.

Let me then reformulate the three stages of Cawelti and Rosenberg's analysis into the terms of our argument. First, the existence of a secret is acknowledged to be vital to the maintenance of a particular order of things. The metaphysical presupposition of the genre is that the world possesses a secret: one of the objects in this world is no longer a mere object, but an element that establishes the unity of the world. But its dependence on this object questions the autonomy of the world. If the unity of the world depends on a secret, the world can only be successfully constituted as "one" if the secret does not fail to perform its unifying role. In other words, if the secret remains in a relation of heteronomy to the world it maintains, the role of the secret is to make up for the failed unity of the world by supplementing its identity with an unknown yet necessary component. This is why the secret is never fully within the law it helps to establish.

Second, this heteronomy of the secret leads to the constitution of another world. Since the function of the secret is to sustain the normal world, the other world is "more real" than the normal world and exempt from the laws that govern it. The impossible closure of the normal world is supplemented by the supposed authenticity of the clandestine world. Although things might not be working according to plan in our world, those participating in the other world "know" what is really going on, and their authentic knowledge is opposed to the lack of authenticity (and the ignorance) of the normal world. While the manifest world is not one, the "real" other world is supposedly fully constituted as one.

But the final stage of clandestinity marks the reduplication of the logic of secrecy. The secret world that was supposed to provide the consistency of our incomplete world is itself revealed to be incomplete. The logic of secrecy turns against itself and makes it impossible to establish a fully functioning totality. Since the function of the foundational principle of this alternative world (secrecy) is precisely to establish alternative worlds, its effects cannot stop on the level of a first, fully constituted world. As a result of this basic principle, this alternative world will also be at least two. The arithmetic of the reduplication of the worlds cannot be a simple addition of two independent units: a world that is not quite one is supplemented by another incomplete world. We can, thus, see that rather than two fully separated independent worlds existing side by side, we get two incomplete worlds that completely intertwine each other.

We are therefore confronted with the question: How does the secret relate to the field of narration it founds? The very form of this question suggests the answer, since it demonstrates the reduplication of the role of the secret. In the fictional field of these novels, the figure of the secret assumes a double role: it is both one of the formulaic elements that make up the world of the novel and the signifier of the totality of the formula. First, we have to point out that the secret designates a limit of representation: the very term acknowledges the existence of a particular object, yet at the same time announces that it is without public representation. The figure of the secret marks the location where something could appear in the field of representation without actually doing so. In fact, it is a figurative "crease" on the surface of the form that marks the site of a possible yet absent content. There is something in our world that cannot be identified publicly yet holds this whole world together. The withdrawal of this object from the field of representation results in the creation of a site where its mere existence has to be marked. This process of withdrawal, however, establishes a field of representation within which a particular set of relations can now be represented.

Second, the split in the identity of the figure (since it stands for something other than itself) guarantees that it is primarily the figure of the consistency of the narrative. The reason why a particular story comes about in a given form and, so to say, "makes sense," is that the secret is acknowledged to be of vital importance for the characters. On the level of the narrative, the secret accounts for the very possibility of the story (there is a story to narrate, since there is a secret); on the level of the represented world, it accounts for the possibility of a given social order (the secret must be secured in order to guarantee the stability of our world). The condition of narration has to appear in the field of narration, but it can do so only in this displaced form, as the split identity of one of the elements of the narration. In his analysis of the thriller, Jerry Palmer makes a similar point when he speaks of the "absolute structural necessity" of conspiracy in the following terms: "it is the conspiracy that drives the plot into action. Without it, there would be no reason for the hero to act."[9]

So Cawelti and Rosenberg are right to compare the ideological figure of the secret to Alfred Hitchcock's "MacGuffin," the secret that is simultaneously vital and "beside the point." They quote Hitchcock to illustrate this point: "And the logicians are wrong in trying to figure out the truth of a MacGuffin, since it is beside the point. The only thing that really matters is that in the picture the plans, documents, or secrets must seem to be of vital importance to the characters."[10] The point is not that the MacGuffin is absolutely irrelevant. Rather, while its actual content is insignificant for the audience, it occupies a significant position for the characters. We are speaking of a structural position that could be occupied by virtually any object. This is why Hitchcock insists that we cannot logically deduce its central position from its content. When the secret is withdrawn from the field of representation, and an object is invested with marking its existence in the "picture," this withdrawal allows the particular configuration of characters and their various relations to be represented. Hitchcock's comment, ultimately, points toward the same conclusion we reached earlier: the secret has to signify the very condition of narration.

In the previous chapter, we defined the fundamental paradox of atomic holocaust fiction by saying that the genre is made possible by the imagination of conditions under which it would be impossible to write fiction. We could, then, speak of a similar complication in the case of the spy thriller as well. On the level of the narrative constitution of the world, we find that the secret appears in the field of narration to mark the very condition of the narrative. In this, it is very similar to the figure of the catastrophe, which fulfilled a similar narrative function. They both sustain a field of representation and appear in it to mark the very limits of what is representable in this field. On the level of the represented world, however, the secret marks the very condition of the constitution of the world. Here the fundamental paradox of spy fiction can be expressed by the formula we already mentioned: in order to be one, the world must be divided.

The question concerning the exact relation and position of the two worlds with regard to each other leads us to a familiar problem, since we find that the clandestine world is neither fully inside nor completely outside the normal world. Jerry Palmer's analysis of the figure of the hero as a "paradoxical figure" clearly highlights this problem. Palmer argues that, on the one hand, "the hero is typically a man who participates fully in the life of the community"; on the other hand, however, "he can never participate fully in the community."[11] This impossible position, caught between the inside and the outside of the community, however, is not a simple exclusion from the community, but the very definition of another dimension of the community whose relative autonomy has to be established as an actual place. Someone or something must occupy this position, since it is vital to the integrity of the community that he does so. And by occupying this position, the hero puts himself in the position of a sovereign instance: "in each novel *he re-founds the state*, he prevents society from returning to the wilderness from which it supposedly came."[12] The secret establishes a fictional field in which another figure, the hero, can emerge as the sovereign instance necessary to maintain the symbolic framework of our world in face of a grave crisis.[13]

Modernism and Secrecy

The historical fact that the "metaphysics of modernism" was based on an internal reduplication of the world has long been recognized.[14] The question we need to raise now concerns the different ways modernism and mass culture articulated this metaphysical condition. The conclusions we reached in the previous chapter apply to the figure of the secret as well as to the ideological figure of catastrophe.[15] Previously, I argued that the historical experience of modernity was translated into a set of aesthetic standards and that catastrophe provided the ideological consistency of formal fragmentation. But whereas authentic art maintained an indirect (that is, figurative) relation to the historical experience of catastrophe, mass culture literalized this ideological content and, thereby, merely offered the simulacrum of catastrophe. In a similar fashion, we could argue that in modernity the category of the secret came to denote a move beyond representation that was essential both for politics and aesthetics.[16]

It is in this context that I want to revisit the historical link between political realism and aesthetic anti-realism characteristic of Cold War liberalism. We have to point out that the liberal "imagination of disaster" is also an imagination of conspiracy. Although the exploration of secrecy remains seemingly underdeveloped in Trilling's *The Liberal Imagination*, conspiracy and revolution do play a central role in Trilling's reading of Henry James, since Trilling singles out *The Princess Casamassima* (1886) as the only text by James to be examined in detail. The role of secrecy in *The Liberal Imagination*, thus, has to be interpreted on two levels: the metaphysical and the ideological (which includes politics as well as aesthetics). Trilling's project can be clearly inscribed in a larger, typically modern problematic. His goal is to deduce a politics (liberalism as the imagination of disaster) and an aesthetics (moral realism as a form of modernist aesthetics) from a metaphysical condition (the constitutive split between the hidden and the manifest). For Trilling, the metaphysical foundation of Cold War liberalism and anti-Communist modernism is an inherent limit in reality which is best represented by the figure of the "secret."

As we have already seen, Trilling defined the "American metaphysics" as an inadequate form of realism.[17] Although he never uses these terms, his criticism of Parrington and Dreiser suggests that what he finds objectionable in these authors is precisely the elimination of a particular kind of secrecy from their metaphysics. Vulgar materialism and religious pietism (the shortcomings of the early and the late Dreiser in Trilling's eyes) are equally unacceptable, since the former simply eradicates secrecy, while the latter reduces it to the mysticism of "Something behind It All."[18] In a world like this, aesthetic mediation must be a fully transparent process. The opacity of art can only be a mistake or, even worse, deliberate deception. Therefore, art can have no secrets. It must be fully identical with the proper representation of a simply self-disclosing reality. For Trilling, this kind of vulgar realism is the art of a world without secrets.[19]

Trilling finds the cure to this flawed American metaphysics in Freud. Speaking of Freud's "tragic realism," he explains how psychoanalysis could contribute to a more appropriate conception of reality.[20] Claiming that psychoanalysis is the continuation of the Romantic tradition, Trilling speaks here of the "perception which is to be the common characteristic of both Freud and Romanticism, the perception of the hidden element of human nature and of the opposition between the hidden and the visible."[21] In fact, this split appears here as the foundational notion of modernity: "the idea of the hidden thing went forward to become one of the dominant notions of the age. The hidden element takes many forms and it is not necessarily 'dark' and 'bad.'"[22]

But this is the point where Trilling parts ways with Freud. According to Trilling, although it does not necessarily follow from the logic of psychoanalytic thought, Freud had a reductive view of art in his writings explicitly devoted to aesthetic matters. Simply put, Trilling accepts the therapeutic validity of a stark separation of illusion and reality, but he argues that the metaphysical conclusion of psychoanalysis should be more radical than this therapeutic pragmatism: "Indeed what may be called the essentially Freudian view assumes that the mind, for good as well as bad, helps create its reality by selection and evaluation."[23] But, as Trilling is quick to point out, if reality is not simply given but created, the full pathologization of illusions is misguided, since reality itself is constituted by illusions. He wants to convince us that "the illusions of art are made to serve the purpose of a closer and truer relation with reality."[24] Since for Trilling reality itself is constituted by necessary illusions, realism in art is also only possible as an illusion rather than a mere reflection of reality: art should be the realism of the illusion that organizes reality.

This redefinition of realism becomes a political principle in Trilling's reading of *The Princess Casamassima* as the new center of the modernist canon. For Trilling, the negative contemporary reception of the novel is precisely the unmistakable sign of James's unfailing prescience, his very modernity: he could pinpoint something in the experience of modern politics that came to be fully appreciated only in the aftermath of World War II. This special element is the conspiratorial nature of modern politics and the unavoidable moral ironies of political secrecy.

In his preface to the novel, Henry James provides a compelling version of the two-world thesis we have been examining. The basic argument is that, because of the constitutive unevenness of the social, "exclusion" is an unavoidable part of modern experience and the role of imagination is to fill in the holes produced by these exclusions. More precisely, the specific experience that James wants to examine is a particularly modern contradiction. By turning society into a spectacle, modernity allows universal access to experiences previously denied to the masses. At the same time, however, this new freedom comes with severe restrictions. James located the specificity of the modern experience in the common availability of urban space. In the first sentence of the preface, he bluntly states that the most important source of *The Princess Casamassima* was "the habit and interest of walking the streets" of London.[25] James fashions himself as a modern flâneur and describes his exposure to the metropolis as "a mystic solicitation, the urgent appeal, on the part of everything to be interpreted and, so far as may be, reproduced."[26]

Thus, there is an essential similarity between the author and his protagonist: they are both walking the city under the spell of this mystic solicitation and they observe and compulsively interpret the same complex reality. But, James hastens to add, there is "one little difference": Hyacinth has access to the same urban world (and the same universal spectacle of the pleasures of modern life) as James does, only he is excluded from a full enjoyment of the city since all access to power is denied to him.[27] Similarly, James has access to the same world that is haunted by the envious Hyacinth, but while to him the doors of privilege are open, he is ignorant of the underworld that is Hyacinth's home. This is why at one point James adds: "Truly, of course, there are London mysteries (dense categories of dark arcana) for every spectator, and it's in a degree an exclusion and a state of weakness to be without experience of the meaner conditions, the lower manners and types, the general sordid struggle, the weight of the burden of labour, the ignorance, the misery and the vice."[28] The fundamental contradiction of modern experience is that it renders visible a wide range of social experiences but, since the social structure is maintained by a set of exclusions, at the same time this spectatorship also necessarily produces "dark arcana." Conspiratorial fantasies are, therefore, constitutive of modern experience.

This contradiction between visibility and exclusion, however, is simultaneously a political issue and an aesthetic one for James. He defines the social as a field of visibility structured by a set of exclusions, and the role of the imagination is to provide the consistency of the social by filling in the holes produced by these exclusions. Close to the end of the preface, James formulates the defense of his art in the following terms: "the effect I wished most to produce were precisely those of our not knowing, of society's not knowing, but only guessing and suspecting and trying to ignore, what 'goes on' irreconcileably, subversively, beneath the vast smug surface."[29] The lack of knowledge inscribed in the social structure is immediately turned into a set of aesthetic categories. This is why James describes his book in the following terms: "My scheme called for the suggested nearness (to all our apparently ordered life) of some sinister anarchic underworld, heaving its pain, its power and its hate; a presentation not of sharp particulars, but of loose appearances, vague motions and sounds and symptoms, just perceptible presences and general looming possibilities."[30] The limits of perception are thus immediately tied to a system of social exclusions in such a way that they can provide the foundations of a whole theory of aesthetic representation (the presentation of loose appearances as an "impressionism" of secrecy).

These passages show us that the role of the imagination is simultaneously aesthetic and political. If social exclusion leads to a lack of knowledge, conspiracy theory is a constitutive part of modern experience. The reproduction of this experience in art is a form of modernist aesthetics which makes this secrecy into a formal principle: "a presentation not of sharp particulars, but of loose appearances, vague motions and sounds and symptoms, just perceptible presences and general looming possibilities."[31] This is a poetics of the limits of experience which tries to imagine the way something appears within experience without ever assuming a full presence. Thus, rather than producing an accurate picture of a "sinister anarchic underworld" based on knowledge, this realism is that of the lack of knowledge about the world. James is not giving us a novel of social realism. Quite to the contrary, his aesthetics of not-knowing is a realism of the limits of representation as they are a constitutive part of social existence. In place of a naturalism of base instincts, James offers us a modernism of conspiracies.

Needless to say, Trilling found *The Princess Casamassima* so appealing because, as James puts it in the preface, its central focus is the "dilemma of the disillusioned and repentant conspirator."[32] At the time Trilling wrote the essays collected in *The Liberal Imagination*, a whole generation of Americans perceived themselves to be a group of disillusioned revolutionaries, if not exactly repentant conspirators. The three central characters of the novel represent for Trilling the inherent weaknesses of liberalism. Paul Muniment and the Princess account for the reason why the novel "was not understood in its own day": "But we of today can say that they and their relationship constitute one of the most masterly comments on modern life that has ever been made."[33] These two characters embody the basic ironies of modern politics. Paul Muniment represents the possibility that an honest idealism can coexist "with a secret desire for personal power."[34] The Princess, on the other hand, represents "political awareness that is not aware."[35] As Trilling explains, in her quest for reality, the closer she believes she comes to reality, the farther away she is in actuality. The final irony of liberalism emerges between this corruption of idealism and the false realism of the secret center of things: Hyacinth Robinson falls in love with the beauty of the world that he himself conspires to destroy. Trilling perceives in Hyacinth's character a crucial predicament of Cold War liberalism: political progressivism cannot be fully justified by aesthetic conservatism.

This is why we have to conclude that the "liberal imagination" is fundamentally conspiratorial. As I argued in Chapter 2, Trilling deduced the necessary aestheticization of anti-Communist politics from the constitutive paradox of liberal democracy. Since liberal democracy attempts to institutionalize freedom by limiting it, there will always be a gap between what Trilling called "the primal imagination of liberalism" and its "present particular manifestations."[36] Imagination here means the imaginary constitution of social reality itself, which is always structured by exclusions. The role of the liberal imagination of disaster is to manifest this gap between primal imagination and particular manifestations. But if no particular manifestation can be identical with the primal imagination, the liberal imagination always has to be suspicious of itself and imagine the dark underworld of its own particular manifestations. In short, to the degree that liberal politics remains irreducible to its present manifestations, its source of authenticity will remain something hidden in principle.

Although the modernist imagination is fundamentally conspiratorial, according to modernist ideologies, mass culture can only offer us the simulacrum of the secret. Edmund Wilson, for example, in a famous article entitled "Who Cares Who Killed Roger Ackroyd?" (1950), dismissed detective fiction in the following terms:

> The addict reads not to find anything out but merely to get the mild stimulation of the succession of unexpected incidents and of the

suspense itself of *looking forward* to learning a sensational secret. That this secret is nothing at all and does not really account for the incidents does not matter to such a reader. He has learned from his long indulgence how to connive with the author in the swindle: he does not pay any real attention when the disappointing dénouement occurs, he does not think back and check the events, he simply shuts the book and starts another.[37]

Wilson does show some appreciation for Raymond Chandler, Alfred Hitchcock, and Graham Greene when he writes that in their works it is "not simply a question . . . of a puzzle which has been put together, but of a malaise conveyed to the reader, the horror of a hidden conspiracy that is continually turning up in the most varied and unlikely forms."[38] But in order to be a legitimate artistic subject, the problem of the secret has to be elevated to the level of the metaphysical horror of historical existence. As the consumption of mass culture is mere addiction, it is the repetition of the experience that counts, not its authenticity. The real point is not the secret itself, but looking forward to learning it.

When Wilson declares that "this secret is nothing at all," he effectively purges popular culture of its secrets. The terrain of cultural simulacra is a mere surface without any depth and, therefore, without any authentic secrets. As a matter of fact, the false promise of revelation is the most effective way of avoiding secrets in an infinite repetition of the reading experience. In Wilson's reading, if the secret "does not really account for the incidents," we could say that these novels fail to connect their ideological foundation with the field of representation that the first establishes. The reduction of this ideology to a formula corresponds to a formal failure to capture this organizing figure (the secret). This formal failure thus reduces the genre to the status of a mere puzzle, rather than a complex expression of a conspiratorial epochal consciousness.

Trilling's work, therefore, illustrates in a compelling way that the ideological figure of the secret functions as the foundation of liberal anti-Communism on three distinct levels. First, it is a metaphysical principle which guarantees that reality is irreducible to what merely appears to us. Second, it is also a political principle, since the politics of liberalism is irreducible to its particular manifestations beyond which we always have to posit a more primary form of liberal imagination. Finally, in the case of art we find that it is irreducible to the field of representation, since it must transcend the mere realistic rendering of the world. The function of true art is precisely to represent the internal split in the world between what is representable and what is not. This is why, if mass culture literalizes the ideological content of modernism, its ultimate failure is that it reduces the secret to the field of representation. From the point of view of the aesthetic ideology of modernism, in mass culture the hermeneutical attitude is replaced by a literal rendering of secrets and conspiracy precisely in order to avoid any hermeneutical encounter. The secret appears on the surface of the narrative because the narrative no longer has any secrets. In modernism, however, the secret cannot be reduced to a plot element on the level of the represented world, since it enters the very process of representation. In "authentic art," the secret is not simply represented but is itself internal to the principle of representation.

Necessary Secrets

In order to establish the basic components of what we could call an aesthetic ideology organizing the world of the modern spy thriller, we have to raise two questions: first, we have to inquire after the principle that establishes the field of visibility specific to this world; then, we need to establish the relationship of this field to art. In spite of the significant differences among individual authors, this double concern with visibility and art is a persistent structuring force of the genre. The most basic assumption at the heart of this problem is that the field of visible experience and the autonomous field of aesthetic experience are both sustained by certain limits. The division of the two worlds (the normal and the clandestine) is established by a theory of representation that includes a reflection on constitutive limits: since there are inherent exclusions, the underworld of secrecy is necessary to maintain the principle of public representations. At the same time, the division of aesthetic production between mass culture and high art is also one of the constantly recurring elements of spy novels. The juxtaposition of these two divisions, then, allows us to raise the question of how particular forms of aesthetic practice are correlated to the constitutive division of the social.

John Buchan's *The Thirty-Nine Steps* (1915)—often referred to as one of the foundational pieces of the modern spy story—offers itself as a perfect example of this double concern with representation. Richard Hannay, "the best-bored man in the United Kingdom," is an ordinary citizen sucked into the tumultuous world of international politics.[39] As it happens, an American agent (Franklin P. Scudder, whom he tried to protect from his German pursuers on a gentlemanly basis) is murdered in Hannay's apartment. Before his death, Scudder entrusts Hannay with a wildly anti-Semitic tale of a "big subterranean government": "Capital, he said, had no conscience and no fatherland; besides, the Jew was behind it."[40] As the story progresses, it becomes clear that Scudder (probably trying to be careful) did not tell the truth to Hannay, but the story is convincing enough and contains enough truth to set Hannay on his personal quest to save the Empire. A considerable amount of the story is, then, devoted to Hannay's attempts to mislead his pursuers as he first flees to Scotland and tries to make his way back to London to reach the capital on a specific day in order to prevent the final catastrophe.

The significance of the story for us is that it presents a perfectly dialectical argument about the reduplication of the world. The three steps of the dialectic are constituted by two reversals. First, the observing subject realizes that he is an object of observation. At this stage, the novel establishes an external split between two different perspectives. But this initial stage is followed by an internal split within the subject's perspective. In the course of the story, we move from the unified perspective of the observing subject to a split between two independent perspectives and, finally, to a split within the original perspective itself. This final reversal teaches us an important lesson about the reduplication of the world: it shows us that the world of secrecy and the world of publicity take place in essentially the same social space, only one has to learn to look at the same scenario differently to perceive both of them.

At one point in the story, Hannay strategically positions himself on the top of a hill so that he can easily spot his enemies. As he surveys the landscape from his "sanctuary," he concludes: "I was on the central boss of a huge upland country, and could see everything moving for miles."[41] But what Hannay has to learn soon is that rather than being in the privileged position of the observer, he is himself being observed. As he is standing on top of the hill, he all of a sudden hears the engine of an airplane: "Then I realized that my vantage ground might be in reality a trap."[42] The lesson of the episode is clear: it is precisely by positioning himself as the observer that he exposes himself to observation.

At this point already we can highlight the central thesis of the novel: a given field of visibility is always established by a split of perspectives. In order to be able to define it as a field, we need at least two perspectives. On the one hand, we are presented with Hannay's horizontal view, which exposes the world to him as everything that he can see. But a seemingly unified, isolated perspective will always be deceptive as it cannot construct the whole picture. In Hannay's case, at least one element is absent from the world as it displays itself to him: Hannay himself. This is why the vertical perspective is introduced: it not only redoubles (and contextualizes) the first perspective but also inscribes the passive state of "being looked at" into the very act of active observation. And what "you" see and what "they" see can never be exactly the same. The field of visibility constitutes itself at the intersection of these two irreconcilable perspectives, but at this point both of the perspectives are imagined to be fully constituted autonomous perspectives.

Hannay's main problem thus becomes that of trying to hide on a flat surface fully exposed to surveillance from above: "How on earth was I to escape notice in that tablecloth of a place?"[43] The answer to this question, however, is not to escape the field, but to become one of its elements: "You must stay in the patch, and let your enemies search it and not find you."[44] Hannay spots the only human being in this field (a roadman) and through perfect imitation becomes this man. He escapes his enemies not by running or by hiding in the ordinary sense, but by exposing himself to full view through mimicry. This same logic is repeated later in the novel, when Hannay recalls a hunting story in which both he and his dog were fully deceived by a rhebok: "that buck simply leaked out of the landscape."[45]

The central theory of deception put forth by the novel concerns precisely this "leaking out of the landscape," as the pure spectacle is punctuated by invisible sites of escape. Hannay quotes his friend, Peter Pienaar:

> Peter once discussed with me the question of disguises, and he had a theory which struck me at the time. He said, barring absolute certainties like finger-prints, mere physical traits were very little use for identification if the fugitive really knew his business. He laughed at things like dyed hair and false beards and such childish follies. The only thing that mattered was what Peter called "atmosphere." If a man could get into perfectly different surroundings from those in which he had been first observed, and—this is the important part—really play up to these surroundings and behave as if he had never been out of them, he would puzzle the cleverest detectives on earth. . . . A fool tries to look different; a clever man looks the same and *is* different.[46]

This is how you move between two worlds: you do not rely on external disguises, you change your own being. The passage suggests a new definition of secrecy: if secrecy is a change in the very being of the object and not a change of appearance of this object, we could also conclude that secrecy should be defined as a specific mode of visibility rather than exclusively as a form of invisibility. In other words, secrecy is not a different location physically separated from the visible world of publicity. As the example shows, it inhabits the very same social space as the normal world. Rather, the task outlined by Peter Pienaar's theory is to disappear between two perspectives.

But the closing chapter of the novel completely revises this theory. Hannay finally figures out how the German spies are trying to leave the country with the stolen secrets, but when he hurries to their villa with the "thirty-nine steps," to his utter consternation he finds only a completely "innocent spectacle," "the happy home of three cheerful Englishmen."[47]

In spite of the fact that according to Hannay's reasoning these three men should be the infernal spies (whom Hannay actually encountered face-to-face before), the spectacle they present are fully at odds with their supposed identity. Once again, Hannay is in the position of the observer and cannot believe his eyes: "The house stood as open as a market-place for anybody to observe. . . . Everything was as public and above-board as a charity bazaar."[48] In spite of his own theory of deception, however, Hannay fails to grasp the spectacle as a performance: "These men might be acting; but if they were where was their audience?"[49] The question betrays a surprising degree of naivety: Hannay misrecognizes the fact that his position of observation is structurally part of the spectacle (in other words, that he is the audience he cannot identify).

The crucial point, however, is that Hannay decides to enter the spectacle: he confronts the three men and accuses them of being spies. But this preposterous proposition appears to be a foolish mistake. Hannay is ready to lose his mind as he is invited to a game of bridge by the three men. Finally a simple little nervous "tick" destroys the whole performance: all of a sudden, one of the men starts tapping on his knees, which leads to "full and absolute recognition" as "the three faces seemed to change before my eyes and reveal their secrets."[50] The moment of revelation depends on the persistence of something real that has the power to interrupt the performance.

The question of literature, as it is discussed in the novel, also involves the problem of visibility. Two scenes are of special interest for us here. First, it is the anecdote of the "literary innkeeper" that introduces the question of literature to the narrative. Hannay at one point seeks refuge at a vacant inn run by a young man who happens to be an aspiring writer. The innkeeper complains that there is no longer any romance left in his profession, as in modern days only vulgar everyday people visit his inn, which does not provide him with the right kind of material. He wants to travel the world and write novels, as Kipling and Conrad did. To which Hannay responds: "D'you think that adventure is found only in the tropics or among gentry in red shirts? Maybe you're rubbing shoulders with it at this moment."[51] The episode tells us something important about the world: "The only thing to distrust is the normal."[52] The function of literature is to bring the exotic colonies home and reveal the normal to be absolutely extraordinary.

The second scene occurs after Hannay finally contacted the proper authorities. Sir Walter, however, dismisses Scudder's story in the following terms: "He was half crank, half genius, but he was wholly honest."[53] Sir Walter admits that the story contains some truth, but adds that "it reads like some wild melodrama. . . . The trouble about him was that he was too romantic. He had the artistic temperament, and wanted a story to be better than God meant it to be."[54] But after dismissing Scudder's tale as a "penny novelette," the chapter ends with the arrival of an urgent message announcing the assassination of the Greek politician, just as it was foretold in Scudder's notebook.[55] This ironic interruption is left without further comments, so the reader is left with the conclusion that the novel in the end confers some realistic value on Scudder's melodramatic narrative. As it appears, a certain "artistic temperament" is actually necessary to understand modern politics (to get at the real truth behind mere appearances).

While in the case of the "literary innkeeper" the normal turned out to be the fantastic in disguise, here the fantastic excesses of conspiratorial narratives are revealed to be true. To put it differently: while reality, in its banality, is always going to appear merely normal, and while conspiratorial narratives are always going to appear unrealistically romantic, the self-reflexive message of the novel establishes an equivalence between the two extremes. The apparent aesthetic failure of spy fiction is a political merit to the degree that it stages the fantasy that sustains the world of bourgeois boredom. Although spy fiction is mere mass entertainment, in reality it is the "necessary melodrama" (or aesthetic excess) that reveals the truth about modern politics.

What is it, then, that this novel tells us about the modern spy thriller? It teaches us to consider the juxtaposition of the problems of visibility and art as constitutive of the genre. It shows us that the split of perspectives is internal (since we are not dealing with a "perspectival relativism" which would claim that everybody sees something different, but rather with the supposition that seeing always presupposes a moment that is different from itself), which also means that a field of visibility is always established by this internal reduplication of perspectives. Therefore, the possibility of deceit is structural, since things simply leak out of the landscape, whether we like it or not.

In addition, it also shows that the internal limit of social visibility establishes a particular self-reflexive moment in the spy thriller. This is what Bruce Merry called the "internal embarrassment" of the genre caused by the fact that it is relegated to a secondary status in the standard hierarchy of cultural production and it is "aware" of this status.[56] In other words, it is impossible to write a modern spy thriller without the full and conscious assimilation of the "great divide" characteristic of modernist culture. This cultural hierarchy is an explicitly thematized formal principle which is by definition part of the ideological foundations of the whole genre. As a result, the spy thriller often legitimizes itself by renouncing its own generic characteristics. Yet the supreme surprise of the genre is when reality reveals itself to be structured by a mere romance, and the melodramatic imagination is declared to be necessary to understand modern politics.

Bypassing some of the history of the genre, let us now move to three paradigmatic representatives of the Cold War spy thriller: John le Carré, Ian Fleming, and Mickey Spillane. I chose these three authors because they clearly correspond to the threefold cultural hierarchy characteristic of Cold War aesthetic ideology: le Carré (along with Graham Greene) is usually considered to be the most artistic and literary representative of the genre; Fleming's works are quintessential kitsch; while Spillane is the prototypical author of lowbrow mass culture. What will be of interest to us is the way the positions of these authors in this cultural hierarchy are reflected on the level of the aesthetic ideology that their works propagate.

It is customary to refer to le Carré and Fleming as representatives of two different traditions of the genre: Fleming is usually considered to be a master of the "sensational" thriller, while le Carré is commonly cited as the heir of the "realistic" spy story. Whereas in le Carré we are confronted with an explicitly aesthetic problematic that opposes art to the ambiguous visibility of the social, Fleming formulates an "anti-aesthetic" for the society of spectacle, in which the image annihilates the original.

Le Carré's "realism" is most often explained as a representation of "moral ambiguity" and not necessarily the accurate representation of the secret service. This moral ambiguity is often depicted as a peculiar characteristic of the Cold War, which often necessitated unethical acts in the name of the defense of freedom. The literary character of le Carré's writing is already obvious in his first novel, *Call for the Dead* (1961), in which art occupies a central position. In this text, the division of the world into two separate fields (the normal and the clandestine) clearly corresponds to a division of cultural production into two distinct fields (mass culture and individualistic artistic achievements). But while the political division is rather problematic in le Carré's fiction, the second cultural division is treated as self-evident. The result of this double division is that le Carré's ethical critique of Cold War politics is tied to his cultural conservatism. In other words, the aesthetic division establishes the conditions of the critique of the political division.

In the famous opening pages of *Call for the Dead*, George Smiley is introduced to us as a "breath-takingly ordinary" person.[57] This ordinariness is in direct opposition to the common "romantic" view of his chosen profession, the secret service, and frames the whole narrative as it is simultaneously thematized on the first and last pages of the novel. In the closing chapter, entitled "Between Two Worlds," we find Smiley on an airplane en route to Zurich to meet his estranged wife. The concluding moment of the text is described as "a glimpse of eternity between two worlds."[58] Once again, however, the division of worlds becomes a question of perspective: "Smiley presented an odd figure to his fellow passengers—a little, fat man, rather gloomy, suddenly smiling, ordering a drink. The young, fair-haired man beside him examined him closely out of the corner of his eye. He knew the type well—the tired executive out for a bit of fun. He found it disgusting."[59] From the perspective of his fellow travelers, Smiley appears to be disgustingly ordinary. But the book also established another perspective that the reader can share now. Seen from this angle, the breathtakingly ordinary is revealed to be extraordinary without being external to the ordinary world.

This social phenomenology of normalcy also establishes the impossibility of the full separation of worlds. Close to the opening of the novel, the freshly widowed Mrs. Fennan (who will eventually turn out to be a Communist agent) establishes one of the central concerns of the text when she attacks Smiley with the following words: "It's an old illness you suffer from . . . and I have seen many victims of it. The mind becomes separated from the body; it thinks without reality, rules a paper kingdom and devises without emotion the ruin of its paper victims. But sometimes the division between your world and ours is incomplete; the files grow heads and arms and legs, and that's a terrible moment, isn't it?"[60] The failed and impossible separation of the two worlds is the very source of the moral ambiguity that is at the center of the text. The novel, if it is to be realistic, needs to manifest precisely the overlap of the two worlds, the ambiguous zone of indistinction, where they become impossible to separate.[61]

As a matter of fact, it is more than just a coincidence that before joining the secret service, Smiley was a scholar "devoted to the literary obscurities of seventeenth-century Germany."[62] In Smiley's case, secret service is a continuation of literary criticism by other means. In a telling passage, for example, intelligence work is essentially defined as a particular form of applied literary criticism: "It also provided him with what he had once loved best in life: academic excursions into the mystery of human behaviour, disciplined by the practical application of his own deductions."[63] In the case of intelligence work, the critical and theoretical conclusions about human behavior are not mere abstractions, since they are directly channeled into the practice of everyday espionage. This seemingly perfect marriage of theory and practice forms the basis of an aestheticized theory of intelligence: the complexity of the world is like that of a work of art. Intelligence work implies the discovery of a narrative structure behind seemingly unconnected and inconsistent set of facts.

But while the internal separation of the world is an impossible but necessary project, the separation of the opposing fields of cultural production is discussed without any ambiguity: "[Smiley] hated the Press as he hated advertising and television, he hated mass-media, the relentless persuasion of the twentieth century. Everything he admired or loved had been the product of intense individualism. That was why he hated Dieter now, hated what he stood for more strongly than ever before: it was the fabulous impertinence of renouncing the individual in favor of the mass."[64] In the rest of the chapter, mass culture is aligned with Communism and art with the individualism of the free world. In a certain sense, while the internal division of the two worlds remains an ambiguous project, the external division of ideological enmity can be formulated in clear terms, to the degree that it corresponds to the division of the aesthetic field into mass culture and high art. Thus, the political function of art is double: on the one hand, it allows us to distinguish ourselves from our external enemies (who are identified with the logic of the masses); on the other hand, it provides a defense against the ambiguity of the internal division of the world as it comes to signify the last stable value in an ambiguous world.

The ideal aesthetic object at the heart of the novel is the so-called "Dresden group," a tiny statue which is one of Smiley's prized possessions: "He loved to admire the beauty of those figures, the tiny rococo courtesan in shepherd's costume, her hands outstretched to one adoring lover, her little face bestowing glances on another. He felt inadequate before that fragile perfection."[65] As a matter of fact, the solution to the mystery is directly tied to this little statue, since it is a moment of "aesthetic experience" that finally brings order to the whole story: "As he stood gazing at the little shepherdess, poised eternally between her two admirers, he realised dispassionately that there was another quite different solution to the case of Samuel Fennan, a solution which matched every detail of circumstance, reconciled the nagging inconsistencies apparent in Fennan's character."[66] The little shepherdess, "poised eternally between her two admirers," becomes an allegorical representation of the suspended state between two worlds. The universalization of moral ambiguity leads to the aestheticization of ambiguity.

Needless to say, Ian Fleming was also aware of the ambiguities of secrecy, but he rejects both the rhetoric of moral ambiguity and the aestheticization of intelligence. In Umberto Eco's words, Fleming's first novel, *Casino Royale* (1953), evokes "the salutary recognition of universal ambiguity" only to dismiss it once and for all as an unnecessary annoyance and mere sophistry.[67] In the chapter entitled "The Nature of Evil," we find Bond in a hospital bed in a particularly philosophical mood. As Bond explains to his French colleague, Mathis, he is ready to resign from the secret service because, as you grow older, "The villains and heroes get all mixed up."[68] At the end of the novel, however, when Bond realizes that the woman he was planning to marry was actually a Communist double agent, he accepts Mathis's moral philosophy: "How soon Mathis had been proved right and how soon his own little sophistries had been exploded in his face."[69] Fleming thus evokes moral ambiguity only to excise it through the formulation of an unequivocal program.

The move toward the unambiguous foundations of ambiguity, however, is tied to the redefinition of the meaning of art, which is no longer the final redemptive value in an unstable universe. Art is actually a sign of a pathological obsession: as such, it becomes the unambiguous sign of evil. It does not save us from the enemy, since it is the enemy who is an "artist." In Fleming's second novel, *Live and Let Die* (1954), for example, the arch-villain Mr. Big (an African-American voodoo priest Communist agent) explicitly aestheticizes his own criminal activities:

> Mister Bond, I take pleasure now only in artistry, in the polish and finesse which I can bring to my operations. It has become almost a mania with me to impart an absolute rightness, a high elegance, to the execution of my affairs. Each day, Mister Bond, I try and set myself still higher standards of subtlety and technical polish so that each of my proceedings may be a work of art, bearing my signature as clearly as the creations of, let us say, Benvenuto Cellini. I am content, for the time being to be my only judge, but I sincerely believe, Mister Bond, that the approach to perfection which I am steadily achieving in my operations will ultimately win recognition in the history of our times.[70]

For Mr. Big, the model of conspiratorial activity is "the self-negation of the anonymous artist."[71] He sees himself "as one of those great Egyptian fresco painters who devoted their lives to producing masterpieces in the tombs of kings, knowing that no living eye would ever see them."[72] This redefinition of conspiracy as an art is therefore based on a constitutive division of human perception (as there are certain things that no living eye can ever see). The question is: What lies beyond these limits?

We can, then, say that le Carré and Fleming represent two opposing paradigms of the aestheticization of the internal division of the world. For le Carré, as we have seen, the greatest threat would be an "audience without art"—that is, a spectator who can no longer come to terms with the ambiguity of the world, since without the aesthetic principle, it would be impossible to make sense of this world. For Fleming, on the other hand, the threat to the social order is the exact opposite: an "art without audience." Instead of the aestheticization of intelligence that characterized Le Carré's vision, Fleming provides us the paradigmatic case of the opposite tendency: the aestheticization of conspiracy.

Umberto Eco's classic article on James Bond, however, is also significant because it demonstrates the standard liberal rejection of Fleming's fiction in its most sophisticated form. What concerns us the most is that

Eco detects a strange contradiction in Fleming that takes us right away to the problem of kitsch. As Eco points out, Fleming's prose pleases "sophisticated readers" who find "aesthetic pleasure" in the discovery that Fleming uses "the purity of the primitive epic" and maliciously translates it into "current terms."[73] This sophisticated reader, however, becomes a "victim" of this strategy "for he is led on to detect stylistic inventions where there is, on the contrary . . . a clever montage of *déjà vu*, a dressing up of the familiar."[74]

Two of the motives that formed the basis of our analysis can be detected in this reading: on the one hand, kitsch is the deceptive imitation of art without true (modernistic) innovation ("Fleming simulates literature by pretending to write literature"); on the other hand, as a result of this mere imitation, midcult has no secret, since its essence is the repetition of the known ("And, again, the pleasure of reading is not given by the incredible and the unknown but by the obvious and the usual").[75] Eco's interpretation suggests that the move beyond ambiguity is simultaneously a political and aesthetic program for Fleming. But a different way of presenting the problem would be to argue that what Fleming excises on the level of political content (Communist simulation) returns on the level of the aesthetic constitution of his work according to the logic of kitsch (aesthetic imitation of art). Thus, if according to the basic tenets of Cold War liberalism, the problem with mass culture is that even if its politics is correct, it cannot successfully translate it into an aesthetic principle, we find that that the problem of spy fiction is that it tries to establish the political necessity of secrecy, but as an art it is without secrets.

"Jehovah's Messenger": Mickey Spillane and the Democratic Paradox

One of the first things that comes to mind at the mention of Mickey Spillane's name is the extremely violent nature of his fiction. The vulgarity of this violence is often understood to be especially repulsive as it is the source of "sadistic" pleasures. The eternal middlebrow, Philip Wylie, for example, found this aspect of Spillane's fiction especially odious and concluded his review of his works (aptly entitled "The Crime of Mickey Spillane") with the following judgment: "If Spillane's millions of readers suddenly began acting like Spillane's detective, Mike Hammer, the Soviets could take us over without dropping a bomb—because the U.S.A. would be in chaos."[76] And if we consider, for example, the following passage, it is understandable that someone of Wylie's moral commitments would feel uncomfortable with Mike Hammer's version of anti-Communism: "But some day, maybe, some day I'd stand on the steps of the Kremlin with a gun in my fist and I'd yell for them to come out and if they wouldn't I'd go in and get them and when I had them lined up against the wall I'd start shooting until all I had left was a row of corpses that bled on the cold floors and in whose thick red blood would be the promise of a peace that would stick for more generations than I'd live to see."[77] Anti-Communism with a vengeance, to say the least.

But Wylie's conclusion seems to miss a crucial point about Spillane's fiction: Mike Hammer's exceptional status. Spillane's point is not to convince every reader to act as Mike Hammer does. Rather, Spillane wants his readers to accept the fact that Mike Hammer's position with regard to the law is that of a structurally necessary supplement. Instead of formulating a universal injunction, Spillane claims that "at least one" element must act like Mike Hammer.[78] The split of the two worlds in Spillane's works is caused by this "at least one" which functions as the exception to the rule it helps institute. As a matter of fact, we could even say that Mike Hammer's violence remains (in an ambiguous fashion) external to the field it helps establish: he is violent so that Spillane's millions of readers won't have to act as he does.

In order to explain the meaning of this exception, we have to remember that in Spillane's fiction, the ideological figure of the secret emerges at the intersection of two generic traditions: the spy story and hard-boiled detective fiction.[79] The latter is important for us, since at the same time that British spy fiction established the standard cultural reaction to the decline of empire, the hard-boiled novel emerged as a specifically American tradition. The hard-boiled explicitly thematized the gap between law and justice. To use an expression from John D. Macdonald's novel, *The Executioners* (better known as *Cape Fear*, 1957), the figure of the private detective emerged as "a supplement to the law."[80] In other words, the constitutive gap between law and justice opens up an intermediary field of dubious legal and ethical value. Ideally, the task of the private detective is to uphold justice even if the law inherently fails to do so.

Spillane's fiction picks up this motive of the "supplement to the law" and derives a particular form of anti-Communist politics from it: Spillane tries to establish a sovereign agency outside the law that nevertheless serves the spirit of the law (beyond the mere letter of the law). But the articulation of this agency is intimately tied to a reflection on the role of enjoyment in politics. We encounter here a democratic paradox in one of its most basic forms: in order to maintain the democratic framework of democracy, certain elements must be excluded from participating in democracy. We could speak of two exclusions here: the sovereign element is simultaneously inside and outside the field it rules over (it withdraws itself from the sphere of democracy to a third domain); but this sovereign instance establishes its rule by excluding others (in a nondemocratic fashion) from participating in democracy. And since the enemy is guilty of a "theft of enjoyment," this sovereign agency has to make up for this lack of enjoyment by way of its extralegal activities: it has to find enjoyment in breaking the law in the name of the law. (In fact, this enjoyment is no longer a sign of its illegal nature, but the guarantee of its legitimacy.)

The clearest example of this logic is to be found in Spillane's 1951 novel, *One Lonely Night*. The story is framed by a direct confrontation with the law, as in the beginning we find Mike Hammer publicly humiliated by a judge for being a murderer. The figure of the judge keeps reappearing in the story which, in the final analysis, is Hammer's attempt to clarify for himself his relation to the law. The central question that Hammer poses for himself is whether he enjoys killing, and if this enjoyment is pathological. But on the very first pages of the novel, the question of law and enjoyment is contextualized by the problem of war: "[The judge] had to go back five years to a time he knew of only secondhand and tell me how it took a war to show me the power of the gun and the obscene pleasure that was brutality and force, the spicy sweetness of murder sanctified by law."[81] For Mike Hammer, therefore, the militarization of anti-Communist politics aims at a recovery of this "spicy sweetness of murder sanctified by law," the "obscene pleasure" of obeying the call of duty. The paradoxical project behind this militarization is, thus, to restore the unity of enjoyment and duty.[82]

But the contradictory foundation of this redefinition of duty is that the logic of obeying and disobeying the law are no longer clearly distinguishable: the new law demands the violation of the law. The starting point of the novel is the opposition between war and law: war is the exceptional situation in which killing is a duty rather than a crime. And this is the primary meaning of the exceptional situation: whereas the law banned certain forms of enjoyments, the exceptional situation is not simply the removal of all such bans (a chaotic situation in which everything is allowed, as Wylie seems to have understood it), but rather the reversal of the logic of the previous ban—what was normally denied is now a duty (and what was normally allowed can now come under a new ban). As official anti-Communist propaganda put a ban on the enjoyment of anti-Communism, Mike Hammer's character concentrates in itself this forbidden joy as he is the only one legitimately (even if not legally) enjoying anti-Communism. Thus, the militarization of anti-Communism is based on this reversal of the banned into a duty which provides the foundations of the joys of anti-Communism.

The problem, however, is that the "normal law" is weak and it cannot protect itself from the new enemy. Mike Hammer clearly pinpoints the failure of the law (which, for him, is the inherent failure of democracy) when he demonstrates that the law of democracy cannot distinguish friend from foe. In effect, the problem with the judge is that he cannot tell the difference between Mike Hammer and the Communists, since they are both simply "criminals" in his eyes. He cannot comprehend that in these two cases the violation of the law serves completely different purposes. The literal interpretation of the law fails to live up to the demands of the spirit and opens up little loopholes that the Communist can manipulate to their best advantage: "They use the very thing we build up, our own government and our own laws, to undermine the things we want."[83] Without a violent supplement (which in general terms could be described as "the politics of secrecy"), democracy is constitutively weak and incapable of guaranteeing the survival of the democratic framework of politics.

In the course of the novel, the blueprints of the most deadly American weapons go missing due to a leak in the State Department. So Hammer's mission is "to make sure this country has a secret that's safe."[84] But when he finally gets hold of these secrets, they are in themselves meaningless: "They were photos of a maze of symbols, diagrams and meaningless words, but there was something about them that practically cried out their extreme importance."[85] I would argue that with this particular sentence (no matter how incidental it might appear, and no matter how easily the reader might slide over it), the novel reaches one of its crucial climaxes, as it simultaneously demonstrates the ideological function of the figure of the secret (the quintessential MacGuffin) and reveals, with an almost barbaric intensity, the pure emptiness of its foundations.

This meaningless yet inexplicably significant secret appears in the narrative to mark the unrepresentable center of the order of things. The ultimate guarantee of authentic identity can only appear in this text as a mere "maze of symbols" (empty hieroglyphs of mystical knowledge) whose actual content, in the final analysis, is nothing but this mystical form. But this secret remains a secret not because of Mike Hammer's ignorance, but due to structural reasons. Its function is to mark and isolate a particular site within a text which offers itself in its pure textuality ("meaningless words"), emptied of all other meaning except for a mystical suggestion of significance: its meaning is that it is "meaningful." The stupidity of the text surfaces in this profound ignorance, which functions as the foundation of knowledge and wisdom. To put it differently, what the sentence demonstrates with the utmost clarity is that the guarantee of meaning is a meaningless sign. But this truth, on the ideological level, is translated into its own opposite: the text suggests that the guarantee of the stability of the world is not a lack of meaning but a particular meaning that is, in fact, so meaningful that it simply transcends the field it establishes.

So what kind of a politics is derived from this structure? In order to answer this question, we have to examine the way "politics" as such is depicted in the novel. We must remember that Mike Hammer is repeatedly described as an apolitical person. At one point, for example, this is how he describes his reaction to newspaper headlines: "More about the trials and the Cold War. Politics. I felt like an ignorant bastard for not knowing what it was all about."[86] This ignorance, however, is not condemned in the text at all, as it is precisely the necessary condition of Hammer's independence from the social structures that would restrict his potential sphere of action.

But if the foundation of anti-Communism is the politics of depoliti- cization, the question of the novel is to establish the legitimate limits of politics. It is on this level that the problem of secrecy has to be addressed. For, ultimately, the point of the novel is not to argue for a certain politics of publicity, but to establish forms of necessary secrecy. It is essential that the solution to the problem posed by Communist conspiracy is not a simple revelation of the truth about this conspiracy. Mike Hammer's solution is much more manipulative: it is a revelation of a partial truth that can influ- ence both domestic and international public opinion in such a way that the truth of anti-Communism can triumph. It is enough that Mike Hammer knows the whole truth; the public only has to know what mobilizes it in the fight against Communism. It appears that the revelation of the whole truth would actually be more harmful than its manipulative distortion.

On the last pages of the novel, when Mike Hammer confronts Oscar Deamer and reveals his true identity as Lee Deamer's evil twin usurping his identity, he decides to kill him in such a manner that this Communist will actually be the greatest hero of anti-Communism. Hammer organizes things so that it will appear that Deamer was killed by Communists while he was trying to protect the secrets of his country (rather than steal them). This maneuver serves two purposes. On the one hand, it will incite good Americans to an unprecedented Red Hunt. On the other hand, it will send a confusing message to the Kremlin: "they'll have to revise their whole opinion of what kind of people are over here. They'll think it was a tough government that uncovered the thing secretly."[87] The Russians will think that the American government is not afraid to act in undemocratic fashion when it comes to fighting Communism.

According to the novel, however, anti-Communist anti-politics is full of enjoyment. The most explicit formulation of the problem of enjoyment occurs as Hammer is getting ready for a final massacre of Communist agents with a tommy gun in his hand. He once again revokes the figure of the judge: "*The judge had been right.* There *had* been too many of those dusks and dawns; there *had* been pleasure in all that killing, an obscene pleasure that froze your face in a grin even when you were charged with fear. . . . I enjoyed that killing, every bit of it."[88] And the same argument is repeated in different forms several times throughout the novel. For example, after Mike Hammer's secretary Velda saves him by shooting a Communist agent, he tries to sooth her conscience with the following words: "There is no shame or sin in killing a killer. David did it when he knocked off Goliath. Saul did it when he slew his tens of thousands. There is no shame to killing an evil thing. As long as you have to live with that fact you might as well enjoy it."[89] What should be striking is that the enjoyment of the violation of the law in the name of a higher duty is inscribed in a Biblical language.

Of course, one of the major concerns of the novel is to distinguish this form of enjoyment from the evil enjoyment of Communist conspiracy. The most memorable scene that depicts this type of evil enjoyment is the final torture scene in an abandoned paint factory, in which Hammer's secretary and fiancé, Velda, is being tortured by three Communist agents. As Hammer is about to make his entry into this impromptu torture chamber, he describes the scene in the following terms: "For an eternal moment I had to look at them all, every one. General Osilov in a business suit leaning on his cane almost casually, an unholy leer lighting his face. My boy of the subway slobbering all over his chin, puking a little without noticing it, his hands pressed against his belly while his face was a study in obscene fascination."[90]

The problem of enjoyment leads us to the conclusion that in Spillane "the supplement to the law" is placed on theological foundations. This is the point where Spillane's anti-politics most clearly aligns itself with the anti-Communist political-theology of his times: since anti-Communism had to define the legitimate limits of politics, the American solution was to designate the necessary limit of politics as religion. Although this theology is not an explicitly formulated religious doctrine in Spillane, it is nevertheless clearly a structuring force of his fiction. The reason why it is easy to misrecognize this religious mission is that it manifests itself only on the level of the sacralization of violence. The moral criticism directed against Spillane's vulgar sadism and the opposing tendency to recover a religious content in his works are equally mistaken unless we perceive the essential identity of these seemingly contradictory themes: the religious content of Spillane's work *is* this excessive violence, this repulsive sadism. To put it differently, in Spillane's fiction, rather than being a mere failure, the heteronomy of the law is recoded as a theological principle. The politics of depoliticization is, therefore, not a mere apolitical posturing, but rather the conflict of two laws: while one of them is worldly and fallible (hence heteronomous), the other comes to us from another world and is infallible (and autonomous). The theological principle establishes the necessary limits of politics and justifies a kind of violence and enjoyment the worldly law denies. Thus the political enjoyment banned by the worldly law becomes the apolitical (theological) duty demanded by the higher law.

This is why Charles J. Rolo's 1952 article, "Simenon and Spillane: Metaphysics of Murder for the Millions," a true classic of Spillane criticism, stands out among the contemporary reactions to Spillane's fiction.[91] Unlike Wylie, for example, Rollo moves beyond the clichéd renunciations of sadism in Spillane's fiction to uncover the hidden religious content of this violence. In effect, Rollo shows that rather than a mere case of sadistic identifications, Spillane's success could be explained by "an altogether different, primitively moralistic set of cravings" which take us to the "metaphysical" foundations of Spillane's fiction.[92] As Rollo argues, in Mike Hammer's world, the inherent failure of law (as the police are incapable of guaranteeing justice) necessitates the realization of a higher law: "Hammer is Jehovah's messenger."[93] The move to the theological dimension, then, makes up for the inherent impossibility of a consistent application of the law. Mike Hammer's sadism is not a form of vulgar immorality; it is a theological form of violence that founds a higher form of morality.

Kenneth C. Davis is, thus, right to suggest that "Spillane's Jehovah could be seen as the active principle in his books."[94] But it is not exactly right to call it the "sublime contradiction" of his fiction that religion and violence coincide in this vulgar manner.[95] As long as we consider this duality a "contradiction," we are deprived of an essential insight. The compulsive attempts to separate religion from violence in Spillane's reception shows that liberal anti-Communism's investment in art and religion was founded upon the disavowal of the violence that established its political and cultural domains. In other words, the suspicion emerges that the separation of culture into high art and mass culture, and the concomitant division of politics into democratic and antidemocratic forces, were themselves the results of violent acts. Religion is not just the source of the truth of anti-Communism, but also the source of the violence that establishes its legitimate field. In Spillane's fiction, this violent foundation is put on display with a disturbing simplicity and exaggerated force.

This is why Malcolm Cowley's attacks on Spillane are so revealing, since in Cowley's work the institutionalization of modernism coincides with the deliberate exclusion of mass culture as paranoid, sadistic, and masochistic.[96] This leads us to believe that the institutionalization of modernism during the fifties had to proceed through a denial of the violent content of modernism (primarily, by displacing it to its other, mass culture). *New York Times* critic Hillis Mills's critique of Spillane's fiction is telling as it condenses this ideological complication in one single phase: "violence for violence's sake."[97] We find here an ironic formula, a parody of an avant-garde battle cry, to explain what is wrong with Spillane: art is replaced by violence. Whereas modernism is capable of making art for art's sake, mongrelized mass culture has nothing else to offer in place of art but violence. The assumption is, therefore, that art is the exact opposite of violence (without dialectical mediation). Modernism is opposed to mass culture the way art is opposed to violence.

We can, thus, articulate an obvious difference between Lionel Trilling and Mickey Spillane. What is common to both is that they try to derive a form of anti-Communist politics from a democratic paradox, but they assign fundamentally different roles to violence. As we have seen, for Trilling, the constitutive paradox of liberal democracy is that the primal imagination of liberalism will never coincide with its particular manifestations, since liberalism tries to establish freedom by instituting limits on this freedom. Therefore, it is always at risk of turning into an illiberal form of violence against this freedom. The role of "the imagination of catastrophe" is to test the limits of these particular manifestations by reactivating the original imaginary constitution of the field of the social. But Spillane argues the exact opposite. Since every particular manifestation of democracy is constitutively incomplete, it has to be supplemented by a sovereign agency whose actions are not limited to democratic procedures. For Trilling, the defense against the totalitarian threat inherent in democracy is manifesting the constitutive gap of liberal democracy through a repetition of the original act of imagination. For Spillane, on the other hand, the defense against the anti-democratic enemy consists of filling in the constitutive gap of democracy through a repetition of the original act of violence that instituted the regime of democracy. One represents the liberal dream of an absolutely nonviolent politics of perpetual self-critique; the other the sacralization of nondemocratic violence as the only viable means of security. Appearances to the contrary, however, these two options are not simple opposites, but two aspects of the same foundational moment. The separation of these two moments as mutually exclusive options was made possible by an "aesthetic ideology" that introduced a "great divide" within the social production of culture.

Thus, Mills's formula ("violence for violence's sake") misses the important point that the truly perverted nature of Hammer's violence is not that it is violence for its own sake but that it is violence for the sake of the Other. The perversion at the heart of this violence is that it is in the service of God. In other words, Hammer's violence is not perverted because it is excessive (and moves beyond the legitimate limits accepted by the guardians of liberal democracy), or because it is the source of enjoyment and self-serving. The democratic paradox is that the "due process of law" that characterizes democracy can only be guaranteed if the possibility of nondemocratic violence is kept alive. But this violence has to be distinguished from mere crime or the sadistic enjoyment of the antidemocratic enemy, so it is only justifiable if it is in the service of God.[98]

After a decade-long break following *Kiss Me, Deadly* (1952), Spillane revived his Mike Hammer series in 1962 with the publication of *The Girl Hunters*. This novel opens with the resurrection of Hammer, who, tortured by guilt, went on a seven-year binge after Velda mysteriously disappeared during a routine job. While the intensity of the later text is not comparable to the fury of *One Lonely Night*, it is clear that *The Girl Hunters* is a continuation of the same project. There is, however, a significant difference: Mike Hammer's relation to the law has undergone a decisive change.

One of the central characters of the novel is Art Rickerby, a federal agent seeking personal revenge for the murder of his friend and fellow agent, Richie Cole. Rickerby represents the logic of vengeance that Hammer used ever since *I, the Jury*. But this time, Rickerby puts a little twist on the original formula when he tries to explain to Hammer why he wants to catch the assassin alive:

> A quick kill would be too good. . . . But the law—this supposedly just, merciful provision—this is the most cruel of them all. It lets you rot in a death cell for months and deteriorate slowly until you're only an accumulation of living cells with the consciousness of knowing you are about to die . . . Too many people think the sudden kill is the perfect answer for revenge. Ah, no my friend. It's the waiting. It's the knowing beforehand that even the merciful provisions of a public trial will only result in what you already know. . . . True violence isn't in the deed itself. It's the contemplation and enjoyment of the deed.[99]

After the final showdown with the Communist assassin code named "the Dragon," Hammer's conclusions reflect the correctness of Rickerby's philosophy: "I thought [Rickerby] was nuts, but he could be right. Yeah, he sure could be right. Still, there had to be some indication that people were left who treat those Commie slobs like they liked to treat people."[100] This "indication" is that, rather than killing the Dragon, Hammer nails his hands to the floor so that he can be properly exposed to the true violence of the law. At the end of *The Girl Hunters*, therefore, we find that Hammer moves away from the vigilante logic of the earlier novels in the direction of a more properly law-abiding solution. His compromise between the two extremes (vigilantism and due process of law) is this "indication," this little extralegal bonus, which institutes a sign (in the form of a wound) that nevertheless marks the theological foundation of everyday democracy. Although the law is now "strong" enough to protect itself (since in this later novel it is redefined as an autonomous entity to the degree that it internalizes its own opposite, lawless violence and cruelty), democracy must be marked by the wounds of sacred violence. Mike Hammer's function is now to be the brutal scribe of these holy signs and literally carve them into the sinful bodies of the enemies of democracy: although the law internalizes supreme violence, it is still dependent on this minimal exteriorization in a sacred text, the holy writing of sovereign violence.

So the most important thing about Rickerby's philosophy is not that it tries to correct Hammer's kill-lust by ensuring a proper trial for a criminal. Quite to the contrary, the law is legitimized here only to the degree that it is the cruelest weapon of punishment. In a certain sense, the logic of vigilantism is internalized: the law is just to the degree that in essence it is vigilante. It regains its dignity only if behind the "supposedly just, merciful" façade we perceive a maximum of possible cruelty. But in that case, ensuring the due process of law is not simply just and merciful, but the most "perverted" form of justice as it provides the highest amount of vengeful enjoyment. While in the earlier Hammer novels the heteronomy of the law was exteriorized in the form of a higher law that justified holy pleasures, in the later novels we witness the interiorization of the guarantee of justice through the inherent cruelty of the law. From now on, the law is only just if it is manifestly cruel.

The shift of perspective between *One Lonely Night* and *The Girl Hunters* can be described in the following three steps. In the earlier novels, we start with the contradiction of the law and its outside (crime). But the problem is that Mike Hammer's relation to the law does not fit this scheme. He is not simply in violation of the law; he is fulfilling the spirit of the law. Therefore, in a second step, the opening contradiction between the law and its outside (law and lawlessness) had to be redefined as the contradiction of two laws: the weak law of democracy and the strong law of sacred violence. Finally, in the later novels, this contradiction between two laws is redefined as a contradiction internal to the law. Therefore, it is really no contradiction at all, since what might have first appeared to be the opposite of the law (supreme cruelty) is actually its true essence. This internalization of its own opposite, however, almost fully restores the autonomy of the law. But this restoration is not complete, because there is a minimal remainder of heteronomy: a message must be sent. Therefore, Mike Hammer's mission is no longer to maintain the democratic framework through sacred violence, since now the law itself is capable of administrating this violence. From now on, Mike Hammer's role is to institute the signs of nondemocratic violence. Although the law is supreme, some people might not know that it is so. Thus, the proper process of democratic justice must be constantly marked by the wounds of sovereign violence.[101]

7 / Three Worlds: Global Enemies

Anti-Communist Global Imaginary

So far, I have argued that nuclear holocaust fiction established the unity of the world and spy fiction introduced the idea that, in order to protect this unity, the world of democracy had to be constitutively split between the normal world of publicity and the clandestine world of sovereign violence. If we now turn our attention to popular political novels of the period, we find that the ideological figure of the enemy fulfilled a similar function in that it contributed to the definition of the external limits of this world.[1] To be more precise, in the case of the enemy we can speak of two related functions. As we have already seen in earlier chapters (and this is probably the best-known aspect of Cold War enmity), on the domestic front the enemy introduced the idea of the subversive simulacrum of the normal. On this level, Communism appeared as a threat to the very principle of representation, since it made increasingly more difficult to tell friend and foe apart. At the same time, however, on the level of foreign policy the enemy was also responsible for establishing a peculiar "global imaginary," the threefold division of the world that defined the age of the Cold War.

Thus, the unity and the internal division of the world corresponded to a set of external limits whose structure was defined by a particular ideological configuration of total enmity. The ideological figure of the enemy was, therefore, simultaneously responsible for the articulation of a global totality and its threefold division. Due to the expansionist nature of the enemy, anti-Communist politics had to be by definition a form of global politics. It was this very same enemy, however, that prevented the unification of the globe as a totality. In this context, we can speak of "total enmity" in at least three senses. First, Cold War anti-Communism involved a radical negation of the enemy, since a possible result of the political conflict was imagined to be total annihilation (either of the enemy or the whole world). Second, this enmity structured the totality of society (since the enemy was attacking on all possible fronts). Finally, since the Cold War was a global conflict, this totality went beyond the organization of a particular society and designated the globe itself as the ultimate horizon of politics. Borrowing a term from Fredric Jameson, we could say that the "geopolitical unconscious" of early Cold War anti-Communism was driven by a necessity to define a new kind of political totality (the globe), but the only viable means of the constitution of this totality turned out to be global enmity.[2]

In order to understand the way this total enmity was articulated, we should recall that it was in fact a common motif of Cold War liberalism to argue that the global enmity of the Cold War can be derived from a more fundamental condition: the internal antagonisms of modernity as such. According to this logic, the two major worlds of the Cold War were simply reactions to this internal crisis produced by the contradictions of the industrial age. Arthur Schlesinger, for example, argued that the "crisis of free society has assumed the form of international collisions between democracies and the totalitarian powers; but this fact should not blind us to the fact that *in its essence this crisis is internal.*"[3] This line of argumentation, however, suggests that the imaginary structure of this global enmity was in fact an externalization (or projection) of an internal antagonism.

The problem of this externalized antagonism also explains why the fundamental question of the Cold War political novel was the following: Why does the globe fail to become a world? This question can be interpreted in two different ways. It appears that something prevents the world (the "first world") from fully achieving its own identity. But something also prevents the first world from becoming a global order. These two obstacles (an internal and an external obstacle) can be derived from the same instance of internal antagonism. In order to prove the last point, three logical steps need to be demonstrated: first, it has to be explained how an internal antagonism prevents a world from fully constituting itself; second, we have to show how this internal antagonism is exteriorized in an ideologically constituted form of total enmity; and, third, we need to prove that the threefold division of the globe can be derived from the fact that a supposedly global conflict does not actually constitute a remainderless totality.

Alfred Sauvy's 1952 article, "Trois mondes, une planète" ("Three Worlds, One Planet")—often credited for being the singular site of the invention of the term "Third World"—provides us with the necessary answers.[4] Although the article might appear to be a mere piece of journalism, it nevertheless contains a miniature philosophy of history whose significance goes beyond the idiosyncrasies of an inspired mind. Right at the moment of its inception, the text announces the advent of the concept of the Third World in the form of a critique of contemporary world politics. The opposition inscribed in the title between the unity of a planet and the multiplicity of worlds calls attention to the fact that world politics is sustained by an empirical limit: the oneness of the planet is a mere fact and, as such, it falls outside of the domain of politics.

The problem, however, is that it is impossible to derive logically the idea of a politically united world from the mere fact of the oneness of the globe. There is no natural global political order that could respond to this fact in the form of the complete and perfect realization of its essence. Thus, while the mere fact of the oneness of the planet made world politics possible, at the same time it also formed an insurmountable obstacle. The apolitical foundation of world politics creates the terrain within which world politics takes place; but the planet remains inexorably silent when it comes to the determination of the right kind of world politics. The silence of the planet denies any guarantees and, therefore, constantly threatens to question the legitimacy of any world order. The planet and the world can never fully coincide.

If this is the presupposition encapsulated in Sauvy's title, it is not surprising that his whole argument is framed by a set of reversals. The first and last sentences of the text give us the most memorable formulations of this philosophy. The article opens with the following sentence: "We like to speak of the existence of two worlds, a possible war between them, their coexistence, etc., often forgetting that there also exists a third world, the most important of all three, which is in fact chronologically speaking the first."[5] At the same time, the often-quoted conclusion of the article announces the presence (or the ghost) of a familiar historical force: "But, ultimately, this ignored, exploited, misunderstood Third World, just like the Third Estate, wants to be something."[6]

The opening sentence declares that the least important is the most important and that the third (which is the last) is actually the first. To paraphrase: that which might appear to be an insignificant addition to a world order is actually the primary terrain of the constitution of this order and hence of vital importance. On the other hand, by formulating an analogy between the Third Estate and the Third World, the last sentence exteriorizes a conflict internal to the Western world and projects it onto the developing world: the relation of the first two worlds to the third is similar to the split that separates the three estates. Thus, the content of this projected conflict is precisely class antagonism, the bone of contention between the first and second worlds. Yet Sauvy's language evokes not only the bourgeois revolutions of the past but also the proletarian revolutions of the future, since the Third World "wants to be something"—just as the proletariat, which has for a long time been nothing, "wants to be everything." Sauvy calls this historical force a "mathematical fatality."[7]

The purpose of these reversals is to formulate the historical dialectics of Cold War world politics. As Sauvy seems to argue, the relation between the first two worlds is not a simple negation but a dialectical interdependence: "Western capitalism and eastern Communism support each other. If one of them disappeared, the other would undergo an unprecedented crisis. The coexistence of the two has to be a progression toward some distant and unknown common regime. It would be enough for each to negate constantly this future reconciliation and let time and technology run their own courses." But since this relation is defined as a "war," the post-historical dialectics of the two worlds actually prevents historical progress: "Therefore, the evolution toward the distant and unknown regime has been halted in both of the camps, and the cause of this standstill is not solely wartime expenditures. The point is to rely on the enemy in order to fixate oneself solidly."[8]

That is, the Cold War is a dialectic without the possibility of historical progress or, to be more precise, a dialectic in order to avoid historical change, since the ultimate purpose of Cold War enmity is to consolidate both of the warring political systems. But, as Sauvy insists, time does not stop and continues to "exercise its slow action" through the Third World: "Without this third or first world, the coexistence of the two others would not pose a big problem. . . . What is important for both worlds is to conquer the third or at least to have it on its own side. This is the source of all the troubles of coexistence." Therefore, at the heart of Sauvy's argument, we find a reversal of the classic Hegelian scheme of history: the "lands without history" are no longer to be located in the Third World. Quite to the contrary, the Cold War places the first two worlds in a post-historical (or even anti-historical) dialectic and displaces the force of history to the developing countries.

Thus, the philosophical content of Sauvy's argument could be summarized in the following terms: Sauvy tried to show that the conflict of the first two worlds is in effect the disavowal of the quintessential historical antagonism whose authentic locale is now the Third World. The Third World is revealed to be the very condition of the kind of world politics that is actualized in the conflict of the first two worlds. But the internal conflict of the Western world (class conflict) which produced these two worlds (capitalist and Communist worlds) is actually disavowed in the conflict of the Cold War, since the latter serves the purpose of the internal stabilization of both worlds. According to the logic of this disavowal, the Third World is the unimportant leftover of world politics, which is to be conquered or, at least, integrated into the logic of the dialectics of the two worlds. The problem is that the Third World cannot be reduced to this insignificant remainder: the mere existence of the Third World makes the peaceful coexistence of the two worlds impossible and therefore makes it impossible to reduce the Cold War to the anti-historical dialectics of internal stabilization. As the very condition of world politics, the Third World appears on the globe as the contemporary manifestation of the antagonism that ultimately led to the Cold War.

Sauvy's analysis allows us to provide a schematic view of the logic behind anti-Communist global imaginary. The internal antagonism of the Western world is exteriorized in an international conflict between capitalist and Communist countries. This exteriorization functions as the institution of a particular type of world politics, which reduces the terms of history to the mutual and absolute negation of two deadly enemies. The problem, however, is that this enmity is only theoretically total. In practice, it produces a historical remnant, that part of the planet which remains external to this conflict. The conflict between total enmity and its irreducible outside, thus, produces another antagonism that interrupts the structure of global enmity that supposedly dominates the globe without any leftover. So the problem is that the "leftover" constitutes a world of its own. First, the one world is divided by an internal conflict. Then, this internal conflict is institutionalized as the conflict of two words. And, finally, the conflict of the two worlds itself is interrupted by another antagonism which creates yet another world.[9]

At the same time, we have to keep it in mind that American foreign policy during the Cold War involved two separate politics: the containment of the Communist world and the modernization of the Third World.[10] The foundational opposition of modernization theory between "traditional" and "modern" societies introduces an idea of historical development ("modernization") which leads from one extreme of the opposition to the other. But this opposition also shows that the theory is based on an idea of totality that leads us back to the split between the world and the globe. On the one hand, if societies are *either* traditional *or* modern, modernity is an attribute of social totality. If a society is modern, modernity defines every aspect of the given social order. On the other hand, if the move *from* traditional *to* modern society is a necessary historical move, every society should eventually be modern. Thus, the ultimate goal of modernization is the total modernization of the globe. The aim of modernization is to define a social totality as a "world" and then define it as the ultimate political model for the globe: it aims to identify world and globe under the category of the modern.

The basic coordinates of Cold War enmity can thus be derived from an antagonism internal to "modernity" as such. According to the basic narrative, the historical process of modernization produced a modern world (the first world), but at the same time it led to irreconcilable social antagonisms. It must be emphasized, however, that according to modernization theorists, the United States and the Soviet Union represented two alternative modes of modernity. In other words, the basic antagonism of the Cold War is internal to the logic of modernity and, thus, can be defined as a hegemonic struggle to define "modernity" itself. To put it differently, the antagonism internal to the very logic of modernity was exteriorized in the total conflict of two different types of state. But this global conflict does not yet coincide with the planet, since the logic of modernity has not yet conquered the globe. The discrepancy between the worlds of modernity and the globe, in turn, produces another world. The "leftover" can be defined as a unified world because now it is that part of the globe which lacks modernity. In other words, it is a world precisely because the lack of modernity gives it an identity. It is in this sense that we can derive the three-world division of the globe from the same antagonism: an internal split within modernity produces two opposing worlds, and the split between modernity and the rest of the globe produces a third world.

Modernism and Modernization

In the previous two chapters, we examined the way the "liberal imagination" used the ideological figures of the catastrophe and the secret. The last question that remains to be settled here is whether this anti-Communist liberal imagination was based on a global imaginary structured by Cold War enmity. If we follow the logic of our previous analyses, we can anticipate at least a partial answer. From the point of view of liberal criticism, there were two major problems with mass culture: on the one hand, mass culture literalized the ideological content of modernism; on the other hand, through this reduction, it offered to its audience only the simulacrum of the vital problems of modernity. According to the same logic, therefore, mass culture as the literal representation of global enmity can only give us the simulacrum of the antagonism at the heart of modernity. Modernism, on the other hand, is capable of turning the antagonism at the heart of modernity into a formal principle, and thereby it can provide an authentic expression of contemporary historical consciousness. It is in this sense that the universality of mass culture (as a global culture) was opposed by anti-Communist aesthetic ideology to the universality of true art (which can be derived from the universality of the human condition).

This is why we have to emphasize that anti-Communist liberalism emerged at the meeting point of aesthetic modernism and political modernization. During the fifties, the term "modern" became one of the central categories of political contestation for American anti-Communism. In fact, these political articulations assumed the form of a confrontation between the aesthetic and political meanings of "the modern." Although the contemporary climate of opinion gave rise to a whole series of much more refined positions, the basic coordinates of this debate were predetermined by the conflict between the aesthetic and political definitions of the modern. If we wanted to formalize this discursive terrain, we could speak of a highbrow and a middlebrow consensus. While the first believed in the inherent value of modernist art and entertained an ambivalent relation to political modernization, the second tended to celebrate global modernization and completely rejected modernist aesthetics.[11]

Cold War anti-Communism had a double investment in aesthetic modernism (defined as the apolitical aesthetic expression of human freedom) and political modernization (understood as the production of the material conditions of political freedom). In this sense, political modernization could be understood as the material condition of modernism; and modernism could be defined as the aesthetic expression of the ideological content of this material production. The problem, however, was that modernization could not be easily reconciled with modernism, which to many appeared to be precisely a critique of modernization. But if modernism was animated by an anti-modernist ideology, it was no longer an aesthetic ally of modernization, but rather the only possible escape from it.

From the point of view of cultural criticism, the problem with modernity was that it simultaneously gave rise to mass culture and modernism. The historical emergence of the "culture industry" was considered by many to be a sign of what was wrong with modernization. In the 1950s, the political value of modernism was contested by a middlebrow centrism, so this modernist politics of anti-modernization came up against serious cultural resistance—what we could call a theory of "anti-modernist modernization." According to this position, modernism is neither an ideological expression nor a valid critique of modernization. Although modernization is not without its setbacks, it is still the only viable form of world politics. The role of art, therefore, is to formulate the ethically correct forms of global modernization. The most appropriate artistic channel for this program, according to this position, was middlebrow sentimentalism.

In order to locate the "liberal imagination" in this scheme, we have to return to our juxtaposition of Arthur Schlesinger and Lionel Trilling. First, we must keep in mind that the fundamental thesis of *The Vital Center* was that the political conflict of the Cold War had to be understood in terms of a tension inherent in the very logic of modernity. From the first pages of the book, Schlesinger argues that modernity is the "age of anxiety" because industrialization failed to produce adequate forms of social organization. Modernity freed the individual, but at the same time it abandoned him in an anxious state of depersonalized freedom. As Schlesinger puts it, "Modern technology created free society—but created it at the expense of the protective tissues which had bound together feudal society."[12] The inherent failure of modernity to protect the individual from anxiety, however, does not lead Schlesinger to a full-fledged condemnation of modernity as such. Rather, it forms the basis of a critique of totalitarian politics: "Even if capitalism and Communism are both the children of the Industrial Revolution, there remain crucial differences between the USA and the USSR."[13] Simply put, totalitarianism is a false response to the internal contradictions of modernity.

Modern art plays a special role in this scheme because, contrary to totalitarianism, it is an authentic expression of the anxiety caused by modern freedom. As we have seen, Schlesinger explained the totalitarian attack on modernism precisely in these terms: "The paintings of Picasso, the music of Stravinsky . . . reflect and incite anxieties which are incompatible with the monolithic character of 'the Soviet person.'"[14] In this opposition of democratic freedom and totalitarianism, modernism does not emerge as a critique of modernization. Quite to the contrary, it is actually the fullest expression of the freedom whose material conditions were produced by modernity. Although Schlesinger is aware that the history of industrialization has produced social antagonisms, the function of modernism is not to criticize these antagonisms but to uphold them as the price of freedom in face of a totalitarian challenge. While totalitarianism offers an escape from the anxiety caused by modern freedom, modernism formalizes it into an art.

The assumption behind this modernist critique of totalitarianism is that the logic of modernity is inherently global and, therefore, its tendency is toward global unification. There are at least two reasons for this globalization in Schlesinger's work: as technological development connects the distant parts of the world, modernity threatens humanity with global ecological catastrophe. This double logic (according to which, modernity simultaneously unites the world technologically and threatens to destroy it completely) breeds ambiguity. Although modernity must be criticized for its internal contradictions, it is nevertheless the only thing that can establish a global unity under the sway of freedom. But if the genuine aesthetic expression of modern global freedom is modern art, modernism should also be understood as an inherently global art. Wherever modernization successfully establishes the material conditions of modern freedom, the authentic cultural expression of this global condition will have to be modern art.

In the chapter entitled "Freedom in the World," Schlesinger argues that the politics of the vital center is of necessity a form of global politics: "We are condemned to think in global terms even to justify non-global politics."[15] This politics has two main components: containment and reconstruction (which is defined by Schlesinger as "the removal in non-Communist states of the conditions of want and insecurity which invite the spread of Communism").[16] But this double formula (Truman Doctrine and Marshall Plan) works only in Europe. The Third World poses a special problem, because there Soviet Communism can appear to be an agent of liberation from colonial influences and a champion of racial equality. Once again, the key word is modernization: "We have, in other words, a technological dynamism to set against the political dynamism of the Russians."[17] The modernization of the Third World should produce the type of economic and social stability that effectively renders these countries immune to Communist influence. At this point, however, it becomes clear that modernization carries a double ideological burden in Schlesinger's system. On the one hand, in the West it actually produced the historical conditions of totalitarianism (since it established freedom as an anxious state without corresponding social structures). On the other hand, in the developing countries it is supposed to produce the conditions of the resistance to totalitarianism.

This double historical burden, however, eventually leads to the necessary transcendence of the political conflicts of the Cold War. As Schlesinger argues, in spite of the fact that the Cold War makes "world government" impracticable, the larger historical logic of modernization makes it absolutely necessary. The problem is that modernization establishes the conditions of world government not in the form of a technologically interconnected world, but rather by exhausting the natural resources that formed its (natural) conditions: "Industrial society has disturbed the balance of nature, and no one can estimate the consequences."[18] Ultimately, Schlesinger seems to predict here a global ecological catastrophe that necessarily establishes the universality of the human race as the proper political subject: "In light of this epic struggle to restore man to his foundations in nature, the political conflicts which obsess us today seem puny and flickering. Unless we are soon able to make the world safe for democracy, we may commit ourselves too late to the great and final struggle to make the world safe for humanity."[19] Once modernity has established its real universality over the globe, it will be possible to reestablish premodern (natural and social) conditions on a higher postmodern level. The historical end of modernization will be its dialectical self-overcoming in an ecological (anti-modern) universality: modernization will lead to the emergence of the true universality of the "globe" over the political universalities of warring "worlds."

This modernist politics of global anti-Communism, however, met serious resistance in the form of the contemporary middlebrow attack on modernism. One of the quintessential documents of this middlebrow aesthetics is James Michener's "The Conscience of the Contemporary Novel" (1951).[20] The significance of this little manifesto of aesthetic world revolution is that it explicitly formulates an anti-modernist politics of modernization in the name of a global politics of liberalism. In other words, Michener argues that the corresponding aesthetics of liberal politics is no longer modernism (which he identifies with formal experimentation), but a reinvention of the content of literature to meet the demands of world politics. This is why Michener actually speaks of the contemporary significance of the "world novel" which, in opposition to modernism, is not concerned with formal innovation at all.[21] According to Michener, modernism cannot produce "world novels" because it is devoid of content.

Michener historicizes the problem of modernism by contrasting the literary revolution of the 1920s with that of the 1950s. Although the modernism of the 1920s was historically necessary in that it broke away from the restrictive traditions of the nineteenth century, it stayed within the destructive phase of the revolution without being able to offer anything constructive in place of what it destroyed. As Michener suggests, two major problems followed from this failure: modernism either produced American forms with un-American content or led to unnecessary formal experiments. But, as he adds, the function of great literature is to serve as "the conscience of the world."[22] This expression demonstrates two things: first, it claims that literature takes place within a global totality (that is, literature is always world literature); but it also suggests that the function of this world literature is essentially moral. Michener claims that for this purpose formal innovation is simply unnecessary. He repeatedly speaks of the "artistic tricks and gimmicks" of modern artists and adds that "in almost every case the experiment is unnecessary, proving forcefully that our principal need these days is not for radical new forms into which stale ideas can be poured but for radically more powerful thought, expressed in the simplest practical terms."[23] This is how the representational logic of anti-modernism is inscribed in the global anti-Communism of middlebrow populism.

Michener opposes this "unnecessary experimentation" to the "necessary knowledge" that should be produced by world literature. The ultimate function of art is to become the moral medium in which modernity comes to know itself. For Michener, the purpose of the restoration of content is to produce self-knowledge about America: "We present the anomaly of a nation assuming world leadership before it even knows itself."[24] But he also insists that this national literature cannot be confined within the limits of regionalism, because the coming of age of the American novel coincides with the birth of the "world novel."[25] The historical moment when America could finally become itself also marks an immediate move to another level of its historical identity: America becomes itself when it becomes the leader of the world. Therefore, American literature becomes itself when it transcends the logic of mere regional nationalism and becomes in itself a form of "world literature."

This rejection of modernism prepares the way for a celebration of the "popular" genre of the novel. Michener's anti-elitist attack on high art establishes the novel as the primary means of global communication: "Yet I must insist that a stupendous portion of the humane and liberal ideas which circulate to keep the conscience of the world clean are customarily circulated by novels."[26] The significance of the novel is that, unlike drama and poetry, it appeals to a popular audience: "the novelist is essentially a popular artist, and as such his responsibility is very great."[27] Thus when Michener calls the novelist "the poor man's poet" and "the poor man's dramatist," he tries to establish the conditions of a global middlebrow populism whose primary medium is popular culture. Modernity, therefore, produced two different cultural paradigms: modernism (as the false critique of modernity through meaningless experimentation) and popular culture (as the terrain of meaningful moral communication). In this sense, Michener reverses the terms of elitist critique of mass culture: modernism is actually a mere simulacrum, since it is pure form without content. Whereas the middlebrow metaphysics of the "content" promises authentic knowledge, formalist modernism is the mere simulacrum of knowledge.[28]

As we can see, both of the authors examined here defined liberalism as a necessarily global form of politics. In fact, it is precisely the presupposition that modernity inevitably leads to globalization that binds them together. Their differences come to the surface when they try to articulate the function of modernism in relation to the global politics of modernization: whereas Schlesinger affirmed modern art as the authentic expression of the internal antagonism of modernization, Michener argued that the logic of modernization had entered a new historical phase that moved beyond the logic of formalist experimentation. In other words, although the globalization of modernity was acknowledged to be something "real," its cultural representation became a politically contested issue.

Necessary Knowledge

As we have seen in the previous two chapters, while the literature of atomic holocaust attempted to legitimate the necessity of certain illusions in the name of political realism, spy fiction was primarily concerned with establishing the necessary withdrawal of certain elements from the public world of democracy. In a similar fashion, the third ideological figure of our analysis, the enemy, was employed to establish the vital necessity of knowledge. In the construction of this global imaginary, however, the Third World posed a special problem as it came to mark a limit of representation. The imperative to know was so ubiquitous and so explicitly formulated in the anti-Communist literature about the Third World that we do not need to spend much time establishing its mere existence. Rather, the question we need to raise concerns the way the limits of this knowledge were theorized. For the problem appeared to be that although accurate knowledge of the Third World was crucial in the fight against Soviet imperialism, the radical cultural alterity of the region threatened to completely undermine this project.

Since one of the most important genres of the dissemination of anti-Communist knowledge about the world was the middlebrow world-travel narrative, I will briefly examine here the way these problems appeared in two of its prime representatives: Philip Wylie's *The Innocent Ambassadors* (1957) and James Michener's *The Voice of Asia* (1951).[29] Wylie's book explicitly theorizes unrepresentable human essence as the very source of authentic anti-Communist politics, whereas in Michener's text we find traces of the suspicion (or, as he calls it, the "reasonable doubt") that ultimately the Third World cannot be "known." The juxtaposition of these authors will show us how modernization, religion, and race were brought together in an anti-Communist politics of representation. In effect, both Michener and Wylie argue for a new global politics based on the recognition of the universality of human nature. This universality performs a double role: on the one hand, it counteracts the negative effects of racism; on the other hand, it establishes a generalized "religiosity" as part of human nature. The task of modernization, thus, appears to be the establishment of the universal religion of humankind, which opposes racism and religious intolerance, as well as Communist imperialism.

The Innocent Ambassadors narrates Philip and wife "Ricky" Wylie's actual but somewhat "fictionalized" trip around the world that took them from Florida to Hawaii, Japan, Hong Kong, Thailand, India, Lebanon, and Turkey. In the introduction, Wylie explicitly presents the book as an anti-Communist tract. Since Communism, "acting on the theory of permanent military stalemate, is proceeding to dismember the world," Wylie "tried to tell what Communism is and what it is doing."[30] This claim might be a bit surprising, since we never actually meet a Communist in the book. We only get to see the malicious effects of Communist propaganda. In addition, the seemingly innocent narrative is explicitly politicized in at least two senses. First, before embarking on the trip, Wylie is approached by some people from Washington, who ask him to do certain things while in Hong Kong. By dissolving the dividing line between tourist and secret agent, this mission explicitly politicizes Cold War tourism as a form of international politics: tourists become ambassadors.[31] At the same time, however, Wylie frames the whole trip by an anti-Communist therapeutic narrative. Ever since his brother's tragic death in Poland in 1936, Wylie had been suffering from a terrible phobia: he could not leave the country or leave for extensive trips. In spite of the official verdict that his brother committed suicide, Wylie had been convinced that his brother was murdered by Communists after their trip to Russia, because they "talked too much." By the end of the book, Wylie is cured of this global fear of Communism (which stages a certain psychological overcoming of anti-Communist "isolationism") and once again becomes a citizen of the world.

The fundamental thesis of the book is that Communism is a religion. In order to prove this point, Wylie examines the psychological roots of religion and effectively claims that "our overt prejudice against other races and our partly unconscious prejudice toward other religions" can be derived from the same psychic functions.[32] This juxtaposition of religious intolerance and racism forms the basis of a redefinition of American foreign policy: neither Christian world conquest nor racist imperialism is a viable means of global anti-Communism. Wylie singles out John Foster Dulles as the symbol of what is wrong with America's relations with the Third World, since on his trip he found that "our longtime, much-traveled, clarion-speaking Secretary of State was a symbol of a specific odiousness to millions everywhere we journeyed."[33] According to Wylie, what Dulles represents gives rise to a "psychological continuation of colonialism."[34] He opposes Communism and American foreign policy in terms of a religious conflict. As long as America opposes Communist dogmatism with a religious dogmatism, it cannot offer true freedom to the Third World.

The central question of Wylie's work concerns the representability of the universal foundations of human nature. The book opens with the complaint that, unfortunately, it is always the wrong kind of people who have the means to travel around the world. Anticipating the type that later became known as the "ugly American," Wylie dismisses these vulgar tourists in the following terms: "These people represent one kind of American success. But they do not represent America. They do not represent the knowledge in America, the understanding, the capacity for brotherhood, the willingness to learn, the widespread ability to evaluate truly or the common wish to appreciate correctly."[35] To rectify the situation, as Wylie argues, the right kind of Americans should be sent abroad: "I have said that we should send young Americans abroad in great numbers. As Ricky and I found out and this book will show, it is probably the only way to win a life-or-death struggle we did not seek but cannot evade."[36]

In the same chapter, however, Wylie also raises the problem of representation in a technical sense when he brings up the question of tourism and photography. Tourist photography is discussed here as an inadequate form of representation, since it is merely concerned with what is immediately visible. In a sense, it is representation without knowledge: "The constant photographer at best can bring back unrelated fractions of travel. By his very assiduity, he is removed from the human environment. He has no time to become acquainted even with the people he photographs. He wants a mere picture of them—not any knowledge of who they are, what they think and feel, or how they relate themselves to him. He has to remain immune to relationships and wholes."[37] Apparently, it is the very act of representation (the photographer's assiduity) that makes authentic representation impossible as it distances the photographer from his or her subjects. The act of representation renders the immediacy of experience inaccessible: "For a picture 'says more than thousand words' only to those who cannot truly read, think or make friends—and have a paltry imagination, besides. A man of modest understanding, for instance, can feel what a Japanese feels; but I would like to see a photograph taken by an American *in Japanese*."[38] The sentimental wisdom of this conclusion consists of a shift from the language of representation (a photograph taken in a particular language) to the unrepresentable and the universal language of feelings.

The foundation of this empathy, of course, is human universality, which therefore possesses its own language. As the Wylies are flying above India, Philip looks down upon the ancient land and is shocked by its strangeness: "For a time I felt as if Asia was meaningless to an Occidental: a human spawning-ground that might, in some next ten thousand years replace man—if, say, his civilized minority should blast and ray itself into extermination."[39] But this apocalyptic vision of the impossibility of meaningful communication between the first and the Third World is only introduced here to show that the universality of human nature is capable of bridging the most drastic cultural differences. The idea of radical alterity dissolves in a humane universality:

> For I knew, and I had to see *because* I knew, that those below, and the Red Chinese, men long tundra-bound and the fever-checked blacks were as other men, exactly. As ourselves—exactly. *They are we:*

I knew the genes, chromosomes, and the history, the anthropol-
ogy, the archeology and paleontology. I could not let myself be like
many of my countrymen who also know these truths, yet talk, think,
persecute, praise and have their being as if what they know were
unknown![40]

And this common humanity is not without its own language. This thesis finds a blatantly sentimental expression in Wylie's reaction to the Taj
Mahal. He is so moved by the experience that he breaks down and starts
to cry. But, more important, a strange exchange occurs between Wylie and
his Sikh guide. As Wylie puts it, "He *knew*":

A nonword in the center of his dual vocabulary was perceived as the
same word, phallus-written for me long ago in Massachusetts on the
living parchment of a mother's womb, where he had learned it and
all men learn it but so few remember, or recognize, when they see it
again in any conscious language of whatever loveliness.
So I looked back at Singh with the passive part of the look-that-
understands-the-other. Then I snorted my nose to exorcise the
prelanguage phrase and to restate my mundane maleness. . . . God is
ascetic in thought, in doing aesthetic, but in being—ecstatic.[41]

Rejecting the religion of a John Foster Dulles, Wylie here claims this phal-
lic, ecstatic, universal, "prelanguage" experience (mediated through the
field of the aesthetic) as the essence of true religion. Since it is a "nonword"
which is "the *same* word" for everyone (or, at least, every male subject),
this experience is not completely outside language. It does precede particular languages, but it still partakes of language as its universal theological foundation.

This is why the ultimate objective of the "necessary knowledge" instituted by the anti-Communist imperative to know does not really produce a
lot of new knowledge. Essentially, it is constituted by the recognition within
the strange and the new of what we already knew. This point is well illus-
trated by Wylie's first exposure to Tokyo, which turns out to be a strange
experience precisely because at first it is devoid of all strangeness: "I did
not feel it alien."[42] Wylie is almost disappointed by this familiarity: "though
fascinated, bemused—I could not find much sensation of the bizarre."[43]
But, ultimately, this lack of strangeness is revealed to be the surprise of the
universal: "It doesn't take great differences to create a sense of foreignness
for most tourists, I guess. . . . But what continually surprises me about foreign cities—Paris, Rostov-om-Don, or Tokyo—is the similarity of ways and
cityscapes." In fact, Wylie explicitly renounces the "shock of otherness" in
favor of what we could call the "shock of sameness": "What now impresses

me is the universality of human ends and means and being."[44] Signifi-
cantly, however, Wylie experiences the most shocking experience of otherness through what is supposedly familiar to him, "Frank Llyod Wright's
earthquake-proof Imperial Hotel": "A contemporary architect (however
much Mr. Wright would resent the adjective) would be horrified by the
waste space within; but the Imperial is very comfortable; and I was amused
that my image of the Imperial as an American product was so inaccurate—
that its reality was more strange to me than the strangeness of downtown
Tokyo."[45]

We can, therefore, see that for Wylie the "beyond" of representation
is a universal human nature whose necessary yet impossible representation is the foundation of successful anti-Communism. The wrong kind
of anti-Communism, as we have seen, is based on the disavowal of this
universal foundation through a religious racism. When this "unknown
known" penetrates conscious, everyday human experience, the possibility of a universal language appears, if ever so fleetingly, on the horizon.
Furthermore, we also know that the mode of existence of this universal
foundation is the surprise of the familiar as it disturbs the experience of
the foreign. When the same appears in the foreign, the uncanny strangeness of the universal is revealed. This is why the foundation of anti-Communist global tolerance is not the "shock of otherness" but the "shock
of sameness." The right kind of politics of representation will need to
establish a terrain within which "the shock of sameness" can emerge as
a universal experience.

A very similar set of problems is addressed in Michener's works as
well. As a matter of fact, the very title of his book *The Voice of Asia* clearly
announces its preoccupation with issues of representation. The central
proposition of the book is that Asia had been traditionally misrepresented,
since Americans did not listen to the true voice of Asia. To rectify this
situation, Michener set out on a trip through Japan, Korea, Formosa, Hong
Kong, Singapore, Indonesia, Thailand, Indo-China, Burma, and Pakistan,
and conducted 120 interviews with a wide range of people. This excavation
of Asia's authentic voice from below the rubble of false representations,
however, serves the same ideological purpose that we have been examining
so far: the true voice of Asia promises authentic knowledge. Once again,
this knowledge is simply necessary, and its foundation is universal human
nature. Michener explicitly speaks of his project in terms of knowledge: "I
learned mostly how much I didn't know. America should have some of its
ablest young men doing for months and years what I did for some days. For
unless we know Asia we will never gain the wisdom to make right decisions at the right time. And unless we start making some right decisions,
Asia will become by default our implacable enemy."[46]

Michener's political program can, then, be described in the following terms: his self-imposed task is to establish a field of representation within which a particular object ("the voice of Asia") can successfully appear. This distinction between the establishment of a field within which an object can appear and the act of appearance itself is significant, since Michener does not conceive of his own activity as a "description" of an object, but rather as an active way of allowing the object to appear. The "voice of Asia" can appear to provide authentic knowledge only if the proper conditions of Asia's self-representations are successfully established. The act of representation is defined here as the establishment of a transparent medium of self-representation.

But one of the most compelling images of the book complicates this formula by staging the "silence of Asia" as the only authentic source of knowledge. Apparently, even authentic self-representation has a negative foundation, because an authentic knowledge of Asia should also include those elements that are incapable of self-representation:

> When I think of India I think of the Kashmiri Gate. . . . There was a young woman who haunted this gate and in some ways she spoke for India. . . . And . . . I could never forget that she was India, too. For she was naked. She was completely naked and once I saw a policeman gently advise her that she really must go home and put some clothes on. She pulled away and walked on through the Kashmiri Gate where the conquerors had marched. She was about twenty-two, most attractive in appearance, very wild-eyed. She carried a few filthy belongings in a rotting cloth and was either a madwoman or someone protesting the bitterly high price of cloth. We looked at each other whenever we passed and she seemed to be a living protest. Actually she was merely a naked woman walking through the Kashmiri Gate. No one thought to arrest her. There is much in India that no American can understand.[47]

The most memorable act of this naked woman is her silence, yet "in some ways she spoke for India." The message of the anecdote appears to be that the voice of Asia is dependent on this silence: that which speaks most authentically is actually what does not speak at all, for no representation of India can ever be fully authentic without her. Michener's text oscillates between a desire to invest her with allegorical meaning and the opposing tendency to reduce her nakedness to its literal content. This dual movement (allegorizing the negative foundation of representation at the same time as reducing it to one single element of representation) establishes a political tension between the voice and the silence of Asia. To the degree that her silence becomes a site of protest, there might actually be a tension internal to the voice of Asia that prevents it from achieving authentic self-representation. Although authentic self-representation is supposedly provided by the voice, the silences that punctuate the voice can undermine its performance.

Michener, however, has another lesson to learn in Asia from naked women. This time the act of self-representation is combined with the act of representing America. What Michener tries to show here is that the necessary knowledge about Asia is riddled by equally necessary doubts. In an early chapter of the book, entitled "Reasonable Doubts at a Strip Tease," Michener's text encounters the problem of the simulacrum as a political question.[48] But what promises to be a pleasant experience of cultural exchange actually turns out to be a rather disturbing lesson: "I have heard of men who encountered varied experiences at a strip tease, but I believe I am the first who ever learned a political lesson at one."[49] What makes this lesson political? Just the fact that Michener understands that the "voice of Asia" is not simply an organic expression of a pre-given "Asian" identity but a performance. And if the voice of Asia is not speaking directly from the heart of Asia, the knowledge produced by this voice can be easily consumed by terrible doubts.

In fact, the very first sentence of the chapter initiates a paranoid logic that threatens to undermine the very possibility of authentic knowledge: "The American occupation of Japan has been so successful that any reasonable human being suspects it can't all be true. Inevitably one gets the sinking feeling in his stomach that the whole thing must be a gigantic farce played by clever antagonists." The ultimate logical consequence of this "reasonable doubt" is the complete loss of certainty: "What proof have we that the Japanese are truly our friends? None. We have no proof at all."[50] From this point on, Japanese friendship is a mere performance, a front, or a simulacrum.

Ultimately, Michener's political lesson concerns the modernization of Japan. His primary concern is the simultaneous exportation of American-style modernization and mass culture. Michener's objective here is to respond to an Englishwoman "who knew Japan well [and who] has described our occupation as the imposition by young barbarians of a barren culture upon one of the oldest continuing cultures in the world."[51] Michener is quick to admit that mass culture is not inherently valuable, but he insists that modernization had a positive effect on Japanese history: "1. Liberation of women. 2. A new concept of where authority to govern rests. 3. Better land distribution. 4. Revision of the Emperor's status. 5. Rationalized manufacturing procedures."[52] This separation of the positive effects of modernization from the negative influence of mass culture is the core of the political lesson that Michener learned at the strip tease: "What does seem wrong is to demand credit for other trivial changes which more often than not were either misguided or downright ridiculous. There is no inherent merit to popcorn, American candy bars, new-style movies or jitterbugging. I am thinking especially of that strip tease I saw at Christmas."[53] For what emerges here is that through simultaneously exporting modernization and mass culture, America provided the Japanese with a language to criticize the American occupation and American-style modernization.

So let us see what actually transpired at that notorious strip tease. What is surprising to Michener is that rather than being a pathetic imitation of American culture, the show turns out to be a subversive parody. In fact, at first, the show does appear to be a cheap imitation: "It was as unsexy as one could imagine."[54] But things take a sudden turn when the main event of the evening, a reenactment of Gone with the Wind, is announced: "This playlet was so astonishing, so subversive and so clever that I want to report it in detail."[55] The point is that failed Japanese imitation turns out to be a conscious critique of what is to be imitated: "It was an amazing show. All aspects of American life were ridiculed. There could have been no purpose other than to burlesque life in the South. Every cliché of the communists was dragged out, explained and posed for exhibition."[56] After the play, the evening comes to an end with a Christmas tribute to Americans: "Then appeared a fat and perfectly repulsive young woman who started to do a violent strip tease. I had difficulties associating this with Christmas, but suddenly the orchestra explained it all. They broke rapturously into 'I'm Dreaming of a White Christmas.' The announcer thought it was all very moving, for he stood ramrod straight, saluting."[57] But even this "tribute" to America is obviously a joke: "They were laughing out loud this time, and I had the strange feeling that somebody in that audience was having hell kidded out of him."[58]

Thus, the political lesson revealed at the Japanese strip tease teaches Michener to doubt the success of the American occupation, which now appears to be a mere performance. Apparently, the voice of Asia is simultaneously the source of authentic knowledge and a satiric performance. First, we have seen that the voice depends on a silence that establishes its authenticity. The self-representation of Asia cannot provide full knowledge, unless Americans know how to interrogate the silences of this voice. But Michener suspects an antagonism behind the performance. Silence becomes a "silent protest," and the real content of the American knowledge of the world is not exclusively universal humanity, but protest and antagonism. No matter how much you know about Asia, in the end you must suspect that it is antagonistic toward America. The split between the voice and the silence, however, also introduces the possibility of deliberate deception. At the strip tease, the voice speaks the language of American mass culture. What remains explicitly unsaid, however, is the resistance to the Americanization of Japan even if the message of the show is quite obvious. This time, the voice of Asia is speaking an American language, but it still formulates Communist clichés. The reasonable doubt of global anti-Communism whispers a disturbing message in the middlebrow ear: it is not self-evident that universal humanism is capable of establishing a global community, because the universality of the human bond might be nothing but a mere simulacrum. Precisely because of its constitutive limitations, the necessary knowledge of the Third World is inherently exposed to the paranoid doubt of antagonistic misrepresentation.

Thus, the anti-Communist imperative to produce authentic middlebrow knowledge about the world was based on an explicitly theorized impossibility: universal human essence *must be represented*; yet it *can never be* fully represented. Both self-representation and the representation of the cultural other were caught in this impossibility. This complication introduced the element of doubt, which had serious consequences for the politics of modernization. What Michener discovers is that although modernization can indeed establish the material conditions of freedom, it does not necessarily ensure pro-American attitudes. In fact, modernization can also provide the language of anti-American resistance to modernization. Tortured by this terrible doubt, modernization can never be fully sure of its own success, for it cannot know for sure that its outcome was a pro-American modern society or its mere deceptive appearance.

The Importance of Being Ugly: Anti-Communist Anti-Imperialism

It is common to read William J. Lederer and Eugene Burdick's 1958 bestselling novel *The Ugly American* as a fictionalization of anti-Communist modernization theory.[59] But one of the most surprising things about *The Ugly American* is that the novel does not fully warrant the common usage of the term it had itself created. It is undeniable that the novel gave rise to the popular expression "the ugly American," which denotes a peculiarly American type of arrogance that refuses to engage other cultures on their own terms. And it is also true that Lederer and Burdick's most important objective was to criticize this kind of American attitude toward other cultures. But in the book itself, the term "ugly American" is *not* used in this negative sense at all. As a matter of fact, in *The Ugly American* the expression is used to name the only viable alternative to the politics of what we call today the "ugly American." As a strange quirk of fate, the title of the book was immediately associated with its critical objective, and it was invested with a meaning that happens to be the exact opposite of what it carries within the text itself. Contrary to popular belief, the novel actually tries to show the importance of being ugly. The question for us, then, concerns the meaning of this "ugliness" for anti-Communist politics.

It should be immediately obvious that we are dealing with a strange combination of aesthetic and political categories: "ugliness" is an aesthetic quality (the negation of beauty) which is now applied to the politics of American foreign policy in the Third World. Upon first glance, then, the book recommends a certain aestheticization of politics that turns a negative aesthetic quality into a positive political program. In fact, we can go even further. Since the book is mostly concerned with the politics of modernization, we can also assume that this aestheticization of politics in the name of "ugliness" concerns the meaning of the "modern."

This is why it is significant that the *The Ugly American* argues that the politics of modernization is incomplete without an aesthetic supplement. The text suggests that, in order to succeed, the global anti-Communism of modernization must incorporate a specific strategy of self-representation. Therefore, the meaning of this "ugliness" must be discussed in both a political and an aesthetic sense. On the level of politics, the novel suggests that the right kind of modernization should not be construed as imperialism. Borrowing a term from Walter Benn Michaels, we could even argue that *The Ugly American* is a quintessential example of the ideology of "anti-imperial Americanism," the attempt to found American national identity on an anti-imperialist rhetoric.[60] John Carlos Rowe formulated the fundamental contradiction of this ideology in the following terms: "Americans' interpretations of themselves as a people are shaped by a powerful imperial desire and a profound anti-colonial temper."[61] On the level of aesthetics, however, we find that the novel's rejection of high modernism serves the purposes of a documentary realism that fully participates in the aestheticized politics put forth in the text. Thus, with its redefinition of "ugliness," the novel provides the middlebrow imagination with an aesthetic ideology in which "imperial desire" and "anti-colonial temper" can be reconciled through the aestheticized politics of modernization.

The Ugly American is a series of loosely connected stories about Americans living and working in South East Asia. Most of the stories are set in the fictional country of Sarkhan, although a significant section of the book is devoted to "real" countries like Vietnam and Burma. What is common to these stories is that they all illustrate the same point: America is losing the Cold War in the Third World because of its essentially flawed philosophy of foreign diplomacy. Yet what is common to all of the characters who stand out as positive examples in the book is that they work outside the traditional institutions of "dollar diplomacy" and attempt to effect change in the Third World by direct interactions with the local people.

So it is important to point out that the "ugly American" of the book is actually one of these positive characters and not one of the irresponsible, power-hungry amateurs the book criticizes for misrepresenting America all over the world. In the two chapters, "The Ugly American" and "The Ugly American and the Ugly Sarkhanese," we are introduced to three "ugly" characters: Homer and Emma Atkins, and the Sarkhanese man called "Jeepo."[62] All three of them are described as being physically ugly. When Homer Atkins first appears in the book, he is at an official meeting staring at his own hands in embarrassment, because he knows that his propositions will be turned down by the committee that he is facing. This is when we are told that "His hands always reminded him that he was an ugly man," and that the meeting made him conscious "of his own personal ugliness."[63] A few pages later, when we meet Homer's wife, Emma, we are told quite directly that "Emma, a stout woman with freckles across her nose was, in her way, quite as ugly as her husband."[64] Finally, when Atkins meets Jeepo, the native mechanic who is going to be his future business partner, their ugliness establishes an immediate bond between the two men: "And Jeepo was ugly. He was ugly in a rowdy, bruised, carefree way that pleased Atkins. The two men smiled at one another."[65] Based on their common ugliness, these three characters establish a community that functions as the fundamental model of successful American-native cooperation in the Third World.

The fundamental thesis of the novel can be easily summarized: on the level of official diplomacy, Burdick and Lederer call for the professionalization of the foreign service. This professionalization involves at least three important changes. First, the Americans who represent the country abroad must be self-sacrificing, trained experts who are familiar with the languages and cultures of the countries where they are stationed. Second, a radical change of philosophy is necessary that shifts the focus of attention from "big" military and economic investments to small-scale pragmatic solutions. In other words, the book propagates a shift from the macropolitics of power to the micropolitics of everyday life. Finally, the novel also makes it clear that America needs to develop a new politics of self-representation that takes into account the psychology of the anti-imperialist resistance to modernization. Thus, what the novel effectively shows is that the politics of modernization is necessarily based on a politics of representation. Without this new politics of self-representation, modernization is destined to fail. In a certain sense, the task of this politics of representation is to establish the cultural conditions of economic modernization. The problems of modernization and representation are joined together this tightly because the novel argues that the proper form of anti-Communism in the Third World must be the kind of modernization that does not appear to be modernization.

But the truly provocative and disturbing thesis of the book is not merely that professionalization is necessary, but that "it is possible to learn from an enemy."[66] In other words, the book calls for the conscious and deliberate imitation of the enemy: in order to fight Communism in the Third World, Americans have to act exactly the same way the Communists do, even if their ultimate objectives are radically different. If we follow Lederer and Burdick's argument, on the level of propaganda methods Communists and anti-Communists become virtually indistinguishable. But while Communist deception tricks Third World countries into accepting totalitarianism, the conclusion of *The Ugly American* is that through the same methods they could also be tricked into freedom. As we can see, the philosophical foundation of this program is the strategic separation of the form of political action from its actual content.

In order to examine the problem of representation in the novel, let us start with the first American character we meet in the book who successfully blends into his environment. Father Finian, a Catholic priest, is on a personal crusade against Communism in Burma. Relying on the same split between form and content, Father Finian understood that Communism is a form of religion, only it serves the devil.[67] The structure of this discovery is decisive: it postulates that formally Communism is a simulacrum of religion, but that on the level of ideological content, it is the exact opposite of religion. To put it differently, Father Finian identifies a formal commonality that, nevertheless, gives rise to opposing contents. So Finian gathers around himself eight reliable Burmese men to educate them in the basic know-how of anti-Communism. The most important rhetorical problem for Finian, however, is to convince the Burmese men that they are not being convinced of anything. Finian wants to steer these men in the right direction in such a way that they believe that they are simply acting out their own innermost desires without any external coercion.

The "nine friends" reach the conclusion that anti-Communism is essentially a "process of persuasion": "What we discovered . . . is that men are persuaded of things by the same process, whether the persuading is done by the Catholic Church, Lutherans, Communists, or democrats. A movement cannot be judged by its methods of persuasion for, short of violence, most successful movements use the same methods."[68] Once again, Finian's point is that on a purely formal level, politics is without an inherent value. An exclusively formal analysis of Catholic, Lutheran, Communist, or democratic politics will only show us that they all necessarily rely on the same techniques. On this level, even the deadliest enemies are undistinguishable. This point is, then, used as a justification for the imitation of the enemy. Since Communists imitate organized religion, and since all efficient political persuasion uses the same methods, it is perfectly acceptable and even necessary to fight Communists with their own tactics.

In this regard, the novel examines the same epistemological crisis that formed the basis of the domestic attacks on Communism. At home, the "masters of deceit" undermine democratic procedures by pretending to be normal members of the community. In the Third World, the Communists pretend to be nationalist liberators who disguise themselves as local civilians. Thus, the primary problem of this war is to identify the enemy: "But even more frustrating than constant defeat was the fact that at the end of three weeks of fighting, they had not once seen the enemy. The firefights always took place at night and were over by dawn; the enemy always slipped away, taking his dead with him; and the men felt they had participated in phantom engagements. The only thing that made it real were the dead Legionnaires."[69] In order to render the enemy visible, however, the French should know more about the enemy. The provocative message of the text is that the only way to fight the Communists is actually to learn something new from Mao:

> What Mao said to do is send a couple of agents ahead into any village in which the Communists conceivably might fight. If possible these agents should be men who come from that village. They settle down in the village and live like everyone else, except that they have a few sacks of hand grenades and a few burp guns which they keep hidden. . . . Whenever the Legionnaires go into a village, there are already a half-dozen of the enemy behind them. These enemy don't wear uniforms; they don't even dig their weapons up until the critical moment has arrived. . . . Imagine if you could have a half-dozen of your own men looking exactly like the Communists, operating back of their lines?[70]

The concluding question (even if it is only a wish) already contains an ambiguous program in that it calls for a deliberate manipulation of appearances: if only our men could look exactly like the Communists. Mao's instructions make it clear that Communist warfare involves a tactical misrepresentation of identity that renders Communists indistinguishable from other civilian inhabitants of the native villages. The task for anti-Communism is, thus, to familiarize oneself with these techniques and adopt them. The necessary imitation of the enemy is made clear in the novel when finally Major Monet decides "to cure our illness with the hair of the dog that bit us," and successfully strikes at the Communists for the first time.[71]

But when the invisible enemy finally appears, the experience turns out to be quite shocking. In a lengthy discussion of the fall of Dien Bien Phu and the French presence in Vietnam, the authors ask a simple question: How is it possible that a modern Western army is beaten by a few home-made guns? On the day when the French evacuate Hanoi, our central characters (MacWhite, "Tex" Wolchek, and Monet) cannot help but observe the striking contrast between the departing French army and the just arriving Communist troops. The French depart as if they were celebrating a victory and put up a real military show. After the French military parade, however, the actual victors of the war enter the city:

> They then saw the first regular Communist soldier arrive—an officer on a wobbling bicycle, wearing a padded suit, tennis shoes, and a tiny forage hat. He had a rifle slung over his shoulder. Trotting behind came a platoon of men dressed in a mixture of uniforms. Some merely wore breech-cloths and what looked like captured French blouses. Many of them were barefooted. Perhaps half of them had rifles. . . . Three of the men were actually carrying home-made rifles. Tex had the feeling that he was looking at people who were fighting a war that should have taken place three hundred years before. . . . They looked harmless and innocent, indeed they almost looked comical.[72]

The most difficult thing for the soldiers to accept is that an almost comically premodern army (which should have been fighting three centuries ago) successfully defeated modern military technology. With this story, the novel tries to warn its readers about the limits of modernization. On the one hand, the episode illustrates the strength of the resistance to colonial powers. The lesson is clear: America must not appear as a colonizing power in the Third World. On the other hand, the French defeat also raises questions about the force of modernization, since the resistance to colonization found supremely effective ways to resist modern technology. In accordance with the general thesis of the novel, the text argues here that modernization is ineffective in the Third World if it is not accompanied by special strategies of self-representation. Reversing the formula of Communist deceit and infiltration, the novel claims that modernization has to imitate the tradition it aims to reform.

So, how does the problem of "ugliness" appear in this argument? In order to answer the question, we have to return to "the ugly American" of the novel. Homer Atkins faces the same problem that Father Finian had to overcome: they both know the solution, they just have to find a way to convince people to accept this solution as their own. Atkins realizes that one of the most vital necessities in Sarkhan is to get water to the hillside rice paddies. In order to help the Sarkhanese, he invents a water pump. But there are two problems he needs to solve first. He has to make sure that his modern invention can be assembled from materials already available in

Sarkhan. So he comes up with the idea of propelling the pumps by bicycles. In addition, he has to make sure that the local people accept this invention as a helpful tool rather than a symbol of white oppression. To achieve this goal, he invites Jeepo, "the Ugly Sarkhanese," to be his business partner.

The story teaches us two things about successful modernization. First, rather than being the imposition of modern technology on a traditional society from the outside, it must be an internal development. Thus, Atkins insists that none of the components of the pump can be imported from America. In other words, modernization must start as a "bricolage" of local elements. Modern conditions cannot be simply imported. The reorganization of traditional society itself should create the conditions of large-scale modernization. Eventually, the recombination of traditional elements should create the conditions of a qualitative change. The task of the modernizer is to incite the process of modernization in terms of the culture that needs to be modernized. At the same time, however, the modernizer has to be able to "sell" the modern as something desirable. In other words, the break with tradition has to be couched in terms of the very tradition it tries to reform. The modern has to be represented either as traditional or as a harmless novelty that really does not violate basic laws of the tradition.

To illustrate this point, we can also refer here to Emma Atkins's intervention in Sarkhanese life: she introduced the broom to Sarkhan. At one point, this ugly American notices that all the old people in the village suffer from terrible back problems. After a while, she figures out that the cause of the problem is that they do not have brooms with long handles, so the old people spend their days bending over to scrape the floors clean. Emma, of course, knows the solution, but she also understands that "people don't stop doing traditional things merely because they're irrational."[73] This fact, however, does not stop her from her modernizing mission: "But Emma wasn't bound by centuries of tradition, and she began to look for a substitute for the short broom handle."[74] Eventually the quest turns out to be successful, and the rest of the chapter narrates her elaborate tricks to convince the villagers to use the new tool. The important thing is that she is aware that the modern element can only be introduced into a traditional setting through a series of indirect interventions. She must modernize, but she must not appear to be modernizing. In fact, Emma's tricks turn out to be so effective that when, years after the couple has returned to America, they receive a letter from the Sarkhanese village, the villagers still refer to the long-handled broom as a "lucky accident." Emma's response: "What does he mean 'lucky accident'? . . . Why I looked all over for three months before I found those long reeds. That was no accident."[75] But the point, of course, is that Emma's project of modernization could succeed only because she deliberately represented it as a "lucky accident" and not as a direct intervention into a long-standing tradition. Although she feigns incomprehension, we know that her search for the most appropriate kind of reed was as deliberate as her misrepresentation of modernization as a lucky accident.

We can now clarify the meaning of "ugliness" in the novel. Jonathan Nashel argued that *The Ugly American* "was written to directly counter Graham Greene's *The Quiet American* (1955), and to refute his supposed anti-American and anti-interventionist sentiments."[76] Two paradigms of American foreign politics emerge here: the quiet and the ugly. And while the "ugly American" is a deliberate attempt to overwrite the anti-Americanism of the "quiet American," what is common to both paradigms is that in both cases Americans *appear* to be doing something in the Third World and in reality they are doing something else. Greene's novel addresses the conflict between the old and new colonial powers in Vietnam through an allegorical love triangle involving the world-weary British journalist Thomas Fowler, the naively idealistic American foreign aid worker Alden Pyle, and the Vietnamese woman Phuong. The novel turned out to be especially offensive to American sensibilities because its basic argument appeared to be that American idealism in the Third World is at best ineffective, but at its worst, it is actually destructive. In Greene's novel, the naively idealist politics of modernization (rather than building a new country) is turned into violent destruction. The modernizer becomes a terrorist.

The Ugly American, therefore, attempts to show that modernization is possible if America is willing to reform its overseas policies. The novel argues that modernization should not be imposed on traditional societies from the outside. Rather, the conditions of modernization have to be introduced in terms of the very culture that needs to be modernized. This is why a real "ugly American" is primarily a master of bricolage rather than the importer of Western technology. At the same time, however, the novel also argues that this modernization must not appear to be Westernization. Even if the final results supposedly serve Western interests, in order to be successful, modernization must be represented as a "lucky accident." Unlike *The Quiet American*, then, Lederer and Burdick argue that the imitation of the enemy is necessary, but it does not always lead to terrorism. If modernization is successfully disguised as the inexorable pull of the history of the Third World, it will provide the only viable means of global anti-Communism.

The question of why the central characters of the novel have to be ugly thus concerns the self-representation of the modern. As we have seen, "ugliness" denotes here the necessary split between form and content: it names the possibility that a negative form can hide a positive content. Therefore, in the world of the novel "ugly" designates *the modern that does not appear to be modern*: successful modernization is always preceded by an act of aestheticization. And if we wanted to give a specific ideological content to modernity, we could also add: ugliness denotes the Western that does not appear to be Western. Edward Shils's words come in handy at this point: "'Modern' means being western without the onus of following the West. It is the model of the West detached in some way from its geographical origins and locus."[77] With *The Ugly American*, therefore, we run into the same ideological problem that Christine Klein observed in connection with the musical *The King and I*: "the entire narrative revolves around achieving some of the ends of imperialism through non-imperial means."[78] This is the most disturbing ideological complication of modernization theory in general and of *The Ugly American* in particular.[79]

Ugliness can, therefore, be interpreted on at least three different levels: the empirical, the aesthetic, and the ideological. First, ugliness appears in the novel as a meaningless empirical fact: Homer, Emma, and Jeepo happen to be ugly. The term designates a real condition which, in the course of the novel, is transformed into a "lucky accident." But we should not underestimate the significance of the fact that Lederer and Burdick chose an aesthetic category (the negative condition of the beautiful) to name the central political concern of their text. On this level, ugliness is not just a mere fact, but a mode of appearance inscribed into a system of values. As it appears, anti-Communist politics depends on this aesthetic articulation of empirical facts. On this level, the aestheticization of the empirical provides the primary terrain within which modernization can take place. Modernization is thus fully dependent on this aesthetics. But the aesthetic value of ugliness is also immediately politicized. This is the level of the ideological inversion through which a negative aesthetic category is reformulated as a positive ideological content.[80] For the reader is led to believe that the ugly bodies of the novel hide beautiful souls, and that physical ugliness is the historical mode of appearance of its own opposite (since "beautiful Americans" supposedly posses ugly souls). The split between essence and appearance, however, is necessary, since without it no real community could have been established between Americans and Sarkhanese. In fact, this split is the very condition of a global anti-Communist community whose foundation is now revealed to be a deceitful modernization.[81] In the world of the novel, ugliness is something "real" (merely given and unchangeable) that functions as the very condition of successful (self-)representation. It is, after all, merely an empirical fact that becomes the site of an ideological inscription. Therefore, through its concept of ugliness, the novel tried to name the real conditions of a global modernization that does not appear to be imperialism.

As a conclusion, we can raise the question whether *The Ugly American* itself is actually an "ugly" book? Does the book participate in the same political aesthetic that it so clearly defines in its pages? And if it does, what does this fact tell us about the aesthetics of middlebrow anti-Communism in general? In fact, we do not have to search too long for the first indications that the book does what it preaches: the whole narrative is framed by an introductory note and a "Factual Epilogue," which make it abundantly clear that the documentary content of the text is necessarily mediated through an act of fictionalization. We encounter here a paradoxical drive toward documentary that can achieve its goals only if it fictionalizes its narrative. The first line of the book is this: "This book is written as fiction; but it is based on fact. The things we write about have, in essence, happened."[82] But as we have seen, what the narrative revealed was precisely the inherent weakness of facts. Facts are not enough. They must be supplemented by a preliminary act of aestheticization that establishes the field within which these facts can appear as effective facts. In the case of the book, the documentary can only achieve its political goals if it abandons its proper aesthetics. The book is composed with the same truth in mind: the best documentary is the right kind of fiction.

This aesthetics of ugliness, then, strikes at the very heart of the middlebrow aesthetics of the absolute priority of content over form. For it is rather difficult to take at face value the claim that content is everything and form is nothing, so the suspicion emerges that the very act of the renunciation of form might be a principle of formalization. The novel showed us something similar. In order to be effective, even the best of contents must be formalized in a particular way: as if it were not formalized at all. The ugliness of this self-effacing form is the central aesthetic force of the middlebrow. The point is not that the middlebrow is effectively without form, but rather that it formalizes itself in a way as if it were formless or at least lacked a concern for form. This is why when middlebrow formal clumsiness is considered to be a moral triumph, the formal shortcoming is not just an artistic deficiency but an ideological program. When modernists renounced the middlebrow as mere simulacrum, they claimed that the middlebrow appears to be art when it is not art at all. But the middlebrow reversed this formula: it claimed that although it might not appear to be art at all, in reality the middlebrow presents the universal content of art as such. According to this logic, the best art would be the kind that does not appear to be art at all. We could then formalize the aesthetic ideology of middlebrow anti-Communism in the following terms: its aesthetics was that of an art which did not appear to be art, and its politics was that of a global modernization which did not appear to be imperialism.

Conclusion

Close to the end of Philip Roth's 1998 novel, *I Married a Communist*, in a characteristically straightforward fashion, the text raises a self-reflexive question: Why would anyone write a novel about the American 1950s at the dawn of the new millennium? The question, thus, concerns the relevance of the fifties for the post–Cold War era, and it translates into the enigmatic simplicity of an honest provocation: Why now? Roth's answer is quite clear. The primary narrator of the book is the ninety-year-old retired English teacher Murray Ringold, who relates his brother Ira's tragic demise during the McCarthy era to his one-time student, Roth's recurrent character, Nathan Zuckerman. At one point, the following dialogue takes place between Murray Ringold and Nathan Zuckerman:

> "Nathan, I've never had a chance to tell this story to anyone this way, at such length. I've never told it before and I won't again. I'd like to tell it right. To the end."
>
> "Why?"
>
> "I'm the only person still living who knows Ira's story, you're the only person still living who cares about it. That's why: Because everyone else is dead." Laughing, he said, "My last task. To file Ira's story with Nathan Zuckerman."
>
> "I don't know what I can do with it," I said.
>
> "That's not my responsibility. My responsibility is to tell it to you."[1]

Upon first glance, this passage reads as a blatant tract on the transmission of historical knowledge. By calling attention to the singularity of the act of transmission, the novel speaks of the ethical duty of the witness to tell it, to tell it right, and to tell it all. At the same time, however, the passage also highlights the unique responsibility of the listener, which is drastically separated from that of the witness. At the heart of this tautological logic (the responsibility of the witness is to speak out, while the responsibility of the listener is to listen), a gap opens up that functions as the very condition of the ethical dimension of historical narration. But in a more specific sense, besides being an ethical allegory, the passage is also a reflection on a concrete historical situation. Murray Ringold's words are, indeed, revealing: "I'm the only person still living who knows Ira's story, you're the only person still living who cares about it." What the passage and the whole book records, then, is the final and irrevocable "becoming-history" of the American 1950s. In a certain sense, the special experience that the book diagnoses is that the lived reality of the fifties is disappearing as we are reading the novel. Soon, no one will be alive who actually saw it, and only a very few who still care.

But today, more than a decade after the publication of Roth's book, we are facing a slightly different situation. Since the novel predates the events of September 11, 2001, obviously it does not raise the question of the actuality of the Cold War from the perspective of the global war on terrorism. But the last couple of years have clearly shown that the war on terrorism can hardly be fully understood without a reflection on the persistence of the rhetoric of the Cold War. Today, however, another kind of generational question can be raised in addition to the one discussed by Roth. For us, it is not only the beginning of the Cold War that is irrevocably fading into history. More than two decades after the fall of the Berlin Wall, we find ourselves at a historical turning point: we are now at least a whole generation away from the end of the Cold War. The first generation has come of age for which the entirety of the Cold War is pure history. One possible consequence of this obvious historical fact will be that, more than ever before, we will be able to see the history of these four long decades as a more or less unified "episode" within a set of broader developments.

From this perspective, then, it becomes clear that the most striking feature of the history of Cold War studies is that from the day of its inception, the discipline has been an integral part of the very field that it studied. It is common to discuss the history of Cold War studies by distinguishing three distinct waves, with the time elapsed since the end of the Cold War counting as the fourth. During the 1950s, the historiography of the Communist question was dominated by liberal anti-Communists. The second, so-called "revisionist" period, which got underway in the late sixties, was a reaction against the fervent anti-Communism of the fifties and was therefore primarily centered around a critique of American anti-Communism. The third period, which coincides with the conservative political turn of the eighties, saw the continuation of the debate between "traditionalists" and "revisionists," with the latter (liberal) position dominating American academia. While traditionalist scholars formulated a critique of Communism based on the methodologies of political history, diplomatic history, and international relations, revisionist scholars critiqued anti-Communism by relying on a "new social history" that always insisted on particular contextualizations of local problems at the expense of more general questions relating to the Cold War. After the collapse of Russian Communism, however, the revelations provided by KGB files and the infamous Venona intercepts severely damaged the credibility of revisionist accounts. Discussing this fourth wave of Cold War historiography, scholars speak of the clash of traditionalist "triumphalism" (which celebrates its final victory over critiques of anti-Communism) and the revisionist myth of a "lost cause" (which is a set of more or less desperate attempts to salvage the revisionist heritage).[2]

The point I want to underline here is that for most of its history, Cold War studies was structured by Cold War politics—even after the end of the Cold War. The split between "orthodox" and "revisionist" scholars was simply a displaced reflection of the ideological conflicts of the era, which survived (in the form of an institutional hangover) well into the 1990s. In other words, the political conflict of the Cold War defined the limits of the discipline. But the most important question of our times is the following: How will post–Cold War politics rewrite the history of the Cold War and thereby redefine the basic structures of the whole discipline? For some time now, one of the most urgent tasks of contemporary scholarship has been to move beyond these old paradigms.[3]

My analysis of anti-Communist aesthetic ideology was intended to be a contribution to this reconfiguration of the field. First, it aimed to inscribe the discussion of the Cold War in a much boarder theory of modernity. My argument was based on the assumption that the Cold War institutionalized a "limit case" or "limit experience" of modernity. This is why, for example, it was within the framework of the Cold War that the move toward post-modernism took place. I chose to focus on the 1950s because I perceived this decade to be the period during which an inherent tendency of modernity assumed an extreme form. The long history of this modernity starts with the circumnavigation of the world and ends with the perfect tripartite division of this world into inimical camps by the Cold War. To put it briefly, the underlying idea of the previous chapters was that the Cold War represents the birth of a new kind of global politics, a breaking point in the history of power and the law: it was a phase in the history of Western political institutions during which the exception increasingly became the norm.[4] Without dismissing all the previous political experiments that were necessary to reach this point of development, we could say that the Cold War represented one of the first successful efforts to impose a global order through the full consolidation and institutionalization of a perpetual crisis. In fact, the paradox captured by the very name "Cold War" makes it clear that the primary means of this transformation was the indefinite suspension of the dividing line between war and peace.

This approach to the Cold War, based on a broader historical perspective, will allow us to expand our arguments in two opposing directions. First, it makes it possible to ask new questions about the ideological prehistory of the Cold War. As is often the case, historical events create their own histories by making visible new constellations of the past in a retroactive fashion. For if the aesthetic ideology that we have examined here and the four figures that it relies on to designate the limits of representation do in fact constitute a more general tendency of modernity, the discursive analysis carried out here can be applied to earlier periods as well. The world, the enemy, the secret, and the catastrophe haunt the modern imagination because they are historically contingent figures produced by a set of constitutive exclusions. In this sense, we could even argue that the Cold War brought about an extreme (maybe even a reductive but most certainly a quite rigid) manifestation of this aesthetic ideology. But by giving shape to an extreme form of this ideology, it put something on display that had been hiding for a long time in the dark laboratories of modernity.

At the same time, we can now also ask new questions about the consequences (and not only the "origins") of the Cold War. Our experiences today seem to confirm the assumption that some of the basic coordinates of this aesthetic ideology remained operational even after the end of the Cold War. In this regard, for example, we can easily detect a direct connection between the Cold War and the war on terror, which bears witness to a certain rhetorical as well as an institutional continuity between the two eras. Nothing would be easier today than to image that the contemporary companion piece to *The Naked Communist* and *The Naked Capitalist* would bear the title "The Naked Terrorist." But this emphasis on continuity should not make us blind to the decisive historical differences that define every singular historical situation. Of course, the point is not necessarily to identify a "perpetual cold war" at the heart of modernity, but it would be equally shortsighted to deny the demonstrable persistence of a structure that gives shape to the very worlds that we inhabit. The analysis of these breaks and transformations, however, is mostly a task still ahead of us.

NOTES

Introduction

1. W. Cleon Skousen, *The Naked Communist* (Salt Lake City: Reviewer, 1983).

2. J. Edgar Hoover, *Masters of Deceit: The Story of Communism in America and How to Fight It* (New York: Henry Holt, 1958).

3. Skousen, *The Naked Communist*, n.p.

4. W. Cleon Skousen, *The Naked Capitalist* (Salt Lake City: Reviewer, 1970).

5. For a definition of "post-Althusserian" political philosophy, see Slavoj Žižek, *The Ticklish Subject: The Absent Centre of Political Ontology* (New York: Verso, 2000), 127–28.

1 / The Aesthetic Unconscious

1. For a brief overview of the debate and the argument that aesthetic ideology should not always be taken to be a negative category, see Martin Jay, "'The Aesthetic Ideology' as Ideology; or, What Does It Mean to Aestheticize Politics?," *Cultural Critique* 21 (Spring 1992). In fact, the start of my argument is Jay's conclusion that the "wholesale critique of 'aesthetic ideology' . . . can thus be itself deemed ideological if it fails to register the divergent implications of the application of the aesthetic to politics. For ironically, when it does so, it falls prey to the same homogenizing, totalizing, covertly violent tendencies it too rapidly attributes to 'the aesthetic' itself." See ibid., 56. In other words, I want to argue here that our task today is to deconstruct the concept of "aesthetic ideology" by highlighting the essentialist residues that still determine its common usage. This deconstruction, however, does not necessarily lead to the elimination of the concept itself.

2. For a famous discussion of these issues, see Michel Foucault, *The Order of Things: An Archaeology of the Human Sciences* (New York: Vintage, 1994).

3. Walter Benjamin, "The Work of Art in the Age of Its Technological Reproducibility," in *Selected Writings: Volume 3, 1935–1938*, ed. Howard Eiland and Michael William Jennings (Cambridge: Harvard University Press, 2002), 122.

4. Louis Althusser, *Lenin and Philosophy and Other Essays*, trans. Ben Brewster (New York: Monthly Review Press, 1971), 171.

5. Ibid., 173.

6. Ibid., 223.

7. See Paul de Man, *Aesthetic Ideology* (Minneapolis: University of Minnesota Press, 1996); and Terry Eagleton, *The Ideology of the Aesthetic* (Malden, Mass.: Blackwell, 2000).

8. Paul de Man, *The Resistance to Theory* (Minneapolis: University of Minnesota Press, 1986), 11.

9. de Man, *Aesthetic Ideology*, 106.

10. de Man, *The Resistance to Theory*, 8.

11. Ibid., 7.

12. Ibid., 11.

13. Ibid., 8.

14. Eagleton, *The Ideology of the Aesthetic*, 28.

15. Ibid., 93–94.

16. Étienne Balibar, *Politics and the Other Scene*, trans. James Swenson Christine Jones and Chris Turner (New York: Verso, 2002), 1.

17. Jacques Rancière, *Aesthetics and Its Discontents*, trans. Steve Corcoran (Malden, Mass.: Polity, 2009), 64.

18. Jacques Rancière, "What Aesthetics Can Mean?," in *From an Aesthetic Point of View: Philosophy, Art and the Senses*, ed. Peter Osborne (London: Serpent's Tail, 2000), 33.

19. Jacques Rancière, *The Politics of Aesthetics: The Distribution of the Sensible*, trans. Gabriel Rockhill (New York: Continuum, 2006), 13.

20. Rancière, *Aesthetics and Its Discontents*, 24.

21. Rancière, *The Politics of Aesthetics*, 13.

22. Jacques Rancière, *Disagreement: Politics and Philosophy*, trans. Julie Rose (Minneapolis: University of Minnesota Press, 1999), 6.

23. Ibid., 23.

24. Ibid., 9.

25. Rancière, "What Aesthetics Can Mean?," 17.

26. Ibid., 16–17.

27. Ibid., 19.

28. Rancière, *The Politics of Aesthetics*, 50.

29. Ibid.

30. Rancière, *Disagreement*, 68.

31. Ibid., 82.

32. Rancière, *The Politics of Aesthetics*, 21.

33. Jacques Rancière, "Aesthetics, Inaesthetics, Anti-Aesthetics," in *Think Again*, ed. Peter Hallward (New York: Continuum, 2004), 219.

34. We could add a fourth political and aesthetic regime to Rancière's list: postpolitics and antiaesthetics. The "postdemocracy" of postmodern identity politics is considered by Rancière to be the final elimination of politics in the form of the all-consuming ideology of "consensus." This antipolitical fervor of the age of postmodernity corresponds to the theoretical enterprise of antiaesthetics, the contemporary attempt to liberate artistic practices from the "straightjacket" of speculative philosophy.

35. Rancière, *Disagreement*, 58.

36. Rancière, *The Politics of Aesthetics*, 62.

37. Ibid., 26. Emphasis in original.

38. Rancière, *Disagreement*, 32.

39. Alain Badiou, *Metapolitics*, trans. Jason Barker (London: Verso, 2005), 115.

40. Ibid., 116.

41. Alain Badiou, *Being and Event*, trans. Oliver Feltham (New York: Continuum, 2005), 24.

42. Ibid., 57–58. Emphasis in original.

43. Ibid., 57.

44. Ibid., 58.

45. Ibid., 59.

46. Ibid., 93.

47. Ibid. Emphasis in original.

48. Ibid., 99.

49. Ibid., 109.

50. Ibid., 109–10.

51. Ibid., 128.

52. Ernesto Laclau and Chantal Mouffe, *Hegemony and Socialist Strategy: Towards a Radical Democratic Politics* (New York: Verso, 2001), 97–105.

53. Ibid., 104.

54. Ibid., 107, 15.

55. Ernesto Laclau, *On Populist Reason* (New York: Verso, 2005), 69–70.

56. Ibid., 71.

57. Slavoj Žižek, *The Sublime Object of Ideology* (London: Verso, 2001), 124.

58. Ibid., 214. Emphasis in original.

59. Ibid., 180.

60. Ibid., 175.

61. Laclau, *On Populist Reason*, 116.

62. Ernesto Laclau, *Emancipation(s)* (New York: Verso, 1996), 38–39.

63. For example, in Nazi anti-Semitic ideology, the Jew represents pure negativity, the Nazi represents being, and the Führer or the Fatherland represents pure Being.

64. Although the concept of the "political unconscious" is most often associated with Fredric Jameson's works, my target here is a more general interpretive phenomenon characteristic of our times that was no doubt inspired by his works as well. Similarly, while Rancière happens to be the author of a book which has the term "the aesthetic unconscious" in its title, my arguments here do not directly follow his example.

2 / Anti-Communist Politics and the Limits of Representation

1. For more information on the history of American anti-Communism, see: M. J. Heale, *American Anticommunism: Combating the Enemy within, 1830–1970* (Baltimore: Johns Hopkins University Press, 1990); Richard Gid Powers, *Not without Honor: The History of American Anticommunism* (New York: Free Press, 1995); Peter H. Buckingham, *America Sees Red: Anticommunism in America, 1870s to 1980s* (Claremont: Regina Books, 1988); and Markku Ruotsila, *British and American Anticommunism before the Cold War* (Portland, Ore.: Frank Cass, 2001).

2. Powers, *Not without Honor*, 17–42.

3. Following Michael Kazin's analysis of American populism, we could say that the novelty of early Cold War anti-Communism was that for the first time in American

history a "conservative populism" emerged. See Michael Kazin, *Populist Persuasion: An American History* (New York: Basic Books, 1995), 167. In other words, anti-Communism provided the basic form of populist identifications, but at the same time it gave politics a particular conservative content. As populism moved from the margins of American politics to its very center, its political orientation seemed to be completely reversed.

4. John Earl Haynes, *Red Scare or Red Menace? American Communism and Anti-Communism in the Cold War Era, 1941–1960* (Chicago: Ivan R. Dee, 1996), 3.

5. Powers, *Not without Honor*, 192.

6. Daniel Bell, *The End of Ideology: On the Exhaustion of Political Ideas in the Fifties* (Cambridge: Harvard University Press, 1988), 123, 19.

7. Michael S. Sherry, *In the Shadow of War* (New Haven: Yale University Press, 1995), 123–26.

8. Ibid., 139.

9. Gregory Mitrovich, *Undermining the Kremlin: America's Strategy to Subvert the Soviet Bloc, 1947–1956* (Ithaca: Cornell University Press, 2000), 181.

10. Kenneth A. Osgood, "The Unconventional Cold War," *Journal of Cold War Studies* 4, no. 2 (2002): 86.

11. If war is the continuation of politics by other means, in the Cold War, culture is the continuation of war by other means. Walter L. Hixson explains the significance of cultural diplomacy during the Cold War in the following terms: "Because the Cold War was a military stand-off, neither nuclear-armed superpower could risk direct conflict with the other (although proxy wars were, of course, intrinsic to the East-West Struggle). Furthermore, animosity between the two superpowers inhibited trade and economic relations. As a result of these limitations, national security planners ultimately discovered that cultural interaction offered an effective way to influence the evolution of the CP [Communist Party] regimes." See Walter L. Hixson, *Parting the Curtain: Propaganda, Culture, and the Cold War, 1945–1961* (New York: St. Martin's, 1997), xii.

12. Lionel Trilling, *The Liberal Imagination* (Garden City, N.Y.: Doubleday Anchor Books, 1950), xi. Emphasis added.

13. See ibid., and Arthur Schlesinger, *The Vital Center: The Politics of Freedom* (New York: Da Capo, 1988).

14. Trilling, *The Liberal Imagination*, xii–xiii.

15. Thomas Hill Schaub evaluates Trilling's opposition of democracy and totalitarianism in the following terms: "Here democracy is the more artful of the two systems because it is a more adequate political representation (or response) to the inherent nature of reality itself. This both reproduces and extends the typical polarities of new liberal discourse between totalitarianism and democracy, utopianism and politics, certitude and ambiguity, resolution and conflict or contradiction. In Trilling especially these polarities become indistinguishable from aesthetic categories, as both politics and art must subscribe to or recognize the complexities and difficulties of life." See Thomas Hill Schaub, *American Fiction in the Cold War* (Madison: University of Wisconsin Press, 1991), 21.

16. Trilling, *The Liberal Imagination*, 10.

17. Ibid., 9.

18. Ernesto Laclau, *On Populist Reason* (New York: Verso, 2005), 137.

19. In 1987, Sidney Lens defined the Cold War as a "permanent war" in the following terms: "Since 1945 the United States has been engaged in a permanent war. It is not

permanent in the sense that it will never end, for all things must eventually end but, rather, permanent in the sense that it is fought every day on every continent and there is no single day when either side can claim definitive victory. This permanent war is unique because it takes two forms: one is the kind of war we have known throughout history, with armies, navies, and air forces confronting each other in open battle; the other is a new type of war fought by subversion, dirty tricks, secret manipulation, coups d'état, even assassinations." See Sidney Lens, *Permanent War: The Militarization of America* (New York: Schocken Books, 1987), 3.

20. Giorgio Agamben, *State of Exception*, trans. Kevin Attell (Chicago: University of Chicago Press, 2005), 2.

21. Whittaker Chambers, *Witness* (Washington, D.C.: Regnery, 2002), 7.

22. Schlesinger, *The Vital Center*, 7.

23. Ibid., 244. Emphasis added.

24. Ibid., 7.

25. Ibid., 6.

26. Ibid., 7.

27. Ibid., 6.

28. Timothy Melley, *Empire of Conspiracy: The Culture of Paranoia in Postwar America* (Ithaca: Cornell University Press, 2000), 7–16.

29. Schlesinger, *The Vital Center*, 143–44.

30. C. Wright Mills, *The Power Elite* (Oxford: Oxford University Press, 2000), 3.

31. David Riesman et al., *The Lonely Crowd: A Study of Changing American Character*. Rev. ed. (New Haven: Yale University Press, 2001), 176.

32. Ibid., 175–76.

33. Ibid., 176.

34. Frederick M. Dolan, *Allegories of America: Narratives, Metaphysics, Politics* (Ithaca: Cornell University Press, 1994), 80.

35. Ibid., 75.

36. Ibid., 68.

37. Jack Finney, *Invasion of the Body Snatchers* (New York: Scribner, 1998), 17.

38. J. Edgar Hoover, *A Study of Communism* (New York: Holt, Reinhart and Winston, 1962), 170.

39. The same argument is clearly legible in George F. Kennan's "Long Telegram" as well as Paul Nitze's NSC-68. Nitze, for example, writes: "Every institution of our society is an instrument which it is sought to stultify and turn against our purposes. Those that touch most closely our material and moral strength are obviously the prime targets, labor unions, civic enterprises, schools, churches, and all media for influencing opinion. The effort is not so much to make them serve obvious Soviet ends as to prevent them from serving our ends, and thus to make them sources of confusion in our economy, our culture and our body politic." See Thomas H. Etzold and John Lewis Gaddis, eds., *Containment: Documents on American Policy and Strategy, 1945–1950* (New York: Columbia University Press, 1978), 413. Nitze's solution, however, is the properly democratic one: rather than suppressing diversity, he argues for the public dissemination of "sufficient information." At the same time, George F. Kennan described unofficial Soviet policies in the following terms: "Efforts will be made in such countries to disrupt national self-confidence, to hamstring measures of national defense, to increase social and industrial unrest, to stimulate all forms of disunity. All persons with grievances, whether economic or racial, will be urged to seek redress

not in mediation and compromise, but in defiant violent struggle for destruction of other elements of society. Here poor will be set against rich, black against white, young against old, newcomers against established residents, etc." See ibid., 59.

40. As Dolan points out, one of the most unsettling effects of the politics of simulation is that it "casts a terrible ambiguity on the institutions American government is established to preserve: Are they vital emblems of freedom, or illusions concealing a deeper work of corruption?" See Dolan, *Allegories of America*, 72. In other words, democracy itself becomes suspicious, since it becomes one of the "impediments to a full-scale mobilization against Soviet subversion." See ibid., 73.

41. Etzold and Gaddis, eds., *Containment*, 62.

42. J. Edgar Hoover, *Masters of Deceit: The Story of Communism in America and How to Fight It* (New York: Henry Holt, 1958), vii. Emphasis in original.

43. Fred Schwarz, *You Can Trust the Communists (To Be Communists)* (Englewood Cliffs, N.J.: Prentice Hall, 1960), 1.

44. W. Cleon Skousen, *The Naked Communist* [1958] (Salt Lake City: The Reviewer, 1983), n.p.

45. Hoover, *Masters of Deceit*, vii.

46. Edward Shils, *The Torment of Secrecy: The Background and Consequences of American Security Policies* (Chicago: Elephant Paperbacks, 1996), 12; Reinhold Niebuhr, *Moral Man and Immoral Society* (New York: Scribners, 1952), 221.

3 / The Enemy, the Secret, and the Catastrophe

1. One of the clearest formulations of this thesis can be found in Daniel J. Boorstin, *The Genius of American Politics* (Chicago: University of Chicago Press, 1953). See also W. Cleon Skousen, *The Naked Communist* [1958] (Salt Lake City: Reviewer, 1983). Skousen claims that the major fallacy of Marxist philosophy was that it "misinterpreted the nature of man" and "turned man against himself." See ibid., 327, 88.

2. Whittaker Chambers, *Witness* (Washington, D.C.: Regnery, 2002), 16. Emphasis added.

3. George Kennan, "The Sources of Soviet Conduct," *Foreign Affairs* 25 (July 1947): 572–73.

4. J. Edgar Hoover, *Masters of Deceit: The Story of Communism in America and How to Fight It* (New York: Henry Holt, 1958), 148.

5. Ibid., 194.

6. Thomas H. Etzold and John Lewis Gaddis, eds., *Containment: Documents on American Policy and Strategy, 1945–1950* (New York: Columbia University Press, 1978), 63.

7. Clinton Rossiter, *Constitutional Dictatorship: Crisis Government in the Modern Democracies* (New York: Harcourt, Brace and World, 1963), 6.

8. Richard Hofstadter, *The Paranoid Style in American Politics and Other Essays* (Cambridge: Harvard University Press, 1996), 32.

9. Michael Rogin, *Ronald Reagan, the Movie, and Other Episodes in Political Demonology* (Berkeley: University of California Press, 1987), 284.

10. Peter H. Buckingham, *America Sees Red: Anticommunism in America, 1870s to 1980s* (Claremont: Regina Books, 1988), 50.

11. See also Leslie K. Adler and Thomas G. Paterson, "Red Fascism: The Merger of Nazi Germany and Soviet Russia in the American Image of Totalitarianism, 1930's-1950's," *American Historical Review* 75 (1970).

12. Etzold and Gaddis, eds., *Containment*, 50–63.

13. Kennan, "The Sources of Soviet Conduct," 567–68.

14. Etzold and Gaddis, eds. *Containment*, 53. Arthur Schlesinger reached a similar conclusion in his *The Vital Center* (1949): "The mixture of legitimate and psychotic elements in Soviet Communism—the question of deciding what is Russian and what is totalitarian—make enormously difficult the problem of estimating its own potentialities and of devising an effective democratic policy toward Russia." See Arthur Schlesinger, *The Vital Center: The Politics of Freedom* (New York: Da Capo, 1988), 66. In other words, Schlesinger explicitly pathologizes Russian national identity and considers Soviet Communism to be the perversion of some legitimate motives of Marxist criticism by this national component. Accordingly, the difficulties of democratic anti-Communism can be accounted for in this mixture of the legitimate and the pathological, social critique and national identity.

15. Etzold and Gaddis, eds., *Containment*, 55.

16. Alan Nadel, *Containment Culture: American Narratives, Postmodernism, and the Atomic Age* (Durham: Duke University Press, 1995), 15–16.

17. Chambers, *Witness*, 350. Chambers joined the Communist Party in 1925, went underground in 1932, and served from 1934 to 1938 as a key figure of the Washington underground. After he broke with the Communist Party in 1939, he first emerged in public in 1948 when he appeared before HUAC naming underground members of the Party, including Alger Hiss.

18. Ibid., 351. Emphasis added.

19. Ibid., 351–52.

20. Similarly, Howard Fast describes his break with the Communist Party in his *The Naked God* by reference to the tale of the Emperor's new clothes: "I had a god who walked naked, but nobody among those I loved said so; for even as the innocent wisdom of Hans Christian Andersen held that those who could not see the king's clothes were persons of small intellect and unfit for the positions they held, so in my world, it was the conviction of millions of good and wise folk that only those who had lost all honor, dignity, decency and courage would dare to point out that this god whom we worshipped for his noble raiment was indeed naked and ugly in his nakedness." See Howard Fast, *The Naked God: The Writer and the Communist Party* (New York: Praeger, 1957), 1.

21. Chambers, *Witness*, 352.

22. Hoover, *Masters of Deceit*, 102–103.

23. Herbert A. Philbrick, *I Led Three Lives: Citizen, "Communist," Counterspy* (Washington, D.C.: Capitol Hill, 1972), 218.

24. David Riesman et al., *The Lonely Crowd: A Study of Changing American Character*, rev. ed. (New Haven: Yale University Press, 2001).

25. In 1947, Kennan wrote: "Surely, there was never a fairer test of national quality, than this. In the light of these circumstances, the thoughtful observer of Russian-American relations will find no cause for complaint in the Kremlin's challenge to American society. He will rather experience a certain gratitude to a Providence which, by providing the American people with this implacable challenge, has made their entire security as a nation dependent on their pulling themselves together and accepting the responsibilities of moral and political leadership that history plainly intended them to bear." See Kennan, "The Sources of Soviet Conduct," 582.

26. George Kennan, *Memoirs, 1925–1950* (New York: Pantheon Books, 1962), 61–89.

27. Ibid., 65.

28. Ibid., 74.

29. Ibid., 75.

30. Ibid., 83.

31. Ibid., 82.

32. Ibid.

33. See, for example, Guy Oakes's argument that the politics of national security was backed up by a narrative of moral decline, in Oakes, *The Imaginary War: Civil Defense and American Cold War Culture* (New York: Oxford University Press, 1994), 21.

34. See Azza Salama Layton, *International Politics and Civil Rights Policies in the United States, 1941–1960* (Cambridge: Cambridge University Press, 2000); Philip A. Klinker and Rogers M. Smith, *The Unsteady March: The Rise and Decline of Racial Equality in America* (Chicago: Chicago University Press, 1999); Mary L. Dudziak, *Cold War Civil Rights: Race and the Image of American Democracy* (Princeton: Princeton University Press, 2000).

35. See George M. Fredrickson, *Black Liberation: A Comparative History of Black Ideologies in the United States and South Africa* (New York: Oxford University Press, 1995); George Lipsitz, *Rainbow at Midnight: Labor and Culture in the 1940s* (Chicago: University of Illinois Press, 1994); Gerald Horne, "Who Lost the Cold War? Africans and African Americans," *Diplomatic History* 20, no. 4 (Fall 1996); Andrew D. Grossman, "Segregationist Liberalism: The Naacp and Resistance to Civil-Defense Planning in the Early Cold War, 1951–1953," *International Journal of Politics, Culture and Society* 13, no. 3 (2000).

36. Quoted in Stephen J. Whitfield, *The Culture of the Cold War* (Baltimore: Johns Hopkins University Press, 1996), 21.

37. Quoted in Layton, *International Politics*, 55.

38. During the years of the Truman administrations, this conflict played itself out in the conflict between the executive and legislative branches of the government, as the former mobilized the judiciary branch in order to neutralize the resistance of Congress. The executive branch assumed the responsibility of mediating the contradiction of domestic and foreign policy through the measures of the Supreme Court.

39. See, for example, the discussion of the relation of the United States to the UN with regard to the question of racial justice in Layton, *International Politics*, 77–78.

40. Penny M. Von Eschen, *Race against Empire: Black Americans and Anticolonialism, 1937–1957* (Ithaca: Cornell Univerity Press, 1997), 3.

41. Etzold and Gaddis, eds., *Containment*, 226.

42. Ibid.

43. Ibid., 226–27.

44. Ibid., 243.

45. Ibid., 254.

46. Ibid., 249.

47. Christina Klein, *Cold War Orientalism: Asia in the Middlebrow Imagination, 1945–1961* (Berkeley: University of California Press, 2003), 11.

48. Etzold and Gaddis, eds., *Containment*, 259.

49. See NSC 48/2, ibid., 275.

50. Daniel Patrick Moynihan, *Secrecy: The American Experience* (New Haven: Yale University Press, 1998), 59.

51. Ibid., 152.

52. Harold D. Lasswell, *National Security and Individual Freedom* (New York: McGraw-Hill, 1950), 65.

53. Herbert S. Marks, "The Atomic Energy Act: Public Administration without Public Debate," *University of Chicago Law Review* 15 (Summer 1948): 839.

54. David E. Lilienthal, "Democracy and the Atom," *NEA Journal*, February 1948, 80.

55. Harold Urey writes similarly about the consequences of secrecy in the influential collection of essays *One World or None* from 1946: "The citizens of the country will know less and less in regard to vital questions and finally must accept decisions in regard to public affairs blindly and from a few men in power . . . , decisions previously made through their elected representatives. . . . Freedom . . . will be seriously threatened." See Dexter Masters and Katharine Way, eds. *One World or None: A Report to the Public on the Full Meaning of the Atomic Bomb* (New York: McGraw-Hill,1946), 56. Furthermore, according to Paul Boyer, Lilienthal's call for a more open distribution of knowledge, when contrasted with the effectiveness of his actions, appears to be mere lip service to democratic ideals, rather than an effective political program. See Boyer, *By the Bomb's Early Light: American Thought and Culture at the Dawn of the Atomic Age* (New York: Pantheon, 1985), 304.

56. Edward Shils, *The Torment of Secrecy: The Background and Consequences of American Security Policies* (Chicago: Elephant Paperbacks, 1996), 21.

57. Ibid., 226.

58. Ibid., 34, 22.

59. Ibid., 226. Emphasis added.

60. Ibid., 197.

61. Ibid., 26.

62. Ibid., 27.

63. Ibid., 24.

64. Schlesinger, *The Vital Center*, 54.

65. Chambers, *Witness*, 321.

66. Hoover, *Masters of Deceit*, 277.

67. Ibid., 302.

68. Philbrick, *I Led Three Lives*, 283–84. Emphasis added.

69. Ibid., 87.

70. Chambers, *Witness*, 456.

71. Hoover, *Masters of Deceit*, 224–25.

72. Norman Cousins, *Modern Man Is Obsolete* (New York: Viking, 1945), 12.

73. For more detailed discussions of the history of the atomic age, see Boyer, *By the Bomb's Early Light*; and Robert A. Divine, *Blowing on the Wind: The Nuclear Test Ban Debate, 1954–1960* (New York: Oxford University Press, 1978).

74. Norman Cousins, "The Standardization of Catastrophe," *Saturday Review*, August 10 1946, 16.

75. Boyer, *By the Bomb's Early Light*, 294.

76. Ibid., 301.

77. Eugene Rabinowitch, *The Dawn of a New Age: Reflections on Science and Human Affairs* (Chicago: University of Chicago Press, 1963), 156. Emphasis added.

78. "Science Testifies," *New Republic*, June 10. 1957, 3. See also Divine, *Blowing on the Wind*, 146.

79. For a contemporary collection of a wide range of immediate responses to the bomb, see Sydnor H. Walker, *The First One Hundred Days of the Atomic Age: August 6—November 15, 1945* (New York: Woodrow Wilson Foundation, 1945).

80. Ibid., 12.

81. Lasswell, *National Security*, 22.

82. See Philip Wylie, "Doom or Deliverance," *Collier's*, September 29, 1945. See also Lewis Mumford, "Atom Bomb: 'Miracle' or Catastrophe," *Air Affairs* July 1948. For a discussion of this polarized rhetoric, see Boyer, *By the Bomb's Early Light*, 125.

83. Cousins, *Modern Man*, 20.

84. Ibid.

85. Ibid., 23.

86. Ibid., 25.

87. Boyer, *By the Bomb's Early Light*, 37.

88. Ibid., 38.

89. Oakes, *The Imaginary War*, 131.

90. Ibid., 166. Emphasis added.

91. Ibid., 146.

92. Ibid.

93. Ibid., 101.

94. Ibid., 164.

4 / Anti-Communist Aesthetic Ideology

1. The basic coordinates of this political realism (by no means a unified doctrine or a clearly defined political program) could be best outlined by reference to three contemporary phenomena: Reinhold Niebuhr's theology, often called "Christian realism"; the "end of ideology" debate; and what is sometimes called the "new realism" of American foreign policy.

2. See Frederick M. Dolan, *Allegories of America: Narratives, Metaphysics, Politics* (Ithaca: Cornell University Press, 1994), 60.

3. Lionel Trilling, *The Liberal Imagination* (Garden City, N.Y.: Doubleday Anchor Books, 1950), 24.

4. Ibid., 67, 212.

5. Arthur Schlesinger, *The Vital Center: The Politics of Freedom* (New York: Da Capo, 1988), 156.

6. Ibid., 79.

7. Ibid., 80.

8. See Andreas Huyssen, *After the Great Divide: Modernism, Mass Culture, Postmodernism* (Bloomington: Indiana University Press, 1986); and Fredric Jameson, *The Cultural Turn: Selected Writings on the Postmodern, 1983-1998* (New York: Verso, 1998), 123.

9. For a discussion of the Gathings committee, see Kenneth C. Davis, *Two-Bit Culture: The Paperbacking of America* (Boston: Houghton Mifflin, 1984), 219-37.

10. Jane de Hart Mathews, "Art and Politics in Cold War America," *American Historical Review* 81, no. 4 (October 1976): 762.

11. Ibid.

12. To quote two extreme examples: Whereas Serge Guilbaut calls 1948 the year of success and argues that by the early fifties the triumph of modern art was indisputable,

Mathews writes "that by the mid-sixties modern art itself had somehow become inextricably linked with the United States as if only in America could the *avant-garde* 'spirit' truly flourish." See Serge Guilbaut, *How New York Stole the Idea of Modern Art: Abstract Expressionism, Freedom, and the Cold War,* trans. Arthur Goldhammer (Chicago: University of Chicago Press, 1983), 165–94; and Mathews, "Art and Politics in Cold War America," 780.

13. George Biddle, "The Artist on the Horns of a Dilemma," *New York Times Magazine,* May 19, 1946.

14. Ibid., 21.

15. Ibid., 45.

16. Ibid., 21.

17. Ibid., 45.

18. Howard Devree, "Straws in the Wind: Some Opinions on Art in the Post War World of Europe and America," *New York Times,* July 14, 1946.

19. Ibid., 4.

20. Howard Devree, "The Old That Leads to New," *New York Times,* July 21, 1946.

21. Ibid., 8.

22. Ibid.

23. Clement Greenberg, "The Decline of Cubism," *Partisan Review* 10, no. 3 (March 1948): 369.

24. Mathews, "Art and Politics in Cold War America," 782.

25. Trilling, *The Liberal Imagination,* 16.

26. Ibid.

27. For an interesting attempt to give an education to the "layman" in the difficulties of modern art, see the *Life* roundtable discussion organized in 1948 (including such illustrious personalities as Clement Greenberg, Francis Henry Taylor, Felix Frankfurter, and Aldous Huxley). The moderator of the discussion, Russell W. Davenport, summarized their conclusions in the following four points: "1. The layman should guard against his own natural inclination to condemn a picture just because he is unable to identify its subject matter in his ordinary experience. 2. He should, however, be equally on guard against the assumption that a painting that is recognizable in ordinary experience is no good. He should not fall victim to the kind of academicism that insists upon obscurity for its own sake. 3. He should look devotedly at the picture, rather than at himself, or at any aspect of his environment. The picture must speak. If it conveys nothing to him, then he should remember that the fault may be in him, not in the artist. 4. Even though he does not in general like nonrepresentational painting, this open-minded attitude will very much increase the layman's enjoyment of artistic works, ancient or modern." See Russell W. Davenport, "A *Life* Roundtable on Modern Art," *Life,* October 11 1948, 68. We should note that while the first two points establish a centrist aesthetic attitude, the latter two points establish the principles of enjoyment of nonrepresentational art.

28. Edward Alden Jewell, "When Is Art American?," *New York Times,* September 1, 1946.

29. Ibid., 46.

30. Ibid.

31. For a discussion of these moral attacks, see Malcolm Cowley, *Exile's Return: A Literary Odyssey of the 1920's* (New York: Viking, 1964), 190.

32. Guilbaut, for example, describes this process in the following way: "What I argue is this: that from compromise to compromise, adjustment to adjustment, the

rebellion of the artist, born of frustrations within the left, gradually changed its significance until ultimately it came to represent the values of the majority, but in a way
(continuing the modernist tradition) that only a minority was capable of understanding. The ideology of the avant-garde was ironically made to coincide with what was
becoming the dominant ideology, that embodied in Arthur Schlesinger, Jr.'s, book *The
Vital Center* (though this change was not without problems for the artists involved)."
See, Guilbaut, *How New York Stole*, 3.

33. Aline B. Louchheim, "'Modern Art': Attack and Defense," *New York Times*,
December 26, 1948, 11.

34. Howard Devree, "Modernism under Fire," *New York Times*, September 11,
1949, 6.

35. Ibid.

36. Emily Genauer, "Still Life with Red Herring," *Harper's Magazine*, September
1949, 91. For yet another version of the same argument, see also Alfred H. Barr, "Is
Modern Art Communistic?," *New York Times Magazine*, December 14, 1952.

37. Genauer, "Still Life with Red Herring," 89.

38. William Hauptman, "The Suppression of Art in the McCarthy Decade," *Artforum* 11 (1973): 48.

39. Mathews, "Art and Politics in Cold War America," 772.

40. R. B. Beaman, "The Cubist Witch," *South Atlantic Quarterly* 48, no. 2 (April
1949): 211–12.

41. Devree, "Modernism under Fire," 6.

42. Quoted in Hauptman, "The Suppression of Art in the McCarthy Decade," 48.

43. See Lawrence H. Schwartz, *Creating Faulkner's Reputation: The Politics of Modern Literary Criticism* (Knoxville: University of Tennessee Press, 1988), 73–98, 113–41.

44. For a discussion of New Criticism, see Mark Jancovich, *The Cultural Politics of the New Criticism* (Cambridge: Cambridge University Press, 1993). For a
standard discussion of the New York intellectuals, see Alexander Bloom, *Prodigal
Sons: The New York Intellectuals and Their World* (New York: Oxford University
Press, 1986).

45. For a more detailed analysis of the status of the novel, see "The Politics of Realism: Novelistic Discourse in the Postwar Period" in Thomas Hill Schaub, *American
Fiction in the Cold War* (Madison: University of Wisconsin Press, 1991), 25–49.

46. René Wellek and Austin Warren, *The Theory of Literature* (New York: Harcourt,
Brace, 1949), 288.

47. Ibid.

48. Ibid., 297.

49. Ibid., 298.

50. Ibid., 38–45.

51. Ibid., 41.

52. Ibid., 43.

53. Ibid., 44.

54. Ibid., 291.

55. Ibid., 220.

56. Ibid., 28.

57. Ibid., 26.

58. Ibid., 27.

59. Trilling, *The Liberal Imagination*, 275.

60. For Trilling's critique of Wellek and Warren's theory of pure art, see the essay "The Meaning of a Literary Idea" in Trilling, ibid., 274–75. Furthermore, in this discussion of the revaluation of the novel, we could also invoke Leslie Fiedler, who opens his *Love and Death in the American Novel* (1960) with the following assertion: "We are living not only in the Age of America but also in the Age of the Novel. . . . The notions of greatness once associated with the heroic poem have been transferred to the novel." See Leslie Fiedler, *Love and Death in the American Novel* (Champaign: Dalkey Archive Press, 2003), 23.

61. Trilling, *The Liberal Imagination*, 214.

62. Ibid., 286.

63. Irving Howe, *Politics and the Novel* (New York: Horizon Press, 1957), 20.

64. Ibid., 22.

65. Ibid., 23.

66. Richard Volney Chase, *The American Novel and Its Tradition* (Baltimore: Johns Hopkins University Press, 1957), 2, 4, 7.

67. Ibid., 19.

68. Ibid., xi.

69. For a discussion of the category of the romance in terms of Cold War cultural politics, see Geraldine Murphy, "Romancing the Center: Cold War Politics and Classic American Literature," *Poetics Today* 9, no. 4 (1988).

70. Bernard Rosenberg and David Manning White, eds., *Mass Culture: The Popular Arts in America* (Glencoe, Ill.: Free Press,1957), 3.

71. Ibid., 545.

72. A more general formula, however, would have to include a different distribution of the terms as well: highbrow = extremism; middlebrow = liberalism; lowbrow = extremism. Defenders of modernism, however, argued the opposite: highbrow = liberalism; middlebrow = conservatism; lowbrow = extremism.

73. Van Wyck Brooks, *America's Coming of Age* (New York: B. W. Huebsch, 1915), 27.

74. Ibid., 39.

75. Ibid., 112.

76. Ibid., 119.

77. Van Wyck Brooks, *On Literature Today* (New York: E. P. Dutton, 1941).

78. Dwight Macdonald, "Masscult and Midcult," in *Against the American Grain* (New York: Random House, 1962).

79. Ibid., 4.

80. Ibid., 37.

81. Ibid., 50.

82. Ibid., 54.

83. Ibid., 37.

84. Ibid., 38.

85. Ibid., 40.

86. Ibid.

87. Ibid., 45.

88. Clement Greenberg, *Art and Culture* (Boston: Beacon, 1961), 10.

89. Ibid., 11.

90. Ibid.

91. Ibid., 12.

92. Ibid., 19.

93. Charles I. Glicksberg, "Anti-Communism in Fiction," *South Atlantic Quarterly* 53 (October 1954): 492.

94. Ibid., 492.

95. Ibid., 495–96.

96. Ibid., 496.

5 / One World: Nuclear Holocausts

1. For useful discussions of the idea of the world, see Alexandre Koyré, *From the Closed World to the Infinite Universe* (Baltimore: Johns Hopkins University Press, 1957); Hans Blumenberg, *Die Lesbarkeit der Welt* (Frankfurt am Main: Suhrkamp, 1981); and Jean-Luc Nancy, *The Creation of the World, or, Globalization*, trans. François Raffoul and David Pettigrew (Albany: State University of New York Press, 2007).

2. Martin Heidegger, "The Age of the World Picture," in *The Question Concerning Technology and Other Essays* (New York: Harper, 1977), 129.

3. This formulation is intended to be a reference to the theoretical argument of Chapter 1 according to which every totality is constituted in such a way that particular elements or "objects" in this totality will have a double identity: on the one hand, they are random components of this totality; on the other hand, they also represent the limits of this totality.

4. Joseph Schumpeter, *Capitalism, Socialism and Democracy* (New York: Harper, 1975), 82–85.

5. Walter Benjamin, "Theses on the Philosophy of History," in *Illuminations: Essays and Reflections* (New York: Schocken, 1955), 257.

6. For more detailed discussions, see: Martha A. Bartter, *The Way to Ground Zero: The Atomic Bomb in American Science Fiction* (New York: Greenwood Press, 1988); Paul Brians, *Nuclear Holocausts: Atomic War in Fiction, 1895–1984* (Kent, Ohio: Kent State University Press, 1987); David Dowling, *Fictions of Nuclear Disaster* (Iowa City: University of Iowa Press, 1987); Bruce H. Franklin, "Fatal Fiction: A Weapon to End All Wars," in *The Nightmare Considered: Critical Essays on Nuclear War Literature*, ed. Nancy Anisfield (Bowling Green, Ohio: Bowling Green State University Popular Press, 1991); Martin H. Greenberg, and Eric S. Rabkin, Joseph D. Olander, ed. *The End of the World* (Carbondale: Southern Illinois University Press,1983); Warren W. Wagar, *Terminal Visions: The Literature of Last Things* (Bloomington: Indiana University Press, 1982).

7. Wagar, *Terminal Visions*, 26.

8. Susan Sontag, "The Imagination of Disaster," in *Against Interpretation and Other Essays* (New York: Farrar, Strauss, Giroux, 1966), 224.

9. Ibid.

10. Ibid., 225.

11. Ibid., 224.

12. William J. Scheick, "Post-Nuclear Holocaust Re-Minding," in *The Nightmare Considered: Critical Essays on Nuclear War Literature*, ed. Nancy Anisfield (Bowling Green, Ohio: Bowling Green State University Popular Press, 1991), 71. The worlds disclosed in these narratives through the catastrophe, however, can differ drastically, which suggests that the relation of the "world" and the "catastrophe" cannot be reduced to a simplistic "end of the world" scenario. Even in the period we are concerned with, the catastrophe can be equally responsible for the total annihilation of the human race and

for the institution of utopia. The following are some of the basic types of this relationship: (1) *Total extinction of the human race*: The peculiarity of this type of fiction is that although it is extremely rare (as if most of the writers had been scared by the very possibility), nevertheless it produced one of the few bestsellers of atomic holocaust fiction in general: Nevil Shute's *On the Beach* (1957). But probably the most memorable image of extinction was provided by Ray Bradbury's "There Will Come Soft Rains" from his *Martian Chronicles* (1950), which depicts the collapse of a fully automated household as it keeps its operation up even after its occupants are long dead. Other examples include: Jefferson Farjeon's *Death of a World* (1948) and Jack Danvers *The End of It All* (1962). (2) *The last man or the last couple*: "Last man" narratives like Pat Frank's *Mr. Adam* (1946) are usually satirical takes on the male fantasy of the possession of all the women in the world. "Last couple" narratives tend to be modern versions of the story of Adam and Eve, and suggest either the extinction or the rejuvenation of the human race. 3. *Neo-barbarian anarchy*: These stories are usually "survivalist" fantasies of the war of all against all. In Richard Foster's *The Rest Must Die* (1959), we witness the wars between survivors of atomic attack living in New York subway stations. In William Golding's *Lord of the Flies* (1954) and Dean Owen's *End of the World* (1962), the story ends with the abrupt restoration of military order, which shows that the catastrophic event reveals something about the inherent aggressiveness of human nature. (4) *Regressive reorganization of society*: In these novels society avoids complete collapse and total anarchy by regressing to more primitive forms of organization. In Philip José Farmer's *Tongues of the Moon* (1961), Athenian democracy is restored, while in Walter Miller's *Canticle for Leibowitz* (1959), the world is inhabited by post-catastrophic medieval monks. In Pat Frank's *Alas, Babylon* (1959), on the other hand, colonial America and the heroic age of the conquest of the West return after a Soviet atomic attack. (5) *Dictatorship*: Atomic catastrophe often leads to the establishment of a totalitarian regime. Most important for us are the Russian occupation novels like Robert Shafer's *The Conquered Place* (1954), in which Russians conquer the Eastern United States and the protagonist invades the conquered land to bring back a scientist before the city is bombed by Americans. Brian Berry's *Born in Captivity* (1952), Jerry Sohl's *Point Ultimate* (1955), and Samuel B. Southwell's *If All the Rebels Die* (1966), all depict similar scenarios. But other forms of dictatorships are also quite common. Of course the most famous example is Orwell's *1984*, but we should also mention here Ray Bradbury's *Fahrenheit 451* (1953), Theodora DuBois's *Solution T-25* (1951), as well as C. M. Kornbluth's *Not This August* (1955). In Edson McCann's *Preferred Risk* (1955), for example, an American insurance firm called "the Company" takes over the world. (6) *Utopias*: The effects of nuclear war are sometimes imagined to be beneficial for humanity, mostly through the recognition of the mistakes of the ancestors. While there is no return to the immediate prewar conditions, these authors see a chance for the rebirth of a more humane civilization. Philip José Farmer's *Tongues of the Moon* (1961), Doreen Wallace's *Forty Years On* (1958), and Ray H. Wiley *On the Trail of 1960: A Utopian Novel* (1950) serve as good examples.

13. Bartter, for example, follows James Gunn and speaks of the postwar period in terms of "a science fiction world." See Bartter, *The Way to Ground Zero*, 116. According to this argument, in the wake of Hiroshima, the world itself has become "unreal" and turned into a science fiction novel.

14. Pascal Bonitzer, "The Silences of the Voice (*A Propos* of *Mai 68* by Guide Lawaetz)," in *Narrative, Apparatus, Ideology*, ed. Philip Rosen (New York: Columbia University Press, 1986), 324.

15. Gary K. Wolfe, "The Remaking of Zero: Beginning at the End," in *The End of the World*, ed. Martin H. Greenberg, Eric S. Rabkin, and Joseph D. Olander (Carbondale: Southern Illinois University Press, 1983), 19. For an attempt to interpret eschatological fictions through the concept of Weltanschauung, see Wagar, *Terminal Visions*, 132.

16. For a direct formulation of the thesis, according to which modernism has an intrinsic relation to catastrophe, see John McCormick, *Catastrophe and Imagination: An Interpretation of the Recent English and American Novel* (New York: Longmans, 1957). We should also mention here a foundational text of American studies, Perry Miller's *Errand into the Wilderness* (1956), which concludes its interpretation of American history through the Puritan heritage with a chapter entitled "End of the World." Miller, thereby, suggests that the very idea of America is apocalyptic in nature—American studies begins where the world ends. See Miller, *Errand into the Wilderness* (Cambridge: Harvard University Press, 1956), 217. To cite a few examples closer to us in time, we could refer to Eric Hobsbwan's history of modernity that calls the period of high modernism "the age of catastrophe." See Eric Hobsbawn, *The Age of Extremes: A History of the World, 1914–1991* (New York: Vintage, 1994), 21–224. And if we follow Frederic Jameson's suggestion that Maurice Blanchot was one of the most effective ideologues of French modernism, then it should be striking that one of Blanchot's books bears the title: *The Writing of the Disaster*. See Fredric Jameson, *A Singular Modernity: Essay on the Ontology of the Present* (New York: Verso, 2002), 183.

17. Gertrude Stein, "Reflections on the Atomic Bomb," *Yale Poetry Review* 7 (1947): 3.

18. Ibid.

19. William Carlos Williams, *The Autobiography of William Carlos Williams* (New York: New Directions, 1967), 174.

20. Ibid.

21. Frank Kermode, *The Sense of an Ending: Studies in the Theory of Fiction* (New York: Oxford University Press, 1968). David Trotter, for example, writes: "Apocalypse was one of the things modern writers imagined most fondly. They saw themselves as inhabitants of a social and cultural system which had stagnated to the point where it was no longer susceptible to reform, but could only be renewed through total collapse of violent overthrow. Without apocalypse, Yeats, Eliot, or Pound would not have had careers." See David Trotter, "The Modernist Novel," in *The Cambridge Companion to Modernism*, ed. Michael Levenson (Cambridge: Cambridge University Press, 1999), 77.

22. Kermode, *Sense of an Ending*, 28.

23. Ibid., 95.

24. Ibid., 98.

25. Ibid.

26. Ibid., 107.

27. Ibid., 109.

28. Lionel Trilling, *The Liberal Imagination* (Garden City, N.Y.: Doubleday Anchor Books, 1950), 66–67.

29. Ibid., 95–96.

30. Ibid., 254.

31. Ibid., 255.

32. Ibid., 254.

33. Brians, *Nuclear Holocausts*, 3.

34. See John Hersey, *Hiroshima* (New York: Knopf, 1946); and Nevil Shute, *On the Beach* (New York: William Morrow, 1957).

35. Ruth Benedict, "The Past and the Future" *The Nation*, December 7, 1946, 656.

36. Quoted in Paul Boyer, *By the Bomb's Early Light: American Thought and Culture at the Dawn of the Atomic Age* (New York: Pantheon, 1985), 208.

37. Michael J. Yavenditti, "John Hersey and the American Conscience," in *Hiroshima's Shadow: Writings on the Denial of History and the Smithsonian Controversy*, ed. Kai Bird and Lawrence Lifschultz (Stony Creek, N.Y.: Pamphleteer, 1998), 298.

38. Dwight Macdonald, "Hersey's 'Hiroshima'," *Politics* 3, no. 9 (October 1946): 308.

39. Mary McCarthy, "The 'Hiroshima' New Yorker," in *Hiroshima's Shadow: Writings on the Denial of History and the Smithsonian Controversy*, ed. Kai Bird and Lawrence Lifschultz (Stony Creek, N.Y.: Pamphleteer, 1998), 304.

40. Ibid., 303.

41. Ibid.

42. Shute, *On the Beach*, 72.

43. Ibid., 115–16.

44. Ibid., 70.

45. Ibid., 88.

46. Ibid., 89.

47. Ibid.

48. Ibid.

49. Ibid., 177.

50. Ibid.

51. Ibid.

52. Ibid., 178.

53. Spencer R. Weart, *Nuclear Fear: A History of Images* (Cambridge: Harvard University Press, 1988), 218.

54. Ibid., 219.

55. Michael Rogin, *Ronald Reagan, the Movie, and Other Episodes in Political Demonology* (Berkeley: University of California Press, 1987), 245.

56. Ibid., 243.

57. For general overviews of Wylie's works, see Clifford P. Bendau, *Still Worlds Collide: Philip Wylie and the End of the American Dream* (San Bernardino, Cal.: Borgo, 1980); and Truman Frederick Keefer, *Philip Wylie* (Boston: Twayne, 1977).

58. As Keefer points out, during the Cold War, this criticism earned Wylie the epithet "anti-American": "during the Cold War of the 1950s, the novel [*Finely Wren*], along with *Generation of Vipers*, was excluded from United States Information Agency libraries in foreign countries as too anti-American." See Keefer, *Philip Wylie*, 73.

59. Philip Wylie, *Generation of Vipers* (New York: Rinehart, 1942), 35.

60. Ibid., 14.

61. Ibid., 23.

62. Ibid., 22.

63. Philip Wylie and Edwin Balmer, *When Worlds Collide* (New York: Dell, 1933).

64. The sequel to the novel, *After Worlds Collide*, already introduces the theme of Communism. As it turns out, a Communist spaceship also escaped Earth in time, so

the reconstitution of the world on the new planet has to face a Communist threat. See Philip Wylie, *After Worlds Collide* (New York: Paperback Library, 1963).

65. Wylie, *When Worlds Collide*, 72–74, 121–22.

66. Ibid., 140–41.

67. See, Philip Wylie, *The Disappearance* (New York: Rinehart, 1951).; Philip Wylie, *Tomorrow!* (New York: Popular Library, 1956); Philip Wylie, *Triumph* (New York: Popular Library, 1961).

68. Wylie, *The Disappearance*, 3.

69. Ibid., 338.

70. For other contemporary novels addressing issues related to civil defense, see: Judith Merrill, *Shadow on the Hearth* (1950); Harold Rein, *Few Were Left* (1955); Martin Caidin, *The Long Night* (1956); Helen Clarkson, *The Last Day: The Day after Tomorrow* (1959); and Richard Foster, *The Rest Must Die* (1959).

71. Wylie, *Tomorrow!*, 39.

72. Ibid., 244.

73. Ibid., 209.

74. Ibid., 286.

75. Wylie, *Triumph*, 105.

76. Ibid., 234.

77. Ibid., 240.

6 / Two Worlds: Stolen Secrets

1. For an analysis of this seemingly contradictory development (the coincidence of full visibility and full invisibility), see Michael Rogin, "'Make My Day!'": Spectacle as Amnesia in Imperial Politics," in *Cultures as United States Imperialism*, ed. Amy Kaplan and Donald E. Pease (Durham: Duke University Press, 1993).

2. For the spy thriller's relation to globalization, see for example Bruce Merry's argument that "the most important feature common to all spy narratives" is the representation of "global simultaneity." See Bruce Merry, *The Anatomy of the Spy Thriller* (London: Macmillan, 1977), 2.

3. Although they do not formulate their conclusions in exactly the same terms, see the following authors for different versions of a similar argument: Eva Horn, "Knowing the Enemy: The Epistemology of Secret Intelligence," *Grey Room* 11 (Spring 2003): 74; Lars Ole Sauerberg, *Secret Agents in Fiction: Ian Fleming, John le Carré, Len Deighton* (London: Macmillan, 1984), 25; Jerry Palmer, *Thrillers: Genesis and Structure of a Popular Genre* (New York: St. Martin's, 1979), 85–87; Michael Denning, *Cover Stories: Narrative and Ideology in the British Spy Thriller* (London: Routledge, 1987), 102–108.

4. John G. Cawelti and Bruce A. Rosenberg, *The Spy Story* (Chicago: University of Chicago Press, 1987), 21.

5. Ibid.

6. Ibid., 15.

7. Ibid., 17.

8. Ibid., 21.

9. Palmer, *Thrillers*, 23.

10. Cawelti, *The Spy Story*, 56.

11. Palmer, *Thrillers*, 82–83.

12. Ibid., 85. Emphasis in original.

13. Michael Denning, for example, concludes his book *Cover Stories* with two observations about the appeals of the spy thriller that are truly pertinent to this analysis. On the one hand, Denning argues that the thriller "serves as a way of narrating individual political agency in a world of institutions and states that seem to block all action and paralyze all opposition." On the other hand, the thriller is an attempt "to restore in the imaginary world of secret services the contradictory processes of the world-system." In other words, the sovereign instance capable of turning a contradictory global system into an ideological totality is an individual. We find here the crisis of representation at the heart of Cold War politics: The individual does not necessary see his or her local interests reflected in the politics of global anti-Communism. The spy thriller, therefore, provides one possible answer to this crisis. See Denning, *Cover Stories*, 151–52.

14. See for example, Michael Bell, "The Metaphysics of Modernism," in *The Cambridge Companion to Modernism*, ed. Michael Levenson (Cambridge: Cambridge University Press, 1999).

15. See also the first chapter of Sauerberg, *Secret Agents in Fiction*.

16. Since in the previous chapter we relied on Frank Kermode's work, let me refer here to his book *The Genesis of Secrecy*, which examines the problem of secrecy through narrative interpretation and biblical hermeneutics. In this book, modernism emerges as a formal principle based on the hermeneutics of the secret. See Frank Kermode, *The Genesis of Secrecy: On the Interpretation of Narrative* (Cambridge: Harvard University Press, 1979).

17. Lionel Trilling, *The Liberal Imagination* (Garden City, N.Y.: Doubleday Anchor Books, 1950), 24.

18. Ibid., 28.

19. For example, discussing Hawthorne and the romance, Trilling writes that "shadows are also part of reality and one would not want a world without shadows, it would not even be a 'real' world." See ibid., 20.

20. Ibid., 64.

21. Ibid., 45.

22. Ibid., 46.

23. Ibid., 53.

24. Ibid., 54.

25. Henry James, *The Princess Casamassima* (New York: Scribner's, 1908), v.

26. Ibid.

27. Ibid., vi.

28. Ibid., vii.

29. Ibid., xxii.

30. Ibid., xxi.

31. Ibid., xxi.

32. Ibid., xvii.

33. Trilling, *The Liberal Imagination*, 93.

34. Ibid.

35. Ibid., 95.

36. Ibid., 10.

37. See Edmund Wilson, "Who Cares Who Killed Roger Ackroyd?" in Bernard Rosenberg, and David Manning White, eds.. *Mass Culture: The Popular Arts in America* (Glencoe, Ill.: Free Press,1957), 153.

38. Ibid., 152.

39. John Buchan, *The Adventures of Richard Hannay: The Thirty-Nine Steps, Greenmantle, Mr. Standfast* (Boston: Houghton Mifflin, 1919), 11.

40. Ibid., 14,17.

41. Ibid., 97–98.

42. Ibid., 92.

43. Ibid., 101.

44. Ibid.

45. Ibid., 215.

46. Ibid., 212–13.

47. Ibid., 209, 12.

48. Ibid., 216.

49. Ibid., 211.

50. Ibid., 226.

51. Ibid., 64.

52. Ibid., 65.

53. Ibid., 167.

54. Ibid., 169.

55. Ibid., 170.

56. Merry, *The Anatomy of the Spy Thriller*, 158.

57. John le Carré, *Call for the Dead* (New York: Walker, 1962), 3.

58. Ibid., 127.

59. Ibid., 128.

60. Ibid., 19.

61. The most memorable scene in le Carré's fiction demonstrating this concern with being caught between two worlds is the closing scene of *The Spy Who Came in from the Cold* (1963), in which we see Alec Leamas dying on top of the Berlin Wall.

62. Le Carré, *Call for the Dead*, 4.

63. Ibid., 4.

64. Ibid., 112.

65. Ibid., 97.

66. Ibid., 98.

67. Umberto Eco, "The Narrative Structures in Fleming," in Oreste del Buono and Umberto Eco. eds., *The Bond Affair* (London: Macdonald, 1966), 36.

68. Ian Fleming, *Casino Royale* (Harmondsworth: Penguin, 2002), 135.

69. Ibid., 180.

70. Ian Fleming, *Live and Let Die* (Harmondsworth: Penguin, 2002), 70.

71. Ibid.

72. Ibid.

73. Eco, "The Narrative Structures in Fleming," 62.

74. Ibid.

75. Ibid., 63, 68.

76. Philip Wylie, "The Crime of Mickey Spillane," *Good Housekeeping*, February 1955, 207.

77. Mickey Spillane, *The Mike Hammer Collection: One Lonely Night; The Big Kill; Kiss, Me Deadly*, vol. 2 (New York: New American Library, 2001), 132.

78. One of the most explicit formulations of the split between the normal and the clandestine world (the underworld of crime) can be found in the opening paragraph

of *My Gun Is Quick* (1950), where Mike Hammer directly addresses the readers: "But remember this: there *are* things happening out there. They go on every day and night making Roman holidays look like school picnics. They go on right under your very nose and you never know about them." See Mickey Spillane, *The Mike Hammer Collection: I, the Jury; My Gun Is Quick; Vengeance Is Mine!*, vol. 1 (New York: New American Library, 2001), 143. In a much later novel, *Survival Zero* (1970), Hammer specifies the exact location of his own world as "the perimeter of normalcy." See Mickey Spillane, *The Hammer Strikes Again* (New York: Avenel Books, 1989), 680.

79. If we consider the products of Spillane's two major periods of literary productivity, we find that it was only during the sixties that he started to write the kind of fiction that could be called spy fiction. Of the seven novels produced during the first period (1947–1952), only *One Lonely Night* (1951) is concerned with Communist espionage. (Unlike Robert Aldrich's *Kiss Me Deadly*, the original novel dealt with the Mafia and drugs, not atomic secrets.) However, during the second period (1961–1973), the move toward spy fiction is obvious on two different counts. First, the resumed Mike Hammer series shows more concern with international politics. Second, Spillane's new hero, Tiger Mann, is a private counter-espionage agent fighting international Communism.

80. John D. MacDonald, *Cape Fear* (New York: Fawcett Gold Medal, 1991), 96.

81. Spillane, *The Mike Hammer Collection*, vol. 2, 6.

82. Kay Weibel, for example, argues that "Mike Hammer does not actually solve his crimes. In fact, Spillane's Hammer novels are not really about crime detection; they are about war. Mike Hammer is a one-man war machine." See Kay Weibel, "Mickey Spillane as a Fifties Phenomenon," in *Dimensions of Detective Fiction*, ed. Pat Browne Larry N. Landrum, and Ray B. Browne (Bowling Green, Ohio: Bowling Green State University Press, 1976), 114.

83. Spillane, *The Mike Hammer Collection*, vol. 2, 78. At one point in the novel, the judge is made fun of for his literal readings of the law in the following way: "He's just a stickler for the letter of the law, the exact science of words. He's the guy that let a jerk off on a smoking-in-the-subway charge. The sign said NO SMOKING ALLOWED, so he claimed it allowed you not to smoke, but didn't say anything about smoking." See ibid., 26.

84. Ibid., 168.

85. Ibid., 147.

86. Ibid., 121.

87. Ibid., 173.

88. Ibid., 159.

89. Ibid., 109.

90. Ibid., 163. This separation of the enemy from the hero is so much the more important as we see Mike Hammer doing almost the identical thing to Ethel Brighton, confused Communist daughter of an American millionaire. Mike Hammer tries to cure her of her ideological follies by simply "teaching her how to be a woman," that is, by having sex with her. But as the story progresses, he mistakenly believes that Ethel betrayed him to the Communists, and he is getting ready to punish her in the old-fashioned way: "A naked woman and a leather belt. I looked at her, so bare and so pretty, hands pressed for support against the paneling, legs spread apart to hold a precarious balance, a flat stomach hollowed under the fear that burned her body a faint pink, lovely smooth breasts, firm with terrible excitement, rising and falling with

every gasping breath. A gorgeous woman who had been touched by the hand of the devil." See ibid., 128.

91. Charles J. Rolo, "Simenon and Spillane: The Metaphysics of Murder for the Millions," in *Mass Culture: The Popular Arts in America*, ed. Bernard Rosenberg and David Manning White (Glencoe, Ill.: Free Press, 1957).

92. Ibid., 169.

93. Ibid., 170.

94. Kenneth C. Davis, *Two-Bit Culture: The Paperbacking of America* (Boston: Houghton Mifflin, 1984), 181.

95. Ibid., 181.

96. Malcolm Cowley, "Sex Murder Incorporated," *New Republic* 126 (February 11, 1952).

97. Quoted in Max Allan Collins and James L. Taylor, *One Lonely Knight: Mickey Spillane's Mike Hammer* (Bowling Green, Ohio: Bowling Green State University Popular Press, 1984), 24.

98. For an interesting reading of the way the potentially emancipatory logic of class conflict is turned into a conservative politics through the logic of perversion, see Tim Dayton, "'The Annihilated Content of the Wish': Class and Gender in Mickey Spillane's I, the Jury," *Clues* 14, no. 1 (Spring/Summer 1993).

99. Mickey Spillane, *The Girl Hunters* (New York: New American Library, 1962), 133.

100. Ibid., 178.

101. This is the point where we could return to the problem of the political theology of the anti-Communist nation. As we have seen in the previous chapter, for Philip Wylie the theological foundation of politics was deduced from the fact that the world is a totality whose absolute destruction and ultimate salvation depend on the same agency. In Spillane's case, however, we find that the theological foundation of politics is the heteronomy of the law, which must be anchored in the autonomy of a higher law. In other words, in both cases the cancellation and ultimate fulfillment of a totality coincide (the salvation of the world is dependent on its utter destruction; the fulfillment of the law is dependent on its violation).

7 / Three Worlds: Global Enemies

1. Accordingly, the threefold division of worlds can serve as a basis for a typology of the Cold War political novel. In this sense, we can speak of "first world" political novels: Robert Penn Warren, *All the King's Men* (1946); Lionel Trilling, *The Middle of the Journey* (1947); Norman Mailer, *Barbary Shore* (1951); Helen MacInnes, *Neither Five Nor Three* (1951); Irwin Shaw, *The Troubled Air* (1951); Ayn Rand, *Atlas Shrugged* (1957); Allan Drury, *Advise and Consent* (1959); Richard Condon, *The Manchurian Candidate* (1959); and Isabel Moore, *The Day the Communists Took over America* (1961). "Second world" political novels include Arthur Koestler, *Darkness at Noon* (1941), and *The Age of Longing* (1951); George Orwell, *1984* (1949); and Noel Sterling, *I Killed Stalin* (1951). Notable Third World political novels include James Michener, *The Bridges at Toko-Ri* (1953); Graham Greene, *The Quiet American* (1955); and William J. Lederer and Eugene Burdick, *The Ugly American* (1958). For discussions of the political novel, see Irving Howe, *Politics and the Novel* (New York: Horizon Press, 1957); Joseph L. Blotner, *The Political Novel* (Garden City: Doubleday, 1955), and *The Modern American Political Novel, 1900–1960* (Austin: University of Texas Press, 1966); Gordon

Milne, *The American Political Novel* (Norman: University of Oklahoma Press, 1966); and Thomas Kemme, *Patterns of Power in American Political Fiction* (Lanham, Md.: University Press of America, 2003).

2. Fredric Jameson, *The Geopolitical Aesthetic: Cinema and Space in the World System* (Bloomington: Indiana University Press, 1992), 9–84.

3. Arthur Schlesinger, *The Vital Center: The Politics of Freedom* (New York: Da Capo, 1988), 244. Emphasis added.

4. Alfred Sauvy, "Trois mondes, une planète," *L'Observateur*, August 14, 1952.

5. Ibid., 14. The quotations from Sauvy's text are my translations.

6. Ibid.

7. Ibid.

8. Ibid.

9. The logic I would like to illustrate here resembles the one we discussed in case of the secret: (1) the world is not one without a secret; (2) the secret produces an alternative world which is more authentic than the normal world; (3) but the world of secrecy fails to constitute itself as a complete world, so we are left with two incomplete worlds.

10. For general overviews of modernization theory, see Michael E. Latham, *Modernization as Ideology: American Social Science and "Nation Building" in the Kennedy Era* (Chapel Hill: University of North Carolina Press, 2000); David C. Engerman, Nils Gilman, Mark H. Haefele, and Michael E. Latham, eds., *Modernization, Development, and the Global Cold War* (Amherst: University of Massachusetts Press, 2003).; and Nils Gilman, *Mandarins of the Future: Modernization Theory in Cold War America* (Baltimore: Johns Hopkins University Press, 2003).

11. For other discussions of the relation of modernism and modernization, see also Gilman, *Mandarins of the Future*, 1–23; Daniel Bell, *The Cultural Contradictions of Capitalism* (New York: Basic Books, 1996); Fredric Jameson, *A Singular Modernity: Essay on the Ontology of the Present* (New York: Verso, 2002).

12. Schlesinger, *The Vital Center*, 51.

13. Ibid., 7.

14. Ibid., 79.

15. Ibid., 220.

16. Ibid., 223.

17. Ibid.

18. Ibid., 241.

19. Ibid., 241–42.

20. James Michener, "The Conscience of the Contemporary Novel," in *The Arts in Renewal*, ed. Lewis Mumford (Philadelphia: University of Pennsylvania Press, 1951).

21. Ibid., 125.

22. Ibid., 116.

23. Ibid., 120.

24. Ibid., 123.

25. Ibid., 125.

26. Ibid., 117.

27. Ibid., 118.

28. This picture would not be complete, however, without a brief reference to the way elitist modernization theorists of the fifties defined mass culture. Unlike Michener, authors such as Harold Lasswell and Edward Shils defended mass culture precisely because it functioned as the "opiate of the masses" and therefore established

the condition of a properly elitist (or even "authoritarian") practice of democracy that excluded the masses from active participation. For a discussion of these points, see Gilman, *Mandarins of the Future*, 26–71, 155–202.

29. Philip Wylie, *The Innocent Ambassadors* (New York: Rinehart, 1957); James Michener, *The Voice of Asia* (New York: Random House, 1951).

30. Wylie, *The Innocent Ambassadors*, xiii–xiv.

31. For discussions of the politicization of Cold War tourism, see also Christina Klein, *Cold War Orientalism: Asia in the Middlebrow Imagination, 1945–1961* (Berkeley: University of California Press, 2003); and Christopher Endy, *Cold War Holidays: American Tourism in France* (Chapel Hill: University of North Carolina Press, 2004).

32. Wylie, *The Innocent Ambassadors*, 16.

33. Ibid., 176.

34. Ibid.

35. Ibid., 14.

36. Ibid., 22.

37. Ibid., 27.

38. Ibid. Emphasis in original.

39. Ibid., 232.

40. Ibid., 234.

41. Ibid., 291.

42. Ibid., 44.

43. Ibid., 45.

44. Ibid.

45. Ibid., 47.

46. Michener, *The Voice of Asia*, 97. The necessary knowledge of Asia is explicitly inscribed in a paranoid global imaginary that posits the possibility of a world conspiracy against America: "Asia is separated from Europe only by a name and some relatively low mountains. Indeed, Europe is merely a peninsula jutting out from Asia as Spain juts out from Europe. Furthermore Eurasia is separated from Africa only by the man-made Suez Canal and the strait of Gibraltar. Americans should from now on think of Asia-Europe-Africa as one land mass; and if that tripartite continent ever consolidates against us we could possibly continue to live within our sea-protected wall, but American life as we know it would vanish." See ibid., 5.

47. Ibid., 214.

48. Ibid., 27–30.

49. Ibid., 28.

50. Ibid., 27.

51. Ibid., 28.

52. Ibid.

53. Ibid.

54. Ibid., 29.

55. Ibid.

56. Ibid.

57. Ibid., 30.

58. Ibid.

59. In order to illustrate the immense popularity of the text, I will quote here Jonathan Nashel: "It was on *The New York Times* best-seller list for seventy-two weeks, sold almost five million copies, was a Book-of-the-Month Club selection, was championed

by Senator John F. Kennedy, and was later made into a film starring Marlon Brando, then Hollywood's reigning male icon. President Eisenhower commented on how much he liked the novel and how U.S. foreign policy would benefit from Lederer and Burdick's prescriptions." See Jonathan Nashel, "The Road to Vietnam: Modernization Theory in Fact and Fiction," in *Cold War Constructions: The Political Culture of United States Imperialism, 1945–1966*, ed. Christian G. Appy (Amherst: University of Massachusetts Press, 2000), 135.

60. Walter Benn Michaels, "Anti-Imperial Americanism," in *Cultures of United States Imperialism*, ed. Amy Kaplan and Donald E. Pease (Durham: Duke University Press, 1993), 365.

61. John Carlos Rowe, *Literary Culture and U.S. Imperialism: From the Revolution to World War II* (Oxford: Oxford University Press, 2000), 3.

62. William J. Lederer and Eugene Burdick, *The Ugly American* (New York: Norton, 1958), 174–80, 81–95.

63. Ibid., 174, 77.

64. Ibid., 181.

65. Ibid., 186.

66. Ibid., 119.

67. Ibid., 40.

68. Ibid., 52, 51.

69. Ibid., 105.

70. Ibid., 107.

71. Ibid., 113.

72. Ibid., 120.

73. Ibid., 198.

74. Ibid., 198.

75. Ibid., 201.

76. Nashel, ibid., 135.

77. Quoted in Gilman, *Mandarins of the Future*, 2.

78. Klein, *Cold War Orientalism*, 208. Klein argues that the modernization of Siam by the governess Anna Leonowens in the popular 1956 Rodgers and Hammerstein musical follows the pattern of "sentimental modernization": "As a sentimental modernizer, Anna Leonowens exercises her influence in Siam not through violence or force or political coercion, but through the power of love and the tools of culture." See ibid., 200.

79. Gilman, for example, argues the following: "Pointing out its reluctance to be a colonial power and its willingness to give up the Philippine colony allowed the United States to imagine itself as different from other colonizing nations, less exploitative and more interested in the welfare of its subjects. This dubious historical self-image blinded Americans to the continuities between the imperious attitudes of former imperialists (including themselves) and their own postwar ideas about the way in which development policy should be analyzed and promoted." See, Gilman, *Mandarins of the Future*, 34. For a similar argument, see also Klein, *Cold War Orientalism*.

80. It is precisely this inversion that the popular reception of the novel could not follow when it misidentified the actual meaning of the term "the ugly American." As a result, the political and aesthetic values have been rearranged in such a way that a negative aesthetic value did not have to correspond to a positive political value: the "Ugly American" was redefined as a figure of political failure.

81. It is interesting to note that the 1965 sequel to *The Ugly American*, originally entitled *Sarkhan* (allegedly repressed by the CIA), was later renamed in 1977 upon its second publication as *The Deceptive American*. The new title seems to emphasize the difference between the politics of 'ugliness' and 'deception.' In the second book, 'deception' names the strategy pursued by Washington bureaucrats, which turns their form of anti-Communism into yet another form of conspiracy.

82. Lederer, *The Ugly American*, n.p.

Conclusion

1. Philip Roth, *I Married a Communist* (Boston: Houghton Mifflin, 1998), 265.

2. John Earl Haynes, "The Cold War Debate Continues: A Traditionalist View of Historical Writing on Domestic Communism and Anti-Communism," *Journal of Cold War Studies* 2, no. 1 (Winter 2000).

3. As early as 1995, for example, Melvyn Leffler argued that the most important task of the discipline is to "enrich and reconfigure realism, revisionism, and post-revisionism, the modes of analysis that have set our interpretive boundaries for many years." See Melvin P. Leffler, "New Approaches, Old Interpretations, and Prospective Reconfigurations," *Diplomatic History* 19, no. 2 (Spring 1995): 193.

4. For a brief overview of this problem, see Giorgio Agamben, *State of Exception*, trans. Kevin Attell (Chicago: University of Chicago Press, 2005).

Bibliography

Adler, Leslie K., and Thomas G. Paterson. "Red Fascism: The Merger of Nazi Germany and Soviet Russia in the American Image of Totalitarianism, 1930's–1950's." *American Historical Review* 75 (1970): 1046–64.

Agamben, Giorgio. *State of Exception.* Translated by Kevin Attell. Chicago: University of Chicago Press, 2005.

Althusser, Louis. *Lenin and Philosophy and Other Essays.* Translated by Ben Brewster. New York: Monthly Review Press, 1971.

Badiou, Alain. *Being and Event.* Translated by Oliver Feltham. New York: Continuum, 2005.

———. *Metapolitics.* Translated by Jason Barker. London: Verso, 2005.

Balibar, Étienne. *Politics and the Other Scene.* Translated by James Swenson Christine Jones and Chris Turner. New York: Verso, 2002.

Barr, Alfred H. "Is Modern Art Communistic?" *New York Times Magazine,* December 14, 1952, 22–23, 28–30.

Bartter, Martha A. *The Way to Ground Zero: The Atomic Bomb in American Science Fiction.* New York: Greenwood Press, 1988.

Beaman, R. B. "The Cubist Witch." *South Atlantic Quarterly* 48, no. 2 (April 1949): 204–12.

Bell, Daniel. *The Cultural Contradictions of Capitalism.* New York: Basic Books, 1996.

———. *The End of Ideology: On the Exhaustion of Political Ideas in the Fifties.* Cambridge: Harvard University Press, 1988.

Bell, Michael. "The Metaphysics of Modernism." In *The Cambridge Companion to Modernism,* edited by Michael Levenson, 9–32. Cambridge: Cambridge University Press, 1999.

Bendau, Clifford P. *Still Worlds Collide: Philip Wylie and the End of the American Dream*. San Bernardino, Cal.: Borgo, 1980.

Benedict, Ruth. "The Past and the Future." *The Nation*, December 7, 1946, 656–57.

Benjamin, Walter. "Theses on the Philosophy of History." In *Illuminations: Essays and Reflections*, 253–65. New York: Schocken, 1955.

———. "The Work of Art in the Age of Its Technological Reproducibility." In *Selected Writings: Volume 3, 1935–1938*, edited by Howard Eiland and Michael William Jennings, 101–33. Cambridge: Harvard University Press, 2002.

Biddle, George. "The Artist on the Horns of a Dilemma." *New York Times Magazine*, May 19, 1946, sec. 6: 21, 44–45.

Bloom, Alexander. *Prodigal Sons: The New York Intellectuals and Their World*. New York: Oxford University Press, 1986.

Blotner, Joseph L. *The Modern American Political Novel, 1900–1960*. Austin: University of Texas Press, 1966.

———. *The Political Novel*. Garden City, N.Y.: Doubleday, 1955.

Blumenberg, Hans. *Die Lesbarkeit der Welt*. Frankfurt am Main: Suhrkamp, 1981.

Bonitzer, Pascal. "The Silences of the Voice (*A Propos* of *Mai 68* by Guide Lawaetz)." In *Narrative, Apparatus, Ideology*, edited by Philip Rosen, 319–34. New York: Columbia University Press, 1986.

Boorstin, Daniel J. *The Genius of American Politics*. Chicago: University of Chicago Press, 1953.

Boyer, Paul. *By the Bomb's Early Light: American Thought and Culture at the Dawn of the Atomic Age*. New York: Pantheon, 1985.

Brians, Paul. *Nuclear Holocausts: Atomic War in Fiction, 1895–1984*. Kent, Ohio: Kent State University Press, 1987.

Brooks, Van Wyck. *America's Coming of Age*. New York: B. W. Huebsch, 1915.

———. *On Literature Today*. New York: E. P. Dutton, 1941.

Browsn, Rome G. Ed. *To the American People: Report upon the Illegal Practices of the United States Department of Justice*. Washington, D.C.: National Popular Government League, 1920.

Buchan, John. *The Adventures of Richard Hannay: The Thirty-Nine Steps, Greenmantle, Mr. Standfast*. Boston: Houghton Mifflin, 1919.

Buckingham, Peter H. *America Sees Red: Anticommunism in America, 1870s to 1980s*. Claremont, Cal.: Regina Books, 1988.

Cawelti, John G., and Bruce A. Rosenberg. *The Spy Story*. Chicago: University of Chicago Press, 1987.

Chambers, Whittaker. *Witness*. Washington, D.C.: Regnery, 2002.

Chase, Richard Volney. *The American Novel and Its Tradition*. Baltimore: Johns Hopkins University Press, 1957.

Collins, Max Allan, and James L. Taylor. *One Lonely Knight: Mickey Spillane's Mike Hammer*. Bowling Green, Ohio: Bowling Green State University Popular Press, 1984.

Cousins, Norman. *Modern Man Is Obsolete.* New York: Viking, 1945.

———. "The Standardization of Catastrophe." *Saturday Review,* August 10, 1946, 16–18.

Cowley, Malcolm. *Exile's Return: A Literary Odyssey of the 1920's.* New York: Viking, 1964.

———. "Sex Murder Incorporated." *New Republic* 126 (February 11, 1952): 17–18.

Davenport, Russell W. "A *Life* Roundtable on Modern Art." *Life,* October 11, 1948, 56–79.

Davis, Kenneth C. *Two-Bit Culture: The Paperbacking of America.* Boston: Houghton Mifflin, 1984.

Dayton, Tim. "'The Annihilated Content of the Wish': Class and Gender in Mickey Spillane's *I, the Jury.*" *Clues* 14, no. 1 (Spring/Summer 1993): 87–104.

De Man, Paul. *Aesthetic Ideology.* Minneapolis: University of Minnesota Press, 1996.

———. *The Resistance to Theory.* Minneapolis: University of Minnesota Press, 1986.

Denning, Michael. *Cover Stories: Narrative and Ideology in the British Spy Thriller.* London: Routledge, 1987.

Devree, Howard. "Modernism under Fire." *New York Times,* September 11, 1949, sec 2: 6.

———. "The Old That Leads to New." *New York Times,* July 21, 1946, sec 2: 8.

———. "Straws in the Wind: Some Opinions on Art in the Post War World of Europe and America." *New York Times,* July 14, 1946, sec. 2: 4.

Divine, Robert A. *Blowing on the Wind: The Nuclear Test Ban Debate, 1954–1960.* New York: Oxford University Press, 1978.

Dolan, Frederick M. *Allegories of America: Narratives, Metaphysics, Politics.* Ithaca: Cornell University Press, 1994.

Dowling, David. *Fictions of Nuclear Disaster.* Iowa City: University of Iowa Press, 1987.

Dudziak, Mary L. *Cold War Civil Rights: Race and the Image of American Democracy.* Princeton: Princeton University Press, 2000.

Eagleton, Terry. *The Ideology of the Aesthetic.* Malden, Mass.: Blackwell, 2000.

Eco, Umberto. "The Narrative Structures in Fleming." In *The Bond Affair,* edited by Oreste del Buono and Umberto Eco, translated by R. A. Downie, 35–75. London: Macdonald, 1966.

Endy, Christopher. *Cold War Holidays: American Tourism in France.* Chapel Hill: University of North Carolina Press, 2004.

Engerman, David C., Nils Gilman, Mark H. Haefele, and Michael E. Latham, eds. *Modernization, Development, and the Global Cold War.* Amherst: University of Massachusetts Press, 2003.

Etzold, Thomas H., and John Lewis Gaddis, eds. *Containment: Documents on American Policy and Strategy, 1945–1950.* New York: Columbia University Press, 1978.

Fast, Howard. *The Naked God: The Writer and the Communist Party.* New York: Praeger, 1957.

Fiedler, Leslie. *Love and Death in the American Novel.* Champaign, Ill.: Dalkey Archive Press, 2003.

Finney, Jack. *Invasion of the Body Snatchers.* New York: Scribner, 1998.

Fleming, Ian. *Casino Royale.* Harmondsworth: Penguin, 2002.

———. *Live and Let Die.* Harmondsworth: Penguin, 2002.

Foucault, Michel. *The Order of Things: An Archaeology of the Human Sciences.* New York: Vintage, 1994.

Franklin, Bruce H. "Fatal Fiction: A Weapon to End All Wars." In *The Nightmare Considered: Critical Essays on Nuclear War Literature,* edited by Nancy Anisfield, 5–14. Bowling Green, Ohio: Bowling Green State University Popular Press, 1991.

Fredrickson, George M. *Black Liberation: A Comparative History of Black Ideologies in the United States and South Africa.* New York: Oxford University Press, 1995.

Genauer, Emily. "Still Life with Red Herring." *Harper's Magazine,* September 1949, 88–91.

Gilman, Nils. *Mandarins of the Future: Modernization Theory in Cold War America.* Baltimore: Johns Hopkins University Press, 2003.

Glicksberg, Charles I. "Anti-Communism in Fiction." *South Atlantic Quarterly* 53 (October 1954): 485–96.

Greenberg, Clement. *Art and Culture.* Boston: Beacon, 1961.

———. "The Decline of Cubism." *Partisan Review* 10, no. 3 (March 1948): 366–69.

Greenberg, Martin H., Eric S. Rabkin, and Joseph D. Olander, eds. *The End of the World.* Carbondale: Southern Illinois University Press, 1983.

Grossman, Andrew D. "Segregationist Liberalism: The NAACP and Resistance to Civil-Defense Planning in the Early Cold War, 1951–1953." *International Journal of Politics, Culture and Society* 13, no. 3 (2000): 477–97.

Guilbaut, Serge. *How New York Stole the Idea of Modern Art: Abstract Expressionism, Freedom, and the Cold War.* Translated by Arthur Goldhammer. Chicago: University of Chicago Press, 1983.

Hauptman, William. "The Suppression of Art in the McCarthy Decade." *Artforum* 11 (1973): 48–52.

Haynes, John Earl. "The Cold War Debate Continues: A Traditionalist View of Historical Writing on Domestic Communism and Anti-Communism." *Journal of Cold War Studies* 2, no. 1 (Winter 2000): 76–115.

———. *Red Scare or Red Menace? American Communism and Anti-Communism in the Cold War Era, 1941–1960.* Chicago: Ivan R. Dee, 1996.

Heale, M. J. *American Anticommunism: Combating the Enemy within, 1830–1970.* Baltimore: Johns Hopkins University Press, 1990.

Heidegger, Martin. "The Age of the World Picture." In *The Question Concerning Technology and Other Essays,* 115–54. New York: Harper, 1977.

Hersey, John. *Hiroshima*. New York: Knopf, 1946.

Hixson, Walter L. *Parting the Curtain: Propaganda, Culture, and the Cold War, 1945–1961*. New York: St. Martin's, 1997.

Hobsbawn, Eric. *The Age of Extremes: A History of the World, 1914–1991*. New York: Vintage, 1994.

Hofstadter, Richard. *The Paranoid Style in American Politics and Other Essays*. Cambridge: Harvard University Press, 1996.

Hoover, J. Edgar. *Masters of Deceit: The Story of Communism in America and How to Fight It*. New York: Henry Holt, 1958.

———. *A Study of Communism*. New York: Holt, Reinhart and Winston, 1962.

Horn, Eva. "Knowing the Enemy: The Epistemology of Secret Intelligence." *Grey Room* 11 (Spring 2003): 58–85.

Horne, Gerald. "Who Lost the Cold War? Africans and African Americans." *Diplomatic History* 20, no. 4 (Fall 1996): 613–26.

Howe, Irving. *Politics and the Novel*. New York: Horizon Press, 1957.

Huyssen, Andreas. *After the Great Divide: Modernism, Mass Culture, Postmodernism*. Bloomington: Indiana University Press, 1986.

James, Henry. *The Princess Casamassima*. New York: Scribner's, 1908.

Jameson, Fredric. *The Cultural Turn: Selected Writings on the Postmodern, 1983–1998*. New York: Verso, 1998.

———. *The Geopolitical Aesthetic: Cinema and Space in the World System*. Bloomington: Indiana University Press, 1992.

———. *A Singular Modernity: Essay on the Ontology of the Present*. New York: Verso, 2002.

Jancovich, Mark. *The Cultural Politics of the New Criticism*. Cambridge: Cambridge University Press, 1993.

Jay, Martin. "'The Aesthetic Ideology' as Ideology; or, What Does It Mean to Aestheticize Politics?" *Cultural Critique* 21 (Spring 1992): 41–61.

Jewell, Edward Alden. "When Is Art American?" *New York Times*, September 1, 1946, 46.

Kazin, Michael. *Populist Persuasion: An American History*. New York: Basic Books, 1995.

Keefer, Truman Frederick. *Philip Wylie*. Boston: Twayne, 1977.

Kemme, Thomas. *Patterns of Power in American Political Fiction*. Lanham, Md.: University Press of America, 2003.

Kennan, George. *Memoirs, 1925–1950*. New York: Pantheon Books, 1962.

———. "The Sources of Soviet Conduct." *Foreign Affairs* 25 (July 1947): 566–82.

Kermode, Frank. *The Genesis of Secrecy: On the Interpretation of Narrative*. Cambridge: Harvard University Press, 1979.

———. *The Sense of an Ending: Studies in the Theory of Fiction*. New York: Oxford University Press, 1968.

Klein, Christina. *Cold War Orientalism: Asia in the Middlebrow Imagination, 1945–1961*. Berkeley: University of California Press, 2003.

Klinker, Philip A., and Rogers M. Smith. *The Unsteady March: The Rise and Decline of Racial Equality in America.* Chicago: Chicago University Press, 1999.

Koyré, Alexandre. *From the Closed World to the Infinite Universe.* Baltimore: Johns Hopkins University Press, 1957.

Laclau, Ernesto. *Emancipation(s).* New York: Verso, 1996.

———. *On Populist Reason.* New York: Verso, 2005.

Laclau, Ernesto, and Chantal Mouffe. *Hegemony and Socialist Strategy: Towards a Radical Democratic Politics.* New York: Verso, 2001.

Lasswell, Harold D. *National Security and Individual Freedom.* New York: McGraw-Hill, 1950.

Latham, Michael E. *Modernization as Ideology: American Social Science and "Nation Building" in the Kennedy Era.* Chapel Hill: University of North Carolina Press, 2000.

Layton, Azza Salama. *International Politics and Civil Rights Policies in the United States, 1941–1960.* Cambridge: Cambridge University Press, 2000.

Le Carré, John. *Call for the Dead.* New York: Walker, 1962.

Lederer, William J., and Eugene Burdick. *The Ugly American.* New York: Norton, 1958.

Leffler, Melvin P. "New Approaches, Old Interpretations, and Prospective Reconfigurations." *Diplomatic History* 19, no. 2 (Spring 1995): 173–96.

Lens, Sidney. *Permanent War: The Militarization of America.* New York: Schocken Books, 1987.

Lilienthal, David E. "Democracy and the Atom." *NEA Journal,* February 1948, 80.

Lipsitz, George. *Rainbow at Midnight: Labor and Culture in the 1940s.* Chicago: University of Illinois Press, 1994.

Louchheim, Aline B. "'Modern Art': Attack and Defense." *New York Times,* December 26, 1948, sec. 2: 11.

Macdonald, Dwight. "Hersey's 'Hiroshima'." *Politics* 3, no. 9 (October 1946): 308.

———. "Masscult and Midcult." In *Against the American Grain,* 3–75. New York: Random House, 1962.

MacDonald, John D. *Cape Fear.* New York: Fawcett Gold Medal, 1991.

Marks, Herbert S. "The Atomic Energy Act: Public Administration without Public Debate." *University of Chicago Law Review* 15 (Summer 1948): 839–53.

Masters, Dexter, and Katharine Way, eds. *One World or None: A Report to the Public on the Full Meaning of the Atomic Bomb.* New York: McGraw-Hill, 1946.

Mathews, Jane de Hart. "Art and Politics in Cold War America." *American Historical Review* 81, no. 4 (October 1976): 762–87.

McCarthy, Mary. "The 'Hiroshima' New Yorker." In *Hiroshima's Shadow: Writings on the Denial of History and the Smithsonian Controversy,* edited by Kai Bird and Lawrence Lifschultz, 303–304. Stony Creek, N.Y.: Pamphleteer, 1998.

McCormick, John. *Catastrophe and Imagination: An Interpretation of the Recent English and American Novel.* New York: Longmans, 1957.

Melley, Timothy. *Empire of Conspiracy: The Culture of Paranoia in Postwar America.* Ithaca: Cornell University Press, 2000.

Merry, Bruce. *The Anatomy of the Spy Thriller.* London: Macmillan, 1977.

Michaels, Walter Benn. "Anti-Imperial Americanism." In *Cultures of United States Imperialism*, edited by Amy Kaplan and Donald E. Pease, 365–91. Durham: Duke University Press, 1993.

Michener, James. "The Conscience of the Contemporary Novel." In *The Arts in Renewal*, edited by Lewis Mumford, 107–40. Philadelphia: University of Pennsylvania Press, 1951.

———. *The Voice of Asia.* New York: Random House, 1951.

Miller, Perry. *Errand into the Wilderness.* Cambridge: Harvard University Press, 1956.

Mills, C. Wright. *The Power Elite.* Oxford: Oxford University Press, 2000.

Milne, Gordon. *The American Political Novel.* Norman: University of Oklahoma Press, 1966.

Mitrovich, Gregory. *Undermining the Kremlin: America's Strategy to Subvert the Soviet Bloc, 1947–1956.* Ithaca: Cornell University Press, 2000.

Moynihan, Daniel Patrick. *Secrecy: The American Experience.* New Haven: Yale University Press, 1998.

Mumford, Lewis. "Atom Bomb: 'Miracle' or Catastrophe." *Air Affairs*, July 1948, 326–45.

Murphy, Geraldine. "Romancing the Center: Cold War Politics and Classic American Literature." *Poetics Today* 9, no. 4 (1988): 737–47.

Nadel, Alan. *Containment Culture: American Narratives, Postmodernism, and the Atomic Age.* Durham: Duke University Press, 1995.

Nancy, Jean-Luc. *The Creation of the World, or, Globalization.* Translated by François Raffoul and David Pettigrew. Albany: State University of New York Press, 2007.

Nashel, Jonathan. "The Road to Vietnam: Modernization Theory in Fact and Fiction." In *Cold War Constructions: The Political Culture of United States Imperialism, 1945–1966*, edited by Christian G. Appy, 132–54. Amherst: University of Massachusetts Press, 2000.

Niebuhr, Reinhold. *Moral Man and Immoral Society.* New York: Scribners, 1952.

Oakes, Guy. *The Imaginary War: Civil Defense and American Cold War Culture.* New York: Oxford University Press, 1994.

Osgood, Kenneth A. "The Unconventional Cold War." *Journal of Cold War Studies* 4, no. 2 (2002): 85–107.

Palmer, Jerry. *Thrillers: Genesis and Structure of a Popular Genre.* New York: St. Martin's, 1979.

Philbrick, Herbert A. *I Led Three Lives: Citizen, "Communist," Counterspy.* Washington, D.C.: Capitol Hill, 1972.

Powers, Richard Gid. *Not without Honor: The History of American Anticommunism*. New York: Free Press, 1995.

Rabinowitch, Eugene. *The Dawn of a New Age: Reflections on Science and Human Affairs*. Chicago: University of Chicago Press, 1963.

Rancière, Jacques. *Aesthetics and Its Discontents*. Translated by Steve Corcoran. Malden, Mass.: Polity, 2009.

———. "Aesthetics, Inaesthetics, Anti-Aesthetics." In *Think Again*, edited by Peter Hallward, 218–31. New York: Continuum, 2004.

———. *Disagreement: Politics and Philosophy*. Translated by Julie Rose. Minneapolis: University of Minnesota Press, 1999.

———. *The Politics of Aesthetics: The Distribution of the Sensible*. Translated by Gabriel Rockhill. New York: Continuum, 2006.

———. "What Aesthetics Can Mean?" In *From an Aesthetic Point of View: Philosophy, Art and the Senses*, edited by Peter Osborne, 13–33. London: Serpent's Tail, 2000.

Riesman, David, et al. *The Lonely Crowd: A Study of Changing American Character*. Rev. ed. New Haven: Yale University Press, 2001.

Rogin, Michael. "'Make My Day!'": Spectacle as Amnesia in Imperial Politics." In *Cultures as United States Imperialism*, edited by Amy Kaplan and Donald E. Pease, 499–534. Durham: Duke University Press, 1993.

———. *Ronald Reagan, the Movie, and Other Episodes in Political Demonology*. Berkeley: University of California Press, 1987.

Rolo, Charles J. "Simenon and Spillane: The Metaphysics of Murder for the Millions." In *Mass Culture: The Popular Arts in America*, edited by Bernard Rosenberg and David Manning White, 165–75. Glencoe, Ill.: Free Press, 1957.

Rosenberg, Bernard, and David Manning White, eds. *Mass Culture: The Popular Arts in America*. Glencoe, Ill.: Free Press, 1957.

Rossiter, Clinton. *Constitutional Dictatorship: Crisis Government in the Modern Democracies*. New York: Harcourt, Brace and World, 1963.

Roth, Philip. *I Married a Communist*. Boston: Houghton Mifflin, 1998.

Rowe, John Carlos. *Literary Culture and U.S. Imperialism: From the Revolution to World War II*. Oxford: Oxford University Press, 2000.

Ruotsila, Markku. *British and American Anticommunism before the Cold War*. Portland, Ore.: Frank Cass, 2001.

Sauerberg, Lars Ole. *Secret Agents in Fiction: Ian Fleming, John Le Carré, Len Deighton*. London: Macmillan, 1984.

Sauvy, Alfred. "Trois mondes, une planète." *L'Observateur*, August 14, 1952, 14.

Schaub, Thomas Hill. *American Fiction in the Cold War*. Madison: University of Wisconsin Press, 1991.

Scheick, William J. "Post-Nuclear Holocaust Re-Minding." In *The Nightmare Considered: Critical Essays on Nuclear War Literature*, edited by Nancy Anisfield, 71–84. Bowling Green, Ohio: Bowling Green State University Popular Press, 1991.

Schlesinger, Arthur. *The Vital Center: The Politics of Freedom*. New York: Da Capo, 1988.

Schumpeter, Joseph. *Capitalism, Socialism and Democracy*. New York: Harper, 1975.

Schwartz, Lawrence H. *Creating Faulkner's Reputation: The Politics of Modern Literary Criticism*. Knoxville: University of Tennessee Press, 1988.

Schwarz, Fred. *You Can Trust the Communists (To Be Communists)*. Englewood Cliffs, N.J.: Prentice Hall, 1960.

"Science Testifies." *New Republic*, June 10, 1957, 3–4.

Sherry, Michael S. *In the Shadow of War*. New Haven: Yale University Press, 1995.

Shils, Edward. *The Torment of Secrecy: The Background and Consequences of American Security Policies*. Chicago: Elephant Paperbacks, 1996.

Shute, Nevil. *On the Beach*. New York: William Morrow, 1957.

Skousen, W. Cleon. *The Naked Capitalist*. Salt Lake City: Reviewer, 1970.

———. *The Naked Communist*. [1958] Salt Lake City: Reviewer, 1983.

Sontag, Susan. "The Imagination of Disaster." In *Against Interpretation and Other Essays*, 209–25. New York: Farrar, Strauss, Giroux, 1966.

Spillane, Mickey. *The Girl Hunters*. New York: New American Library, 1962.

———. *The Hammer Strikes Again*. New York: Avenel Books, 1989.

———. *The Mike Hammer Collection: I, the Jury; My Gun Is Quick; Vengeance Is Mine!* Vol. 1. New York: New American Library, 2001.

———. *The Mike Hammer Collection: One Lonely Night; The Big Kill; Kiss, Me Deadly*. Vol. 2. New York: New American Library, 2001.

Stein, Gertrude. "Reflections on the Atomic Bomb." *Yale Poetry Review* 7 (1947): 3–4.

Trilling, Lionel. *The Liberal Imagination*. Garden City, N.Y.: Doubleday Anchor Books, 1950.

Trotter, David. "The Modernist Novel." In *The Cambridge Companion to Modernism*, edited by Michael Levenson, 70–99. Cambridge: Cambridge University Press, 1999.

Von Eschen, Penny M. *Race against Empire: Black Americans and Anticolonialism, 1937–1957*. Ithaca: Cornell Univerity Press, 1997.

Wagar, Warren W. *Terminal Visions: The Literature of Last Things*. Bloomington: Indiana University Press, 1982.

Walker, Sydnor H. *The First One Hundred Days of the Atomic Age: August 6–November 15, 1945*. New York: Woodrow Wilson Foundation, 1945.

Weart, Spencer R. *Nuclear Fear: A History of Images*. Cambridge: Harvard University Press, 1988.

Weibel, Kay. "Mickey Spillane as a Fifties Phenomenon." In *Dimensions of Detective Fiction*, edited by Pat Browne, Larry N. Landrum, and Ray B. Browne, 114–23. Bowling Green, Ohio: Bowling Green State University Popular Press, 1976.

Wellek, René, and Austin Warren. *The Theory of Literature*. New York: Harcourt, Brace, 1949.

Whitfield, Stephen J. *The Culture of the Cold War*. Baltimore: Johns Hopkins University Press, 1996.

Williams, William Carlos. *The Autobiography of William Carlos Williams*. New York: New Directions, 1967.

Wilson, Edmund. "Who Cares Who Killed Roger Ackroyd?" In *Mass Culture: The Popular Arts in America, edited by* Bernard Rosenberg and David Manning White, 149–154. Glencoe, Ill.: Free Press, 1957.

Wolfe, Gary K. "The Remaking of Zero: Beginning at the End." In *The End of the World*, edited by Martin H. Greenberg, Eric S. Rabkin, and Joseph D. Olander, 1–19. Carbondale: Southern Illinois University Press, 1983.

Wylie, Philip. *After Worlds Collide*. New York: Paperback Library, 1963.

———. "The Crime of Mickey Spillane." *Good Housekeeping*, February 1955, 54–55, 207.

———. *The Disappearance*. New York: Rinehart, 1951.

———. "Doom or Deliverance." *Collier's*, September 29, 1945, 18–19, 79–80.

———. *Generation of Vipers*. New York: Rinehart, 1942.

———. *The Innocent Ambassadors*. New York: Rinehart, 1957.

———. *Tomorrow!* New York: Popular Library, 1956.

———. *Triumph*. New York: Popular Library, 1961.

Wylie, Philip, and Edwin Balmer. *When Worlds Collide*. New York: Dell, 1933.

Yavenditti, Michael J. "John Hersey and the American Conscience." In *Hiroshima's Shadow: Writings on the Denial of History and the Smithsonian Controversy*, edited by Kai Bird and Lawrence Lifschultz, 288–302. Stony Creek, N.Y.: Pamphleteer, 1998.

Žižek, Slavoj. *The Sublime Object of Ideology*. London: Verso, 2001.

———. *The Ticklish Subject: The Absent Centre of Political Ontology*. New York: Verso, 2000.

INDEX

aesthetic ideology, 9–35; and aesthetic unconscious, 32–34; and critique, 9–14; defined, 2–3; and distribution of the insensible, 20–27, 33; and distribution of the sensible, 15–20, 33; and exclusion, 27–32; and ideology, 9–14; and limits of representation, 27–32

Aesthetic Ideology (de Man), 12

aesthetic practices, 15, 17

aesthetics: and art, 82–85; defined, 9–14; of high modernism, 82; and literature, 97; modernist, 85–94; in spy novels, 155; of ugliness, 190, 197, 198, 228*n*81

aesthetic unconscious, 32–34

After Worlds Collide (Wylie), 133–34

Agamben, Giorgio, 43

age of anxiety, 44, 177

allegorization, 116

Althusser, Louis, 11, 27, 29

American exceptionalism, 65

American national identity, 62–63, 65

The American Novel and Its Tradition (Chase), 99

America's Coming of Age (Brooks), 101

"Anti-Communism in Fiction" (Glicksberg), 105

anti-Communist aesthetic ideology: aesthetic components, 3, 82–108; and limits of representation, 36–52; and literature, 94–100; and mass culture, 175; political components, 3, 36–81

anti-Communist politics, 36–38; and anticolonialism, 68; art's role in, 84; and catastrophe, 75; and global enemies, 170–75; internal struggles of, 37; militarization of, 39–40, 162; and modernism, 3, 85–94, 100, 176, 179; naturalization of, 53–54, 60, 83, 164; and popular fiction, 100–108; and religion, 54–55, 166, 192–93, 224*n*101; religious universalism of, 134; and Third World, 173–74

anti-imperialism, 66, 189–98. *See also* colonialism

antirealism, 83, 85, 120

art: aesthetic ideology's relationship to, 2–3; and aesthetics, 10, 82–85; Althusserian theory of, 12; in anti-Communist ideology, 35, 82; conspiracy as, 159; and distribution of the sensible, 16; kitsch vs., 160; and mass culture, 102–3, 121; and modernism, 177, 213*n*27; phenomenology of, 13; politicization of, 10, 40–41, 122; propaganda vs., 82, 106–7; realism in, 146–47; regimes of, 18; and representation, 150–51; role in anti-Communist politics, 84; and secrecy, 146; violence as replacement for, 167

"The Artist on the Horns of a Dilemma" (Biddle), 88